I am me: the lived experienc

is an examination of the 'mixed-race
six people of mixed heritage in inter

f

These accounts are accompanied by in-depth commentary, including a discussion of the implications for psychotherapy, and a thorough critique of racialised thinking and attitudes which will challenge the reader's views on race and the ingrained social attitudes which pervade our world.

In western countries such as the UK and the US, census data shows that people identifying as having a mixed background to be the fastest growing ethnic category. However, there is very little literature shedding light on what having such an identity means, and what little there is can often be brief and simplistic. As prejudice, ignorance and racialised thinking, dating back to times of colonialism and legalised slavery, continue to blight the social psyche, it is clear that a greater understanding is much needed.

Haran Rasalingam is a psychotherapist and coach. In writing I am me, part of his psychotherapy research, he has contributed to filling a gap in the understanding of the 'mixed-race condition'.

Of mixed heritage himself, he explores what it is like to experience life with a 'mixed-race' identity through the fascinating accounts of six people's brave journeys of enlightenment about themselves in their social contexts.

I am me

the lived experience of a mixed-race identity

Haran Rasalingam

I am me: the lived experience of a mixed-race identity
©2019 Haran Rasalingam

ISBN 9781081852146

Cover design by John Woodcock,
Modified by Haran Rasalingam

Published by Amazon

No person on this planet has ever had black or white skin

CONTENTS

ABOUT ME AND THIS BOOK

I am a professional life coach, business coach and psychotherapist. This book is based on the thesis which I completed in 2011 towards my Masters in Psychotherapy and Counselling. It is an exploration of the lived experience of a mixed-race identity and the implications of this for psychotherapeutic theory and practice. As you will see, mixed-race identity is very under-researched, especially within the field of psychotherapy.

Naturally, there are some quite heavily academic sections in this book, but I have included the transcripts of all of the interviews which I conducted, and I think these make for interesting reading for a much wider audience.

As I am someone who considers myself to have a mixed-race identity, this is a subject that I was very keen to explore, and I found the research to be extremely rewarding. By making this work available as a book, I hope that it will be of interest and indeed helpful for others, both within my own family and beyond!

ACKNOWLEDGEMENTS

First of all, I would like to thank my co-researchers. I have huge respect and admiration for you, and I am extremely grateful to you for collaborating with me and sharing your stories with such enthusiasm, honesty and courage. I thank my dissertation supervisor for her truly excellent guidance and encouragement, and I thank those psychotherapists, lecturers, colleagues and fellow students who have been enormously influential and inspiring.

The biggest thanks of all must go to my wife for providing both practical and moral support as well as considerable patience during my 'psychotherapy years'.

I dedicate this work to my children for whom I hope this will be helpful during the next generation where the melting pot has melted still further beyond the old divisions.

ABSTRACT

This research examines the lived experience of six people who self-identified as having a mixed-race identity in some sense. The research methodology used is Interpretative Phenomenological Analysis (IPA). All co-researchers were either qualified or nearly qualified psychotherapists and had thus all experienced psychotherapy as both a client and a therapist and had all had psychotherapy training.

Do therapists understand the mixed-race condition? Although there is now a growing amount of literature and research in the area of cross-cultural counselling, this seems to deal very stereotypically and simplistically with these issues. Within training colleges, little time is devoted to the subject and among therapists, just as amongst the population as a whole, large misunderstandings and confusions remain. It is also a taboo subject which many shy away from. Others believe that they are unaffected by racism and do not feel the need to reflect on the subject.

Given the situation with regard to understanding otherness generally in the racial/ethnic/cultural dimension, where it appears that many therapists do not have a basic awareness of core historical and sociological themes, the prospects are even grimmer for mixed-race people. The lived experience of mixed-race people is extremely under-researched even within social sciences as a whole. There are also many additional confusions – for example, presumptions that mixed-race people are somehow tragic and to be pitied, that 'mixed race' means mixed-up and confused, or that 'mixed' means 'black'.

This work aims to contribute to the understanding of mixed-race issues both within the social sciences in general and especially within psychotherapy. It is hoped that psychotherapists will gain an increased awareness of mixed-race issues and develop a more nuanced awareness of cultural/ethnic/racial issues.

INTRODUCTION

Born in the UK to an English mother and a Sri Lankan father, I have grown up with what I experience as a 'mixed-race identity'. In simple terms, this means that my parents are of different 'races', a concept which requires exploration. This identity has often been difficult to live with particularly because it seems difficult for others to comprehend. It has had a profound impact on my sense of belonging and my way of thinking. I have tried to reach various resolutions to 'stabilise' my identity, but none seems satisfactory.

More recently, I have questioned whether there is some resolution to my identity, one with which I can feel settled and whether, in fact, it may be the illusion that there is one which causes me discomfort. Perhaps I could come to accept a more fluid identity which would include the varied attitudes and ignorances of others and straddle the internal and the external as much as it straddles polarities of black and white. It would include being subjected to presumptuous classification by others. It would include my need to be acknowledged as belonging in some sense to the heritages of both of my parents and it would include a desire for it not to be an issue.

Does one's own understanding of 'race' affect things? To what extent is one's own understanding of 'race' irrelevant if it is dependent on the perception of others? Why do we seem to create a two-way split between black and white, despite the fact that there is a vast array of shades of skin colour from dark to fair? What is the crossover point between 'black' and 'white'?

My mother is considered to be 'white' by all accounts and yet she has some 'black' ancestry from Barbados. My father is a Sri Lankan Tamil, and his skin is very dark and typical of Sri Lankan Tamils. But some of his facial features seem more typical of, say, Europe, than of Sri Lanka. This indicates to me that much of our genetic make-up is completely ignored when we think in terms of 'races' – we become blind to such details.

If racial categories are based on certain characteristics while ignoring others, then a notion of mixed race seems to be based on arbitrarily drawn boundaries which do not cater for the mixed-race person. What is it that tells us that a person is mixed race? Is it that, on seeing a person, we become confused when we are unable to place them in a conventional category? Is it only when we see that person with his/her parents and perceive them to be racially different? What is it that seems particularly significant about skin colour differences as opposed to, say, hair colour or height?

In the context of psychotherapy, a mixed-race client could bring complex issues into the therapy room and could challenge many assumptions of the therapist. I would like to find out how others might experience their own mixed-race identity and what stances they adopt, and what impact, if any, the participation in psychotherapeutic activity has had on them. That is the subject of this research.

LITERATURE REVIEW

Introduction

In this section, I will discuss current literature, theory and research relevant to my work on mixed-race issues and psychotherapy. I have found that, while there appears to be a great deal of literature on the subject of culture/ethnicity/race (more on these terminologies below), particularly in sociological disciplines, I have found much less on mixed-race issues. And while I have come across an established body of writing around culture/ethnicity/race within the field of psychotherapy, referred to using terms such as *cross-cultural counselling* (Pedersen, 1987), *multicultural counselling* (Palmer, 2002) or *transcultural counselling* (Eleftheriadou, 1994; d'Ardenne & Mahtani, 2004), I have managed to identify very little writing within the field of psychotherapy which focuses specifically on mixed-race issues.

I will look at the history of the concept of 'race' which has led us to contemporary views on it, examining the motivations, inherent inequalities and problems related to the concept and the different ways in which it is understood. From here I will turn to the specific issue of mixed race and look at the complexities and paradoxes within this idea. I will look at the history of attitudes towards 'racial mixing' and the way in which this is related to the maintenance of racial concepts.

This will be followed by a discussion of mixed-race issues within the field of psychotherapy. I will argue that they are not merely edge cases within a broader discussion around culture/ethnicity/race, but they can also challenge these ideas and bring up entirely separate questions altogether on more general subjects such as the self and identity.

As a practising existential psychotherapist, my perspective on this discussion will be influenced by existential theory. Existential psychotherapy is primarily grounded in the continental European philosophy of thinkers such as such as Heidegger, Sartre, Nietzsche, Wittgenstein, Kierkegaard and Merleau-Ponty (Cooper, 2003). The therapist working in this way sees each of us as fundamentally and originally embedded in a particular situation at a particular time and resists imposing a pre-existing framework onto a client's experience (van Deurzen, 1988; Cohn 2002; Spinelli, 2007). Since a mixed-race identity also seems to break out of pre-established racial frameworks, existential theory seems particularly relevant to this research.

The Problem with Race

Race is a problematic word which has something of a sordid, and yet seductive, history. In many contexts it is taboo. Theories abound as to what race is and yet it is a concept which has proved to be impossible to pin down. The way in which the concept of race is often reported in the media (e.g.: BBC News Online, 2011) and the way it is used by government and other official institutions (e.g.: National Statistics Online, 2001; National Health Service, 2011) seem to reinforce the idea 'that race is a natural and important way to categorize people' (Gaskins, 1999:46). And yet, the idea of there being a coherent and intrinsic basis for race is largely discredited within academic and scientific circles (Young, 1994; Rattansi, 2007) and so it is, in a sense, puzzling that the concept of race continues to carry so much significance.

Much of the problem seems to be historical and many ingrained attitudes of the past regarding race are still with us today in a completely different context. These attitudes are woven into the language which constructs our world. A perennial problem for anyone writing about the subject, myself included, is the fact that, while attempting to deconstruct or reconstruct any ideas around race, the original ingrained concepts are also reinforced due to the language we use. Dalal (2006) argues that academics often try using other words such as 'ethnicity' or 'culture', in order to clarify the situation, but such a strategy, he argues, and as I shall expand on below, does not appear to make matters any less problematic.

I would suggest that another part of the problem is the modern culture of *scientism*. Due possibly to the high status in which science is held, it has led to the popular belief that science can and should be considered as the discipline which will provide the ultimate explanation for all knowledge (Okasha, 2002; Bennett & Hacker, 2003; Latour, 2005; Legrenzi & Umiltà, 2009). Malik shows the evolution in European thought through the Enlightenment period which gradually moved the idea of different races of the world being something which was fluid, societal and environmental to their being fixed, immutable and primarily biological in nature (Malik, 2009). This culminated in the horrific policy of eugenics by the Nazis in 1930s Germany. After this, race was re-examined and considered once again to be broadly speaking a social construct. However, rapid advances in the field of genetics have made biological notions of race credible again (Obasogie, 2009).

Within the scientific world there exists a school of thought known as *race realism* (Malik, 2009). Amongst scientists of this persuasion we can see a revival of research into supposed racial superiority on, for example, the grounds of intelligence. Lynn (2006), emeritus professor at the University of Ulster and Rushton (2000), a psychology professor at the University of Western Ontario in Canada, claims that there are differences in intelligence due to race, with sub-Saharan Africans thought to be less intelligent than white people and East Asians to be the most intelligent of all. One criticism of the findings was that IQ tests taken by black Americans with much larger proportions of DNA found predominantly in Europe fared no better on average than black Americans with a much lower proportion, thus suggesting that the findings were more related to socio-environmental issues (Channel 4, 2009a).

The tendency to think of race as a biological classification reinforces the implication that it is fixed and permanent and thus a form of *essentialism*, that is the belief that who we are ultimately is some fundamental unchanging essence or fixed set of characteristics (e.g.: Sayyid, 2000; Phillips, 2010). An example of this is the use of ethnic/racial categories (more on the distinction between these words later) in official contexts such as in forms which ask a person to tick a box to indicate the ethnic group s/he belongs to, thus carrying the implication that there are some absolute underlying ethnic types.

The official form scenario where ethnic group questions are asked is an oft-mentioned example of when mixed-race individuals feel 'boxed in' (Olumide, 2002). For example, in the GP Patient Survey questionnaire commissioned by the National Health Service (NHS) in the UK (conducted by Ipsos MORI, 2011), question 49 asks: 'What is your ethnic group?' This type of closed questioning is designed to provide very structured data in response (Aspinall, 2008), but a person feeling boxed-in and the reinforcement of myths about fixed identities are unpleasant consequences of this.

The Problem with Mixed Race

The idea that a person can be of mixed race is predicated upon a prior concept of race, whatever that might mean, and carries the implication that the person in question does not fit into established categories that the majority of people do fit into. The person in question is outside of the norm. The person designated as mixed race, therefore, presents a problem to a society which believes in the racial categories to which it subscribes. Without *a priori* racial categories, there can be no mixed-race category.

However, if there is no biological basis for the concept of race, then race must be derived from observation of perceived similarities between people. It is a descriptive process rather than a prescriptive one. Therefore, sustaining a concept of mixed race requires that we ignore the mixed-race person in terms of developing our description. Major French existential-phenomenological philosopher, Merleau-Ponty (2006), referred to this type of phenomenon as *sedimentation*, where through repeated confirmation of our suppositions of our perception, we come to reify particular configurations and come to think of them as absolutely fixed, failing to accept other possibilities outside of those configurations. The twentieth century Austrian philosopher, Ludwig Wittgenstein, who developed a philosophy of language use, used the term *bewitchment* to describe the way in which the words we use trap us into thinking in certain ways at the exclusion of others, a kind of linguistic sedimentation (Rasalingam, 2009).

Biologically, we might consider that the genetic make-up of a mixed-race person is untypically diverse, because, for example, of combinations of genes typically found in two or more different geographical locations (Channel 4, 2009c). In terms of racial categorisations, the mixed-race person perhaps breaks the pattern of what people in a particular place and time are used to seeing, and our language is built upon what we are used to referring to. A society may be content with its sedimented way of seeing things and to treat mixed-race people as an anomaly, but what effect does this have on the mixed-race person who has been deemed an anomaly in order not to disrupt pre-established boundaries?

The 2001 census (National Statistics Online, 2001) revealed that those describing their ethnicity as 'mixed' constitute the fastest growing 'ethnic minority' group in the UK (e.g. Smith, 2006; Ahmed, 2010). Indeed, it was as a result of this growth that 'mixed' as an ethnic category appeared in its own right on UK census forms for the first time in 2001 and so here we have the paradox that to be of mixed 'ethnicity' is to cross categories at the same time as being a category itself. I should note here that on the 2001 UK census form, the ethnic categories described were identical to racial categories, being as they were a combination of black/white distinctions, such as 'white British, 'white Irish, 'black African', 'black Caribbean' and various types of geographical/national descriptions which have very unique usages, for instance, 'Asian' excluded 'Chinese'.

Language and Terminology

The question of language and terminology on the subject of race is a problem in itself and I have already used racial terms above which I find problematic. It seems that even well-intentioned attempts to use new terms or to redefine existing ones do not clarify the situation at all. Take, for example, Alibhai-Brown's well-intentioned declaration on terminology:

'I do not use the word "black" to mean mixed-race in this book unless this is how my interviewee describes herself or himself. Most other writers use the term "black" to mean mixed-race, and when I quote them I do so too. I prefer the

I am me: the lived experience of a mixed-race identity
by Haran Rasalingam

terms "mixed-race" or "mixed-parentage". At times I use
"black" as a political term and apply it to all British people of
colour. But when it comes to ethnicity, I use the word "black"
to mean of African and African Caribbean origin. The context
makes this clear I hope.'
(2001:xv)

Already, I am thrown into some confusion. Why would the term
'black' be used to describe 'mixed-race'? What does 'all British people
of colour' mean? And when the word 'ethnicity' is introduced, is this
different from colour? If so, why use the colour word 'black' to
describe an ethnicity? If I am from Africa or from the Caribbean, is my
skin colour automatically black? Are Egyptians black? Where would
white South Africans or white Kenyans fit into such a schema? What
is meant by 'origin'? How many generations back does one need to go
to establish 'origin'? If your origin is Caribbean, how can it also be
African? If black people are ultimately deemed to be of African origin
and consequently white people are deemed to be of European origin,
then it is clear that the circumlocutions used are only a thin veneer
superimposed on pre-existing racial premises.

Using Wittgenstein's philosophy (Wittgenstein, 2001), we can
say that the actual word used is irrelevant if put to the same use as the
word it replaces - it is the *use* to which racial terms are put which needs
to be understood (Rasalingam, 2009). Similarly, Dalal (2006), a
psychodynamic psychotherapist and group analyst, emphasises the
need to consider the *function* our words have in order to understand

them, so that where the word 'ethnicity' replaces the word 'race' or where 'culture' replaces the word 'ethnicity', those words are synonymous if put to the same purpose. What similarities and differences are we trying to bring out when we use these terms? Dalal (ibid) gives several examples of authors trying to distinguish between 'culture', 'ethnicity and 'race' and argues that all definitions contradict each other, and all fail to distinguish the three terms simultaneously. Dalal (ibid) argues that there is a strong link between racial categorisations and divisions created by colonialism and that racial constructs were used to maintain these divisions.

Societal and Family Attitudes to Racial Mixing

The focus of this study is on mixed race, but in any case, no account of race seems possible without a discussion of attitudes to racial mixing. Even when tolerance of racial difference exists, there still remains the problem of attitudes towards racial mixing or *miscegenation*. For the racist, the most abhorrent idea is that one race mix with another causing 'contamination' and 'degradation' (Prasad, 2009). As recently as 2009, a justice of the peace in Louisiana refused to issue marriage licenses for interracial marriage, while the leader of the far-right political party, the British National Party, Nick Griffin, believes that mixed marriages are unnatural and that mixed-race children are the tragic victims (ibid).

From my own childhood experience, I will never forget the ferocity with which one passer-by shouted at me: "fucking half-caste!" as if not only my presence in this passer-by's vicinity was an affront to him but that my very *existence* were an aberration. It was my *existence* which seemed to be the primary cause of his wrath. Ali (2005) notes that fear of miscegenation and antagonism towards it was common throughout colonial history. The British colonial approach was to pathologise the cultural and psychological differences of colonised people to reinforce an idea of unsuitability of the British mixing with the colonised. But fear and antagonism also persist in the present day and it is not uncommon for racial mixing to be considered undesirable. For example, Alibhai-Brown (2001) found objections such as the idea that relationships will be problematic if one's partner is not from the same culture, religion or caste, or the fear that the children will lack a strong sense of identity and may be confused and unhappy. Olumide (2002) found that it may be seen as a turning one's back on one's own 'people' or a threat to the continued existence of one's 'people'. She also noted that some people of mixed parentage reported racial tension between their mother and father or hostility by the grandparents towards their daughter-in-law or son-in-law (ibid).

Context, Asymmetry and Dichotomy

The fact that racial categorisations vary from country to country and from context to context indicates that racial concepts have sociological and political dimensions to them. In 2008, the BBC reported that in South Africa, the Chinese community were reclassified as 'black' after complaints from the Chinese that they were being unfairly discriminated against having been classified as 'white' post-apartheid

(BBC News Online, 2008). In Brazil, Pena (2009) notes that the term *pardo*, literally meaning 'brown', is used as an official racial categorisation between *branco* (white) and *preto* (black), but *pardo* and *preto* are grouped more broadly under *negro* (another word for 'black'). Pena (ibid), citing Suarez-Kurtz (2007), found the ancestry within a group of self-defined *pardos* in Rio de Janeiro to be predominantly European (68.1%) and therefore, argues Pena, the reason that *pardos* are grouped more broadly with *pretos* under the grouping of *negros*, rather than with *brancos*, is political.

Historically, a key justification for colonisation by European nations appears to be a presumption of superiority of the colonisers over the colonised (Ali, 2005; Rattansi, 2007) and skin colour was a powerful visual marker to distinguish fair-skinned colonisers from the darker-skinned colonised (Dalal, 2006). In more recent times, such hierarchical divisions can be seen to persist in, for example, laws prohibiting inter-racial marriages (Pheonix & Owen, 2000) and the fundamental asymmetry to the concept of race is evident in the principle of *hypodescent* or the *one-drop rule* (Spencer, 2004) – the principle which assigns a person of mixed parentage to the lower-status racial category – which was a long-standing and legally sanctioned principle in the USA. Ali finds that 'the central concerns within contemporary discussions often still hold echoes of colonial ideologies' (2005:3), while Dalal argues that the concept of race exists to serve a purpose of distinguishing 'between the haves and the must-not-haves' (2006:122).

This would therefore imply that the concept of race, even in the modern era, inevitably carries a fundamental assumption of inequality.

There is certainly evidence to support this. Consider for example the normative status of 'white' implicit in phrases such as 'ethnic communities' as in the following example from the *Daily Mail*, a national newspaper in the UK:

> 'More than half of those under 16 in the cities are now from black, Asian and other ethnic communities'
> (Ellicott, 2011).

Here, there is a strong implication that, while 'black' and 'Asian' constitute ethnicities, 'white' does not. But even the term 'ethnic minority', which seems to imply that there is such a thing as an 'ethnic majority' turns out to be little more than another euphemism to indicate that the group is marked in contrast to the neutral. I tried performing a Google search for 'ethnic majority' as a phrase and this returned 96 results from UK pages within the month. In contrast, a Google search with the same criteria for 'ethnic minority' as a phrase returned 66,300 results (searched 6th February 2011). This strongly suggests that the word 'ethnic' is most clearly associated with those groups who are not considered to be the norm. And that norm is designated 'white' and therefore it could be said that 'ethnic' is a euphemism for 'not white' or 'not the norm'.

The most fundamental categorisation in racial conceptualisations seems to be that of the dichotomy black/white. For example, the former

US President, Barack Obama, is widely described as the first black president of the United States of America, even though his mother is a white American (e.g.: MacAskill et al., 2008; Baldwin, 2008). With such a principle, 'white' seems to represent the gold standard of purity and 'black' represents not only the lowest category of 'black', but anything which is not white, which could include, for example 'Asian' or, of greatest significance here, 'mixed'. The American golfer, Tiger Woods, coined the phrase 'Cablinasian' (a combination of 'Caucasian', 'black', 'Indian' and 'Asian') when asked by journalists to describe his 'race' and was widely criticised for refusing to label himself 'black' and accused of being in denial about his 'blackness' (Gaskins, 1999).

As Rattansi puts it: 'This leads to the racialized anomaly in which a white woman can give birth to a black child, but a black mother's child will always be classified as black or mixed' (2007:172). Rattansi argues that in both the USA and most of Europe the one-drop rule is in operation in some way with regard to what makes a person black and that this 'acts as a powerful *de facto* recognition of the spurious category of race and the special character of whiteness' (2007:172).

The persistence of a black/white dichotomy in our collective social psyche leads to some curious scenarios, such as immigrants to the USA from Latin America finding to their surprise that they are often considered black in the USA when in their country of origin they were considered white (Fears, 2004). A further consequence of this dichotomy can be seen in the concept of *passing* where an individual of mixed descent claims membership of a 'pure' racial category usually to improve life chances (Olumide, 2002; Broyard, 2007). Another form of passing is the passive form where it is others who assign an individual to a 'pure' racial category and is usually experienced as unpleasant pigeon-holing (Olumide, 2002).

Culture, Ethnicity and Race in Psychotherapeutic Literature

I have found an established body of literature within the field of psychotherapy which focuses on cultural/ethnic/racial dimensions of therapeutic work (e.g.: Pedersen, 1987; Eleftheriadou, 1994; Krause, 1998; Palmer & Laungani, 1999; Palmer, 2002; Carter, 2005; Lago, 2006). But although the amount of work in these areas is growing, it seems to me that far more needs to be done to go beyond a largely generalised understanding of the sort of issues that these dimensions might bring up in therapy.

I did not find a great deal of work focusing specifically on mixed-race issues, so I will examine the literature that there is in the subsequent section together with literature from a broader range of fields within the social sciences. Before that, however, I shall discuss a number of areas within a psychotherapeutic context which are pertinent to this research.

Cultural awareness

Awareness that all of us are immersed in a cultural dimension of some kind has long been recognised within the field of cross-cultural counselling as being of paramount importance. Suggestions for modalities which might be most appropriate for cross-cultural or multicultural scenarios share a focus on contextual, environmental and systemic factors and also recognise that some of the most widely established principles of psychotherapy and counselling, such as a non-judgemental attitude and an openness to the client's world view are found to be effective (Rawson et al., 1999; Eleftheriadou, 2002).

Nevertheless, there is research which suggests therapist bias in favour of clients who are more similar to them culturally speaking (Pearce, 2002). Wrenn (1962) coined the term *cultural encapsulation* to describe therapists unable to appreciate that their own cultural bias has a significant impact on the way in which they work with clients.

Lago (2006) argues that a lack of cultural awareness is more of a problem for therapists who have primarily known a mono-cultural context or have lived as part of a majority group. This encourages the sense that one's own perspective is both normative and neutral. Within a Western context, the normality of 'whiteness' causes the white person not even to notice it and so white therapists need to make a special effort to become aware of their 'whiteness' and the impact that it has on others. There also appears to be considerable denial that there is even an issue to examine among white therapists (ibid), and white people generally (Channel 4, 2009b), possibly due to the potentially uncomfortable implications it might bring up.

Lago (2002), citing Katz (1978), proposes the idea of *white awareness*. Lago argues that it is essential for 'white' therapists to become aware of the racial dimension to their existence which bestows on them privilege and power which they might be completely unaware of, in contrast to any 'non-white' client who would be keenly aware of this.

Krause (1998) asserts that therapists need to be wary of essentialising and of viewing clients as cultural/ethnic/racial types. And yet there is considerable debate around the need for *ethnic matching* in psychotherapy, the suggestion being that the best therapist for a client will be someone of the same ethnicity (Rawson et al., 1999). Such a view, Rawson et al. (ibid) argue, stems from concern as to the ability of therapists, mostly of white, middle-class backgrounds to be able to meet the needs of 'ethnic minorities' and also that most 'ethnic minority' clients express a preference for a therapist of the same ethnicity. Once again, such debates appear to be blighted with problems of fixedness, oversimplification and what I would call a kind of 'race fetishism' which persist in a way which cannot be helpful when considering the subtleties around mixed-race issues. Furthermore, the words 'culture' and 'ethnicity' in such discourses appear to be racial euphemisms, since the discourse generally centres on the subject of black versus white.

Mental Health, Culture, Ethnicity and Race

Within psychotherapeutic literature, I found a body of work concerned with mental health issues in relation to matters of culture/ethnicity/race (e.g.: Nazroo, 2000; Fernando, 2002; Eshun & Gurung, 2009; Sewell, 2009). Particularly relevant here was the question of the cultural suitability of models of mental health and mental illness. For example,

Sewell (2009) argues that conceptualisations of mental health and mental illness are culturally dependent and so what may be considered abnormal behaviour in one culture may not be seen so in another. Fernando (2002) argues that this is a significant concern with regard to psychiatry which, due to its dominant status, known as *psychiatric imperialism,* can be used in a far wider set of circumstances than it is perhaps appropriate for. Related to this is the problem that members of 'ethnic minorities' are more likely to be sectioned or otherwise treated as acting abnormally (Sashidharan, 2003).

Eleftheriadou (1999) discusses the psychological issues which may accompany the experience of migration. Issues included guilt at having left home, difficulties in settling into the new country, poverty and social deprivation in the new country, a yearning to return 'home' and the loss and/or guilt which children might feel for not being good enough to keep their parents staying in the new country and then the loss which might be felt on returning 'home' to find that 'home' is very different to how it was remembered.

Laing's existential-phenomenological theories and research regarding ontological insecurity, madness and schizophrenia are pertinent given that Laing emphasises the context-dependent nature of mental illness (Laing, 2010). From Laing's theoretical perspective, it is easy to see how racism and issues around cultural/ethnic/racial identity can have a significant detrimental impact on mental health.

Racism

Dalal (2006) discusses in great detail the psychological processes which need to take place in order for us to develop a view of the world which categorises by race, a process which he describes as *racialization*. Dalal (1997) argues that our racial perceptions are born out of European colonisation around the world when '[c]olour was an important signifier that was used to distinguish the coloniser from the colonised' (Dalal, 1997:203). He argues that this has not only ingrained a firm dichotomy of white as the colonisers and black as the colonised but has consequently embedded the notion of a racial hierarchy with whites at the top and blacks at the bottom. Dalal argues that our internal object world must be *colour-coded* given that we see social objects in the external world in a colour-coded fashion, which we must internalise (Dalal, 1997).

Dalal explains that a child introjects 'a multitude of values and ways of experiencing the world' (1997:204) from the outset via the introjection of aspects of the parents. Since the parents have already been immersed in the world along with its history and social values, it follows that the child's psyche will introject these values. He reminds us of Freud's position that '[t]he child's superego is constructed on the model not of its parents but its parents' superego' (Freud, 2001:67). Or as Fonagy (2001:49) describes: '[for Freud,] morality is tantamount to the internalisation of the child's perception of the parents' value system'.

As a result, Dalal argues, since our society categorises by race and colour, our internal object world must also do so. Therefore, starting from the premise that our internal object world is in some way colour coded, Dalal proposes that a white racial identity involves the introjection of all things white. The superego is white, representing the colour of authority, trustworthiness and sound judgement. In the case of the white racist, by way of projective identification, all undesirable elements of the self are pushed out onto black people. The development of the non-white psyche, on the other hand, while needing to acknowledge the same racial hierarchy, has to come to a different arrangement with regard to its place in that hierarchy. For the non-white, the superego is, nonetheless, still white (Dalal, 1997).

Anthias suggests that the construction of race might link 'ontologically to the wider category of ethnos' (1990:22). From this, I understand that the notion of race must *serve a purpose*, namely, that of creating group identities satisfying the need to belong and the need to exclude in order to reinforce belonging. Dawson et al. (1999:10) describe identity as being formed of both the need for individuality on the one hand and of group belonging on the other. From this viewpoint, racial constructions seem to provide a solution to a fundamental necessity of being.

Identity

Identity development is a key area with regard to mixed-race issues and in relation to psychotherapy, it is worth considering the oft-accepted assumption of a core self (e.g.: Masterson, 1985; Damasio, 2000; Kingsley, 2003; McCormick, 2008). From my own experience, I have been led to question the validity of such an idea and have wondered whether the attempt to find my core self might not *itself* be a problem from a mixed-race perspective. It is useful to turn to existential-phenomenological theory on the self which, as Spinelli (2004) argues, contrasts sharply with the predominant Western view of the self, that it is more or less fixed and provides the source and explanation for our actions. Existential-phenomenological theory argues for the reverse in many respects: that the self is an emergent phenomenon borne of our actions and interactions with the world and that it is fluid and in constant flux (van Deurzen-Smith, 1996; Spinelli, 2004).

A most prominent writer in the field of psychology on the lived experience of a black person living in a colonial context is the psychiatrist and philosopher, Frantz Fanon. Fanon's writings have been described as 'psychopolitics' (Hook, 2004) and considers the external world as an essential part of understanding race and the psychology of racial consciousness (e.g. Fanon, 1986; Fanon, 2004).

Mixed-Race Theory and Research in Social Sciences and in Psychotherapy

Miville has carried out a review of 'biracial' theory and research from 1992 through to 2005 within the social sciences. She concurs with others that little work has been done in this area, and points to 'the sociohistorical context' (Miville, 2005:295) as a key reason for this.

However, since the early 1990s and, in particular, in Root (1992), theory and research have been growing (Miville, 2005).

Miville carried out database searches in the fields of 'psychology, education, sociology/social work, and psychiatry' (2005:295-296) and found in all 'approximately 30 published studies focusing on [biracial issues]' (2005:296). The studies reviewed by Miville were mainly concerned with 'psychological adjustment issues and identity development in biracial people' (ibid) and most employed qualitative methodologies, although more recently there has been an increase in quantitative studies. Acknowledging the benefits and drawbacks of both types of methodology, Miville suggests that for future research more blended methodologies could be used. In examining research results, she notes that common themes include 'ambivalence and fluidity regarding social group and self-definitions, the search for an overarching community, crossing bridges/loosening social boundaries, and transcendence of or use of multiple racial labels as part of one's identity' (Miville, 2005:314). She also believes that qualitative research remains important in order to highlight 'the unique experiences and stories of biracial people' (ibid).

Informed by the last two decades of research, SooJean Choi-Misailidis has proposed a universal framework within which to understand mixed-race identity which she calls Multiracial-Heritage Awareness and Personal Affiliation (M-HAPA). Choi-Misailidis notes that earlier research on mixed-race identity development often concluded that it would always be problematic but that such findings were skewed due to the use of clinical samples. The M-HAPA framework acknowledges an inherent plurality of possible healthy outcomes for identity development and lists the following as actual or hypothesised variables which affect mixed-race identity development: phenotype/appearance, age, name, gender, education level, parents, parents' marital status, extended family and other caregivers, friends and significant others, geographical location, community (Choi-Misailidis, 2010).

Within the field of multi-cultural counselling, some authors touch on mixed-race issues in passing in a rather simplistic way. Rawson et al. focus very briefly on the scenario of: 'African-Caribbean people … intermarrying into the indigenous white British population' (1999:10). Citing Gilroy (1993) they claim that: 'For the growing number of children of mixed origin the experience of belonging to a black identity is a more important feature of their identity than skin colour' (ibid). Quite what is meant by 'belonging to a black identity' is unclear to me. For example, it could be using the term 'a black identity' to mean 'an ethnic-minority identity' or 'an African-Caribbean identity' or 'an immigrant identity'. Furthermore, the statement seems to be a huge generalisation, something which appears to plague the field of cross-cultural counselling.

Eleftheriadou presents a slightly more nuanced account and acknowledges that: 'it is time that [mixed-race] issues were examined more closely' (1999:126) since the number of mixed-race children is increasing (he gives the US context, but as noted above, the trend is also a sharp increase in the UK). Eleftheriadou explains that for mixed-race children the 'ethnic identification process is rather more complicated than children who are brought up in monoracial or monocultural families' (ibid) and that they 'have to integrate two or more racial and cultural backgrounds from birth' (ibid). But again, brevity brings about rather simple generalisations.

More recently, there is much greater recognition of the uniqueness of experience for specifically mixed-race individuals. In Sue and Sue (2008), a chapter is devoted to summarising research findings from social science in which they argue passionately that there is an urgent need for mental health professionals who work with mixed-race people to gain a thorough understanding and awareness of specifically mixed-race issues. For example, they highlight the following: that mental health professionals should examine their own views about race and about racial mixing: advocation of 'an active psychoeducational approach' (2008:402); the value in family counselling; the debunking of stereotypes and myths; the need for 'knowledge of the history and issues related to hypodescent (the one-drop rule), ambiguity (the "What are you?" question), marginality and racial/cultural identity' (2008:403); and other points (Sue and Sue, 2008).

Finally, it is worth stopping to consider the content of Root's *Bill of Rights for Racially Mixed People* (Root, 1996). Sue and Sue describe Maria Root as 'a leading psychologist in the field of multiracial identity and development' (2008:400) and they summarise Root's bill of rights in terms of affirmations and assertions which challenge the status quo, push for a radical upheaval of social sedimentations and resist social forces which would have people with mixed-race identities fragment themselves in order to ease the discomfort of society (Sue and Sue, 2008).

Conclusion

I have found a great deal written about culture/ethnicity/race within the social sciences and there seems to be a general consensus that these are social constructs, reinforced by the mainstream scientific view that there is no correlation between genes and racial categories. Despite this, and despite attempts to use more modern terminologies, the old colonial racial categories still persist and still represent social divisions in society. There appears to be a vicious circle in operation whereby the discriminatory categories are reinforced by the very forces wishing to remove the discrimination.

Within the literature of cross-cultural counselling, the same problem persists and discussions about this are marred by an overly reified attachment to cultural/ethnic/racial constructs. Discussions on mixed-race issues in psychotherapy are often both brief and hampered by over-generalisations and simplifications.

METHODOLOGY

Introduction

Here I will discuss the methodology employed for this research, its characteristics, the reasons for selecting this methodology and the details of its practical application in the current work. Then, I will consider the theoretical assumptions I have made and carry out a critical appraisal of my approach.

The methodology I have employed for this research is Interpretative Phenomenological Analysis (IPA). Firstly, IPA is a qualitative approach as opposed to a quantitative one. The key purpose of a qualitative approach is to explore and reveal deep significance and meaning within the research data with the aim of increasing understanding of lived experience of the selected topic (Moustakas, 1994). Such understandings may be gained through factors which may be unique to individuals. This contrasts with quantitative approaches which are geared towards finding statistically significant factors upon which generalisations and predictions can be made (Langdridge, 2007).

It seems to me that one of the most important factors about mixed-race experiences is the unique nature of each person's experience. I would argue that it is the conflict between society's pull towards racial categorisations and the mixed-race person's unique characteristics which result in a discussion of mixed-race experiences in the first place, rather more than the discussion being one which takes racial categorisations as given with the mixed-race scenario being one where we simply combine or aggregate those racial categorisations.

I believe I have demonstrated in the Literature Review section that the concept of 'race' is one that is phenomenological: if race cannot be explained biologically, it would seem that we need to think about race *as it appears to consciousness*. To grasp the concept of 'race', it seems necessary to consider a combination of a number of factors which are dependent on human interaction, understanding and perception, such as: sociology, politics, history, philosophy, context and psychology. Race resists a definition which falls outside of such human factors and is perceived by people due to a complex interaction of them (Dalal, 2006; Rattansi, 2007; Malik, 2009).

For the reasons of uniqueness of experience and the phenomenological nature of the concept of 'race' outlined above, IPA strikes me as a very suitable methodology, which I will expand on in the sections below. By using IPA, I am setting out to ask questions of my co-researchers which will encourage them to give a rich account of their experience from which I hope to draw out themes both for each co-researcher and across some or all co-researchers in a way that communicates the nature and quality of those accounts. Thus, I am taking the view that to understand the *mixed-race condition* (Olumide, 2002), we need to make an inquiry into what it is like for a person with a mixed-race identity *from the perspective of that person*.

Phenomenological Research

The philosophical foundations of phenomenology

The philosophy of phenomenology was developed at the turn of the twentieth century by Moravian philosopher and mathematician, Edmund Husserl (1859-1938). Husserl (1998) held the view that the scientific community wrongly believed the relation between the world and our perception to be unproblematic and he was concerned with how we arrived at scientific concepts that would become the basis for scientific enquiry. To do this, he believed that it was necessary to understand human experience, consciousness and perception of the world from which the structures of scientific conceptualisations were born. For this reason, Husserl's phenomenology put our consciousness of the world centre stage and from here the *meaning* of scientific concepts could be established. He proposed a number of techniques which were designed to give us a scientific understanding of the world grounded in this philosophical perspective.

If we accept therefore, as Sartre (1985; 1997) explains, that the concept of 'race' is dependent on human perception, then the relevance of phenomenological philosophy to an enquiry into understanding becomes apparent: if we take the view that there is no biological validity to the concept of 'race', it is simply unsafe to enquire about the nature of this concept without understanding that it is a concept borne of the structures of human experience which lead us to see 'races'.

Different strands and evolution of phenomenology

Langdridge (2007) explains that subsequent thinkers developed Husserl's phenomenology along different lines and for different purposes. As a result, not all phenomenological approaches share the same techniques – such as epoché, phenomenological reduction and imaginative variation – to understand experience. Nevertheless, the techniques employed by the various phenomenological approaches all provide various bases for a way of thinking which is different from the everyday way or the natural attitude and all approaches share a fundamental focus on experience.

Husserl developed what is known as *transcendental phenomenology* which was achieved by the phenomenological techniques of *epoché* (or *bracketing*), *description* and *horizontalisation* (Spinelli, 2005). The aim of these techniques was for the practitioner to achieve a suspension of the natural everyday way of perceiving, with all its judgements, prejudices and interpretations, and thus transcend them in order to allow that which is given to perception to be focused on (Zahavi, 2003).

Within the context of the topic of 'race', given that 'race' seems to be entirely grounded in the natural everyday attitude, employing such phenomenological techniques will help us see past the façade of 'race', which blinds us from seeing the specifics of what is before us. In racialised perception we do not see individual idiosyncrasies, but rather generalisations such as 'black', 'white', 'Asian' and so on (Rasalingam, 2009).

I am me: the lived experience of a mixed-race identity
by Haran Rasalingam

With concepts such as the *lifeworld*, our pre-scientific experiencing of the world, it is in the later work of Husserl that the direction of phenomenology can be seen to move towards an understanding of human existence itself (Zahavi, 2003). This is taken up by Husserl's pupil, Martin Heidegger, for whom interpretation was an integral and inseparable part of perception (Heidegger, 2007), and the existential leanings of phenomenology are continued by thinkers such as the French philosophers, Sartre (1943), de Beauvoir (2008) and Merleau-Ponty (2006), and it is in the understanding of human experience, rather than in the philosophical foundations of science, that phenomenological psychology has emerged (Langdridge, 2007).

Existential phenomenologists took issue with Husserl's concept of transcendental phenomenology and rejected the idea that the technique of epoché could enable us to completely suspend the natural attitude and enable us to reach the pure essence of the perceived object of enquiry. Fundamentally, the existential phenomenologists took the view that we are too involved in the world to be able to achieve some kind of neutral position (Sartre, 1943; Merleau-Ponty, 2006). Their approach to the problem was to accept our own interpretation of the world as a necessary and inevitable part of understanding and to *include* it in the analysis (Heidegger, 2007).

For Heidegger (2007), Gadamer (2006) or Ricœur (1997), interpretation was not only an inevitable part of our perception, it was also a necessary part. In accepting this position, it is impossible to adopt the stance of a detached observer trying to understand the object of analysis.   As the analyst, I am inevitably involved: I do not approach the research from a neutral position, but rather, my own understanding of the world cannot be ignored and should be incorporated within an understanding of the research as a whole (Smith et al., 2010).

For Ricœur and Gadamer, the hermeneutic process splits into two broad categories: *empathic hermeneutics* and *hermeneutics of suspicion* (Ricœur, 1977; Gadamer, 2006*)*.   Empathic hermeneutics employs a technique which tries to accept at face value as closely as possible what is being presented.   In terms of research, the researcher strives to gain an understanding of the co-researcher's first-person experience of a phenomenon, to see things from the co-researcher's perspective as much as possible.   Hermeneutics of suspicion attempts to uncover meaning not directly presented (ibid).   Ricœur (1977) found that Marx, Nietzsche and Freud were the three masters of the hermeneutics of suspicion (e.g.: Marx & Engels, 1985; Nietzsche, 1997; Freud, 2001), able to uncover the deeper meaning behind what we do.   By employing the hermeneutics of suspicion in research, we attempt to draw out understandings which are perhaps further from the co-researcher's conscious awareness.

The relevance of phenomenology to psychological research and the relevance of IPA to this particular research

Phenomenology is of particular importance within psychology, the humanities and the social sciences, for it is through phenomenological approaches that we can attend to meaning as experienced by the people who are the subjects of our research (Ashworth, 2006). In order that my research may be of use within the field of psychotherapy, my work needs to communicate successfully to my audience what it is like from a first-person point of view to live with a mixed-race identity.

As I accept interpretation as a fundamental grounding in the understanding of phenomena, I elected to adopt the IPA methodology. Smith (1996), the founder of IPA, originally intended it to be a synthesis of two opposing schools of thought: social cognition and discourse analysis. Within the interview process, I aimed to maintain a focus which would maximise descriptions of lived experience pertinent to the research question, but at the same time my approach was not purely descriptive. For example, my own questions based on personal experience played a part and my own interpretation was a factor. I will say more about this below.

By drawing out themes from the co-researchers' descriptions of their lived experience, IPA tries to access the meaning of that experience. Research conducted using IPA can be described as idiographic because, through deep analysis, the aim is to gain a detailed understanding of the specifics of each participant's lifeworld. Such deep analysis is time-consuming which means that small sample sizes are used – in my case, six participants. The small sample size limits the ability to make large generalisations based on the data analysis, but this is not the aim of an IPA study (Smith & Osborn, 2006).

Research Method

Unlike descriptive phenomenology, which adheres closely to a Husserlian phenomenology, IPA approaches the research from a hermeneutic perspective (Eatough & Smith, 2008). Firstly, IPA takes the position that the researcher is interpreting the data at the same time as interpreting his/her own way of understanding. This is known as a *double hermeneutic* (Giddens, 1987). In the context of this research, it is necessary for me to recognise that I am trying to understand the mixed-race experience of my co-researchers as a mixed-race person myself and all the biases that this brings with it. Secondly, IPA makes use of both empathic hermeneutics and hermeneutics of suspicion and combines them according to the specifics of the research (Langdridge, 2007).

Here, I would like to raise the question of my own unavoidable involvement in the research process, firstly as a researcher with a mixed-race identity myself and secondly as the researcher who will inevitably be impacted by the interviews conducted and by the whole research process in general. In qualitative research, this is known as *reflexivity* (Ashworth, 2006). For example, I am aware that, while I may well find themes which resonate with my own experience, I need to be prepared for the eventuality that the experiences of my co-researchers might well challenge my own beliefs. I will be very interested to see how the interviews with the co-researchers and how the analysis of the research data will affect me, and I will monitor this and take notes. What is both difficult and fascinating about this topic, is that the main concept of the research, namely that of 'mixed race', is impossible to pin down. In carrying out this research, I might conclude, in the extreme case, that the whole concept is completely flawed. It may result in me feeling the need to make major changes to my whole conceptualisation. It could turn out that I come to the conclusion that the life experiences I have had, which I attribute to a mixed-race identity, may have nothing to do with it at all. There is something circular about the concept of race: race exists because people say it does. It is the assumption of race which maintains its existence. Is the conducting of this research itself reinforcing assumptions? Am I creating mixed-race identities by asking who has one? Just in writing this short paragraph, I already find my thoughts turning on themselves and chasing their tails. The circularity and interactivity between myself, the topic and the co-researchers, each feeding off the other with no clear start or end point leave me having no idea where this project will take me!

Recruitment and Selection of Co-Researchers

In keeping with a qualitative approach, my intention was to recruit a small number of co-researchers – between four and six. Keeping to a small number of co-researchers ensures the optimum environment to carrying out a focused and in-depth analysis into the unique story of each co-researcher. My recruitment process was very successful, and I managed to recruit six people in a very short space of time.

Regarding the characteristics of the co-researchers, I was looking for candidates who experience or have experienced a mixed-race identity in some way who were practising therapists, including those in training, and who would thus have had experience of therapy training and of therapy itself both as therapist and client. However, as discussed above, the notion of mixed race is very contextual and subjective. For example, biologically speaking, we can say that everyone is mixed race; or depending on political factors, a person may be considered black or white in one setting but mixed in another. And so, it was not immediately obvious precisely what criteria I could stipulate. What seemed key to me was to bring it back to a person's felt sense of identity, to ensure that it would be possible to study the subject from a lived-experience, and hence phenomenological, point of view. For this reason, the first characteristic of the co-researchers which I was looking for was that they consider *themselves* in some way to have/have had a mixed-race identity. This sense of having a mixed-race identity may have come about for various reasons but is likely to have come about through a combination of self-perception and through the perception of others.

However, I also wondered whether it was important that *I too* perceived a co-researcher as having a mixed-race identity in some way. While the term 'race' can be used in a broad range of ways substituting words such as 'ethnicity', 'cultural background', 'nationality', 'religion' and many more, the likelihood that the perception of others would be a component in giving someone a mixed-race identity increases the likelihood that there would be at least some visual component to this perception combined with an understanding that the co-researcher's parents would look different from each other and perhaps different to the co-researcher. On reflection, however, I feared that such a criterion might be too prescriptive, relying too much on my own assumptions.

Instead, what seemed inevitable was that the question of mixed race would need to be an *issue* for the co-researchers to some extent. Otherwise it would be hard to imagine them coming forward to participate at all. Firstly, such a criterion would distinguish between, on the one hand, all of us as a mix biologically speaking and, on the other, those for whom their particular mix made them *feel* like a mix rather than not, thus leading to a sense of identity in which mixedness played a part. Secondly, without the question of mixed race being an issue, I would theoretically be in the absurd position of trying to convince someone that he/she were mixed race and that he/she should think about it and reflect on his/her identity in the light of it! This therefore means that this research must inevitably involve people for whom a mixed-race identity is not something that just blends unnoticed into the background of their lives. One could argue, in fact, that the very definition of mixed race is that one does not blend in racially speaking.

Two of my co-researchers were therapists with whom I was already loosely acquainted and whom I recruited by word of mouth, one of whom I had met at a psychotherapeutic event and one who contacted me having heard through a colleague about my research. In order to recruit more, I advertised on the noticeboard within my own college and also via an e-mail newsletter of a society for ethnic minority therapists in the UK. The response to the e-mail newsletter was very fast and I received four enquiries within a few days of advertising. All of these enquiries led to the enquirers becoming co-researchers.

Demographically speaking, then, my co-researchers were fairly random, although I recognise that there was a bias in my recruiting some people who had subscribed to a newsletter for a society of therapists with particular demographics. In terms of age, all co-researchers were born before 1980, which means that their stories were all linked to a time in history which may be less applicable to younger generations and also five of the six co-researchers were female, and one was male. However, since the nature of this research does not pretend to make predictive generalisations about anyone defined as mixed race in some objective sense, I was satisfied that I had a group of co-researchers with whom I could carry out research for my particular investigation.

A short description of each of the six co-researchers is given below. In the interests of confidentiality, I have preserved anonymity in this study by substituting the names of all co-researchers (CR) with CR1, CR2, and so on up to CR6. All co-researchers who were interviewed were practising or trainee psychotherapists/counsellors in the UK who self-identified as mixed race:

- CR1 is a psychotherapist in her early thirties. Her mother is black, from Jamaica, but grew up in the UK in care and was fostered by a white family. CR1's father is white British. Her parents separated while CR1 was a child and CR1 grew up with her mother, although now she lives with her father. CR1 describes herself sometimes as black, sometimes as mixed race, sometimes as human race, but never as white. Visually, one can see CR1's black heritage and it is possible to speculate that she is mixed race on account of her being quite fair skinned.

- CR2 is a psychotherapist in her early forties. She grew up in the UK with her white English mother. Her father was a black from a country in west Africa. CR2's parents separated when CR2 was very young after which she had almost no contact with her father. CR2 describes herself as being of dual heritage. Visually, one can see CR2's black heritage and it is possible to speculate that she is mixed race on account of her being quite fair skinned and the curls in her hair are quite loose.

- CR3 is a trainee psychotherapist in his late thirties. CR3 never knew his biological father with whom his mother had had a one-night stand. He describes his mother as white English, but he does not know the cultural, ethnic or racial background of his father and speculates that he might be Mediterranean, Middle Eastern or north Indian. CR3 describes himself as culturally white mixed race. CR3 says he was darker skinned as a child and now he has slightly tanned skin which leads people to speculate that he might not be English.

- CR4 is a trainee psychotherapist in her late thirties. She describes her father as a Sephardi Jew of Persian-Indian origin and her mother as an Ashkenazi Jew of East European-Swedish origin. CR4's parents separated while she was in her teens after which she spent most time with her mother. CR4 feels a much closer affinity to the Ashkenazi side of her heritage and she describes herself first and foremost as Jewish. Visually, CR4 says she was darker skinned when younger and now considers herself 'white, but only just'.

- CR5 is a psychotherapist in her early thirties. She grew up in Spain with her white Spanish mother and her black Nigerian father. Her parents separated while she was in her teens. Culturally, CR5 feels far more European than African. Visually, CR5 is fair skinned with frizzy light-brown hair and she points out that both her hair and her skin have fluctuated in colour over the years. She is generally considered to look unusual.

- CR6 is a psychotherapist in her early fifties and grew up in Malaysia. She describes her mother as white English and her father as Malay. CR6's parents divorced when she was ten, after which she grew up with her father and her half-Chinese, half-Indian-Muslim stepmother. In CR6's family, marrying people from other cultures is very common. Visually, CR6 says she was always taller than other Malaysians, but it is possible to speculate that CR6 has some East Asian or South-East Asian ancestry, due perhaps to her eyes, nose and hair.

Data Collection

There is no hard and fast rule about data collection in phenomenological research as its very philosophy requires that adaptability to the specifics of the subject matter be necessary (Spinelli, 2005). However, as is often the case with IPA, the data was gathered through semi-structured interviews (Reid et al., 2005). The reason for this was to attempt to find a balance between, on the one hand, allowing co-researchers to speak freely and describe their experience without being channelled into any preconceived theoretical framework and, on the other hand, remaining focused on the subject of the research by asking questions as openly as possible that I judged would increase the chance that the data collected would be related to the research question.

By choosing a semi-structured approach in my interviews, I am immediately declaring that I do not come from a neutral position. My questions originate from my own experience of living a mixed-race identity and the issues which this has brought up for me. The way in which the questions were framed however was designed to avoid as much as possible the incorporation of what perhaps my answers and conclusions would be.

To take one example, I have a large degree of scepticism about the concept of 'race' and thus this prompts me to want to find out what my co-researchers think of the concept. To ask this in a way which loads the question towards my view of it would be something like: 'In what ways do you find the concept of "race" problematic if at all?' If the question were phrased in this way, it would be a token gesture towards the idea of an open question, since I am already planting the seed of race being a problem concept. Instead, the question I ended up with was, I think, far less loaded: 'What does the word "race" mean to you?' This way of framing the question invites the co-researcher to start from a clean slate, as it were, with regards to how s/he might want to describe his/her thoughts on this. At the same time, it would be wrong to pretend that the question is entirely neutral. The very act of asking this question subtly calls the word 'race' into question as something that cannot be taken for granted.

Ethical Considerations

In any research which deals with the life experiences and personal and private matters of individuals, the establishment of clear ethical guidelines around confidentiality and informed consent are essential (Gregory, 2003; Israel & Hay, 2006; Oliver, 2010). In the context of the present study, the co-researchers' material was intimately connected with their private family lives on very sensitive and delicate topics which were in many cases connected with emotions of shame, anger or resentment and were often issues of conflict within the families in question. This indicated to me the need for confidentiality and the protection of identity when publishing any details of the co-researchers' stories. Additionally, it was important to hide the identity of any other people in the stories of the co-researchers such as ex-partners, therapists and so on.

The greatest difficulty in concealing identity was in terms of geography which is a significant factor in the mixed-race stories of my co-researchers while at the same time providing a clue to identity which could compromise confidentiality. I took the decision to hide any reference in the co-researchers' material to cities, regional areas or institutions and to restrict geographical descriptions to a country level and in some cases, even a continental level.

Informed consent refers to the idea of co-researchers not only agreeing to participating, but also to understanding just what it is they are agreeing to (Israel & Hay, 2006). Co-researchers needed to be fully aware of the nature of the research and the likelihood that we would probe into intimate details of their lives. This in turn could lead to stirring up emotions which may have been lying dormant, it could cause the co-researchers to have unexpected revelations, to re-evaluate core parts of their understanding of themselves, their loved ones, their place in the world, their upbringing and overall life history. Such issues had the potential to be of great significance and possibly cause discomfort and unhappiness both in the short and the long term.

Given that it is impossible to know if and when such problems could arise for the co-researchers, it was important to make clear that they were entitled to pull out of the research any time up until its final submission. In addition to this, I also offered support if required in the form of possible reading which co-researchers could find beneficial and the option of being referred by me to a counsellor or therapist.

Interview Analysis

The approach I took to analysing the data collected from the interviews was based on that described by a number of authors, such as Colaizzi (1979), Moustakas (1994) or McLeod (2001), which is essentially a question of discovering and drawing out key themes in the data. To do this, I needed to read and re-read the transcripts in order to become familiar with them and try to make summarised notes and tried to stay quite closely descriptive and minimised remarks which were more interpretative.

Then I brought these descriptive notes together under emergent themes, making bolder statements of interpretation and meaning which seemed to me to be more significant from a theoretical perspective. This stage was followed by an organising and regrouping of these themes into a more ordered and structured set of theoretical topics and sub-topics, a task aided by my continual return to the original data. Finally, I created a coherent table of themes each referenced back to specific quotes in the transcripts. This process can be carried out on one transcript at a time or on all transcripts in parallel, although it is important to be flexible as one may need to go back and rework some of the themes built up in light of later analysis and so forth. Personally, I read through all the transcripts twice to gain a strong overview, before proceeding to analyse each in turn gradually building an emerging list of themes which were reinforced, broadened or narrowed as I went along.

Issues of Validity

There are varying perspectives on the importance of validity in qualitative research, what constitutes a good qualitative study and how this can be evaluated (Creswell, 2007; Silverman, 2010). The current focus on validity in qualitative research is in part due to the fact that, compared to quantitative methods, qualitative research within the field of psychology is relatively new and also there is such a diversity of methodologies which come under the general qualitative umbrella that this presents challenges in formulating consistent and coherent criteria (Smith et al., 2010).

Here, I shall discuss briefly the guidelines for assessing the validity of qualitative research proposed by some authors. Polkinghorne (1989) suggests that qualitative researchers should consider a set of five questions of themselves in carrying out the research to determine the degree of validity in their findings. These five questions appear to serve as useful reminders to the researcher to avoid veering away from the data presented while at the same time ensuring that findings can be applicable beyond the specifics of that data. Moustakas (1994) gives an example of a researcher sending his findings to the co-researchers to examine their accuracy, while Giorgi argues that 'phenomenological qualitative research is closer to experimental situations and so the validity issue is not as pressing as is often supposed' (2002:1). The philosophy underpinning these guidelines, however, is Husserlian phenomenology and so they may have more suitability for descriptive approaches, than interpretative ones. For example, from an interpretative phenomenological standpoint, Polkinghorne's guidelines appear to rely on an inherent subjectivity and interpretation which is not accounted for by means of acknowledgement of where the subjectivity and interpretation are coming from, while Moustakas's idea of gaining confirmation of validity from the co-researchers themselves does not allow for hermeneutics of suspicion.

Instead, guidelines proposed by Elliott et al. (1999, cited in Smith, 2006) and Yardley (2000, cited in Smith, 2006 and Langdridge, 2007) represent 'a new maturity … for assessing the quality of qualitative psychological research' (Smith, 2006:232), and which may be more suitable for IPA studies as they appear to recognise the researcher's own interpretations as a continual factor rather better as there is an emphasis on showing the researcher's own process in relation to the research.

Another way of assessing validity is by following the principle of independent audit (Yin 1989, cited in Smith et al., 2010), which is considered to be 'a really powerful way of thinking about validity in qualitative research' (Smith et al., 2010:183). This way of thinking about validity seems to have similarities with Yardley's ideas around transparency and coherence in that the aim is that the reader should be able to follow the journey which the researcher has taken in carrying out the study.

Here, I will outline Yardley's guidelines in a little more detail. Yardley identifies four areas of concern for assessing the validity of qualitative work: i) sensitivity to context; ii) commitment and rigour; iii) transparency and coherence; and iv) impact and importance. I shall look at each of these in turn in relation to the current study (Yardley, 2002).

Sensitivity to context refers to the many possible ways in which a researcher shows an awareness of where his/her study and his/her co-researchers are situated in place and time, for example, sociologically, politically or personally. So for example, I hope that I will be able to show that the current study is relevant within the field of psychotherapy at the present time with the current knowledge and understanding around identity, race, ethnicity and culture within psychotherapy, thus demonstrating an awareness of the current context and how this study might augment in some way the knowledge that is currently there. Also, I hope that this study shows a sensitivity to my co-researchers in terms of understanding their stories from within the context in which they have found themselves historically, linguistically, politically, sociologically and geographically.

Commitment and rigour refer to a sense of taking the work seriously; treating co-researchers and their stories with deep respect and attention; skilful, sustained, systematic and complete analysis; and a clear and maintained focus and relevance to the research question. In this research, I hope to show these qualities, but as an inexperienced researcher, I think the question of skill and achieving a complete analysis are the greatest challenges here.

Transparency and coherence in a research study will ensure that the reader can fully see the development and evolution of the study from its inception to its conclusion all the while being able to follow a consistent, logical argument which is laid out clearly and concisely. For this study, then, the reader should be left in no doubt as to the issue which I am trying to address and be able to clearly see how my findings and conclusions follow from my interpretation of the data.

Impact and importance mean that the study should be engaging, interesting, relevant and informative. It is my task to grab the reader's attention and make him/her aware of the significance of the topic and to take him/her along with me on my research journey.

Conclusion

The method of research analysis used in this study was interpretative phenomenological analysis (IPA) which was originally considered to be an attempt to bridge the gap between quantitative and qualitative paradigms within the field of psychology, with social cognition and discourse analysis being the extreme polar opposites to bridge (Smith, 1996).

Unlike descriptive phenomenological approaches, which subscribe to a Husserlian idea that interpretation can be transcended to reach an objective understanding of the thing in itself (Zahavi, 2003), IPA follows the philosophy of later phenomenologists, such as Heidegger (2007) or Merleau-Ponty (2006), and recognises that, although the interpretations of the researcher complicate the process, interpretation is nevertheless a fundamental necessity in order to gain an understanding of that which is being researched.

INTERVIEW: Which side of the fence?

"...people were always kind of trying to decipher which side of the fence you sat on."

About Co-Researcher #1

Co-Researcher #1 (CR1) is a psychotherapist in her early thirties. Her mother is black, from Jamaica, but grew up in the UK in care and was fostered by a white family. CR1's father is white British. Her parents separated while CR1 was a child and CR1 grew up with her mother, although now she lives with her father. CR1 describes herself sometimes as black, sometimes as mixed race, sometimes as human race, but never as white. Visually, one can see CR1's black heritage and it is possible to speculate that she is mixed race on account of her being quite fair skinned.

Research interview with Co-Researcher #1

[I = Interviewer; CR1 = Co-Researcher #1]

1. I: Right here we go, so I'm gonna ask first how would you describe your family background, your family history?

2. CR1:   Hmm I always think that my family history is quite complex, and I think that maybe everybody else thinks that theirs is complex too? My mum's black, born here, my dad's white, born here, my mum's first generation born here, from like the Windrush ... she was a twin,

however her mum had children back in Jamaica that she still had to support and when she came here I think she couldn't support them so she put them into a home ... so they grew up in – I think they were like the first black kids in a home, so they grew up in a Doctor Barnardo's home, so they were like the first kids, you know like black hair ... my mum never knew how to comb her hair, she never experienced – you know all those kind of cultural things that get handed down, she kind of never had that. So, yeah, so my Dad's .... sister fostered my Mum when she was like 16 and that's how my Mum and my Dad met.

3.   CR1:   Yeah, so my Dad grew up in *[place in England]* and he was exposed to a lot of black people because after the war, black people were, you know, coming to work the buses and so on and so forth, but I think, kind of what I've read from "Small Island" and "the Windrush" by Trevor Philips was like the first generation were quite middle class erm Caribbeans, so it was kind of the people who could afford to come came, and so I think my dad grew up with the concept that he always thought that the black people were better than them? Because of how they kind of did things ... and erm I think he was surprised that people kind of looked down upon them and criticised them ... and whether that's because of the class thing at the time ... you know this is my kind of turn on it ... that the people

were probably better off and maybe did things in a different way to how my Dad had been used to.

4.   Erm, so I think that's where my Dad kind of got his er flavour for black women? Because he was exposed ... I think he used to hang ... go to the other they lived in those called sort of storey houses, flats top middle bottom they had all rooms and I think my dad spent a lot of time with the black families they'd take him in, so ... yeah, so I kind of .... because ... because my other Auntie, she had – my Dad's sister – she also had a black partner, too, so I don't have any white cousins? Does that make sense? It was a sister and a brother and they both had black partners, yeah, so, in terms of white cousins, I don't have any. Yeah so, I think it's quite ... quite ... odd in a way and I think for me as well, because my Mum's black, whereas most, usually it's a black Dad and a white Mum?

5.   I: Right, whereas this is the other way round ... and that's unusual ...

6.   CR1:   Yeah, and a lot of people, well I regard myself as black ... often people regard me as black because I date black men, erm, so, I think they often ... think ...: *(whispers)* "Oh yeah well she's a bit like that because she's got a black Mum!"

7.   So, because I have a black Mum, it's kind of like: well that's why you've kind of gone on that side of the fence? Because I've got a black Mum ... something about that ...

I am me: the lived experience of a mixed-race identity
by Haran Rasalingam

but I have a brother as well who had a white partner and people often – I guess like where we grew up – see there's also like a class thing, too, so my Dad lived in *[place in England]*, all my life he's always lived in *[place in England]*, and I grew up with my Mum in an estate next to *[large store]*.

8. I: So, you didn't grow up with your Dad.

9. CR1: No … no, so I think on the estate I don't think there was many mixed-race kids and then people were always kind of trying to decipher which side of the fence you sat on: whether you was white or you was on the black side and … I guess, while I was growing up as well, my Mum began to … find her black identity and …

10. I: Did you feel that you had to decide on one side of the fence or the other?

11. CR1: Yeah, definitely, in my teenage years … most definitely … definitely … yeah … and I think it was more so at high school – I kind of had a few Asian friends … I don't think I had a lot of white friends, I don't think there was a lot of white kids in the area, actually, probably that whole white feel frightened of everyone, so there wasn't that much white kids, but I think … I don't know when … but I kind of knew that I had decipher like, you know, where I … er … where I anchored myself really.

12. I: So, you felt that you had to 'anchor' yourself ... do you know when you decided that?

13. CR1: *(thinks)* You see, also what happened was, whilst my Mum was discovering her blackness ... what that meant for her, she started to go back to Jamaica to find out where she came from ... so then she'd start sending me there, too, in the summer ... so I think, for me, what also happened was ... or what I realised was that in Jamaica it didn't matter whether you listened to Celine Dion or Michael Bolton ... you're still, like, black or you're still Jamaican. Whereas where I grew up in *[council estate]*, people would regard you as, like: "you don't listen to that and be black" because black people don't listen to that, you listen to hip-hop, rap, you know ... so it was quite perplexing going to the Caribbean and, you know, people openly listened to pop music and there was no deal about it.

14.   Cos, I like did it in secret *(laughs)*

15.   Yeah so I found that quite erm I don't know it was quite freeing and perplexing because I guess they didn't have all that: "you do this, this is what you do", you know, they're they're freer, they seem freer ... to me ... doesn't mean they're less black, less Jamaican, they don't seem to define themselves as such

I am me: the lived experience of a mixed-race identity
by Haran Rasalingam

16. I: And how did that impact on you then when say you came back to England after experiencing that in Jamaica?

17. CR1:   You know what I think for them they say what they see, you know, so, if you're black you're black, if you're brown you're brown and erm I kind of really valued that and erm I don't know, I guess, erm, I guess people felt more …. I think ... I dunno it kind of just got soaked into my bones and I always loved it out there, so I kind of felt more – and I guess that would probably push people to more be inclined to think that I am black anyway

18. I: Because you identified more with that attitude maybe?

19. CR1:   Well, because I'd kind of been to the Caribbean and I got into the Jamaica thing, so erm … but yeah, it did throw up more kind of contradictions if I could openly listen to Celine Dion, because, you know, being black ... I guess where I grew up in the estate ... that wasn't regarded- that's not what we do as such ... we do the stereotypical thing. So, it was a little bit ... I guess throughout my teenage years ... I guess I guess it probably just meant more and more so that I pull onto the black side

20. I: And did pulling over to the black side or anchoring yourself in the black side, did that always make things easier or did it also come with a downside as well?

21. CR1:   I think, historically, there may be the odd few people who were a bit ... I dunno ... I guess my Dad was white and I

guess he was one of the Dads who came round he came every Sunday for us, a lot of the other kids on the estate didn't see their Dads ... what was the question again?

22. I: Erm you said you sort of anchored yourself on the black side and you kind of soaked up the black experience and you sort of saw yourself as black: did that always make life easier for you or did it also have a down side as well?

23. CR1: I think overall it made things easier, but also, I fell into stereotypical rôles, so I didn't do particularly well at school and erm I had children young ... I've got two kids ... not that young, twenty, but I had no kind of plan career wise ... so I kind of erm I kind of hit rock bottom with my kids and I thought "flippin' hell, if I don't fix up I'm gonna be like this for the rest of my life". I knew I had to sort myself out.

24. I: So, you felt it was a black stereotype to have kids early and to not do well at school.

25. CR1: Yeah, I had no ambition, I was listening to the radio the other day ... what's his name?   ... *[name of radio presenter]* ... and they were bringing up the thing about young teenage pregnancies ... and the woman phoned in to say you know I'm so glad that you're not focusing on people getting pregnant young for a council house, because there is the fact that you don't have low expectations for yourself low self-esteem and I think kind

of growing up where I've grown up erm I dunno, boys tended to get in trouble and the girls got pregnant ... and I don't remember having any ... I went to college after that and I did apply for uni, but I didn't really know what I was good at ... I know I enjoyed human resources erm, but I didn't really I guess I you know you find it difficult you grow up on an estate erm and I think I absorbed the kind of- all the negativity around that as well and I think my Mum was also trying to fit herself into what she believed was what black people do, cos she's got her own stuff going on ... you know she'd grown up in care ... brought up by white people

26. I: Do you mind me asking you when you were born?

27. CR1: Seventy-seven ... I'm thirty-two

28. I: Right, OK so you were growing up late seventies ... up-

29. CR1: Well, I guess I'm more like eighties really, aren't I?

30. I: OK, the eighties is your ... sort of ... key ... key period

31. CR1: Yeah ... yeah

32. I: So, what was growing up like? I mean you told me that you saw your father ...

33. CR1: We saw him once a week

34. I: What was it like in terms of parents, in terms of school, all of this ... friends?

35. CR1: Well I guess the class thing also happened because my Dad lived in *[place in England]* ... you know he had the

big house, the kids went to the good school they had a nice whole life going on and erm I guess I didn't … you know … living with my Mum … she was more interested in finding black culture now so like the whole thing was like "Black Culture", so she had like black boyfriends now, the boyfriend she had he used to then beat her up so she went through a kind of- I think she was more interested in trying to find out her identity and then making herself fit because people then found her odd because well I don't think they could work her out … she was particularly well spoken … I guess she had had a middle-class upbringing in the care system erm so I guess for me it was all a bit weird and I guess I was an overweight kid, too, so my sister, by my Dad, she was kind of like a Bonnie Langford type of girl dancing and stuff so I think I was all in awe of her erm

36.   I: Did he *(the father)* marry, did he get together with a black person?

37.   CR1:   Mixed race … she *(the father's new partner)* was mixed race … she was from a home as well … he was churning them out, but she's clueless about her identity, she regards herself as a coconut and she's quite happy to regard herself, my sibling's Mum regards herself as a coconut …

38.   I: And how do you regard yourself now?

39.   CR1:   Well erm it's a very hot topic and I recently had an argument with my sister about it, actually, and she told me

that I wasn't black, and I flipped because there's something about somebody telling me who they think I am ... I can't be dealing with I'm not having it ... it really does ... I was listening, you know I don't get the time to read so much, I drive everywhere so I bought Obama's erm his second book ... *The Audacity of Hope* that's the audio one I'm listening to at the moment and at the beginning he defined himself as: "I'm a black man with mixed-race heritage" ... and you know what? I thought: that's it, I like that, yeah, I like that ... I can work with that ... I don't feel like I ignore my white heritage ... I guess I live in England, it feels like it's the default here ... do you know what I mean?

40. I: Yeah

41. CR1:   Erm ... but ... I don't feel like it's something that I have to research or be conscious of or aware of ... I think that – no matter what – whether you're mixed, whether you want to call yourself white or- I guess it depends as well because "mixed" can mean so many different things, like I think you said that you're mixed as well

42. I: That's right

43. CR1:   Yeah, but I guess, like, for myself ... I think you could either for me like my Mum always brought us up and told us we were black kids, but it's like you could either define

yourself as mixed race or black, but you can't define yourself as white

44. I: You can't

45. CR1:   You can't, so you can jump between the two, you can call yourself black – which people will challenge you about that, why you would call yourself black-

46. I: And you have been challenged?

47. CR1:   Oh yes

48. I: Well, your sister, in fact!

49. CR1:   Yeah, definitely, and I guess she wasn't very tactful about it, so it ended up being an argument

50. I: But you could never be called white, see that's one of my questions: I wonder why that is?

51. CR1:   Mmm

52. I: Why is that?

53. CR1:   Well, because you don't look like that ... right? No? I don't know, maybe with you ... I don't know, you look more Asian ... you look Asian ... I don't know if you're Asian and black, I don't know ...

54. I: Yeah, my Mum's English, my Dad is Sri Lankan, so yeah ...

55. CR1:   Yeah, I guess it's about whether you could- you have a look and you could get away with calling yourself white? I met a – you know I work in a prison and erm I'm always encouraging myself to be open all the time cos people

I am me: the lived experience of a mixed-race identity
by Haran Rasalingam

always say things that you know you still don't want to it happens to all of us and this guy looked white and so he was ticking the diversity box and he said I'm mixed race and I thought oh and he said yeah my Mum's black, she's light-skinned and he didn't look it and I thought that's interesting because he could have said obviously he could have said white - anybody could say white a black man could say white if he wants – erm and I just thought that's interesting but I don't know if there's very few mixed-race people who could say white and get away with it

56. I: or maybe you wouldn't know

57. CR1:   if they were, but then maybe if it was a mixed-race person who say white and they openly look mixed I guess for me I'd wonder what's going on with their cultural identity

58. I: so, for example, if you're sister said "I'm white"

59. CR1:   she is white to me

60. I: she is white to you

61. CR1:   her Mum's mixed and her Dad's white

62. I: right sorry – because she's a half-sister basically, in a sense

63. CR1:   but there's all this three quarter...

64. I: but what about one of your cousins? What if one of your cousins said, "I'm white"? What would you say to that? What would you think? Would it be crazy?

65. CR1: Of course! Listen you could either call yourself mixed or could call yourself black – you might get more challenged with that people might be more happy with medium ground of that you know the middle ground, mixed but imagine if you're calling yourself white there's something you're not facing up to then

66. I: so, there's something about your look which means that you can qualify as black but not as white

67. CR1: you know what I don't even know I don't even think I've pondered that like could I ever call myself white? No.

68. I: just instinctively it's a no

69. CR1: how? Never! I have never. I've got white family and my Dad's white and you know I guess even my Mum now, because my Mum's still living in a separate house and she's had some I guess I don't fit stereotypes anymore she's become a little bit more like you're a bit more white now because you've done a degree and everything else

70. I: so, doing a degree makes you more white

71. CR1: yeah because of the things I come out with now so I challenge my Mum about some of the nonsense she talks about and my Auntie is a therapist as well so kind of my Mum's a lorry driver they grew up together but one went on to be a therapist and my Mum's a lorry driver so I think my Mum thinks that I've become more like my Auntie now … my Auntie dates white men and I think my Mum

has a stereotype that once you start using long words and stuff once you're educated that you're more white because she's tried to make herself and she knows better but because she's tried to fit herself into a narrow mould of what it is to be black because she so wanted to be in with the community she's narrowed herself down so sometimes she jars me

72. I: so, there's something there about being black in England is totally different to being black in Jamaica you know in Jamaica you can listen to Michael Bolton you can do that whereas here you have to kind of make yourself black

73. CR1: I think it's more it's like certain terms don't really exist in Jamaica and when I hear Jamaican people saying it here that word ... HC ... it don't sound right because you don't say that back home. That is a word that you have here. When you're home you say it as you see it, people don't have those terms

74. I: what would they say?

75. CR1: brown, you're brown

76. I: so, it's just a description of skin tone

77. CR1: yeah, I think they say: "you fat brownin'" that's it they keep it simple you know so they have these er words that ... you know like they don't have those words that you can dice it what does that mean? What do those words

mean? They don't have that, there's no kind of bottled language

78. I: yes, what you see is what you get kind of thing basically

79. CR1: yeah so you know it doesn't it's not people just it's not such a deal

80. I: it's like it's not so politicised, in a way it's not political … it's just your skin colour

81. CR1: yeah but then there is the whole thing there because there was, I guess, slavery … you know they do have erm you know even today a man was saying it's because your colour is high that's why

82. I: and what does that mean?

83. CR1: cos I'm fair skinned like that we don't do those sort of things

84. I: oh, high as in high status?

85. CR1: yeah and that's because in Caribbean light-skinned people are seen as a higher status so years back they used to be like …

86. I: so that kind of thing is still ingrained a little bit

87. CR1: it's still there but it's getting better it is still definitely part of the fabric most definitely and I had to say he said it in jest but I had to say to him by telling me that are you trying to say that my Mum's colour is low? You're calling me high er you know it's … you know … good hair all that kind of stuff

88. I: good hair ... so what constitutes good hair?

89. CR1:   being mixed because it's not so Afro it's less the curls are less tighter it's wavy ... you can wash and go you don't have to perm it you don't have to straighten it, so it's regarded as good hair

90.   So I've had my children with a black man so my daughter's hair one of my daughter's hair is more Afro and one is a little bit more like mine so the one with more Afro was talking yesterday cos she's always careful around me she knows I'm gonna start on her and then she's like "yeah Mum my other friend her hair's better than mine" and I looked at her and I thought what do you mean "better"? And she was like "it's just, you know ... it's just longer ... and straighter ..." and I thought it's so ... there

91. I: Everywhere you go

92. CR1:   it's still there and I know she's asked for little pieces in her hair as well like you can buy false pieces to clip on erm I've let her have them a couple of times but within myself I thinking am I teaching her not to value you know what she's got naturally? This western ... erm ... perception of beauty ... you know that whole thing ... I don't know

93. I: and when you say "that western perception of beauty" do
             you ever feel that you're kind of er affected by that as
             well?

94. CR1:   well I guess I guess you know what I think more so I guess
             because I was always overweight that kind of that took
             precedence so I've got other friends who are my skin tone
             who like *[name of friend]* whenever we would go out
             together and she'd go *(whispers)* "have you noticed?
             We're the only light-skinned girls in here" ... I mean I've
             never noticed ... like if we go to a club and there's a lot of
             dark-skinned people- see I've never noticed but she'd
             always notice that we be like the light-skinned girls there
             ... but I guess I was always – growing up – I was always
             overweight, so I don't think I ever got caught up in the
             whole light-skinned dark-skinned thing I think I was
             always more conscious of being overweight

95. I: right, so your skin tone was a secondary issue sort of thing,
             was it?

96. CR1:   yeah because I guess the boys on my estate weren't
             interested if you were fat anyway ... whether I was light-
             skinned or not but when I went to the Caribbean being
             light-skinned was like a flippin' erm like a trophy! I never
             had so much- I mean I always had- you know, you're
             foreign as well so that- there's a whole different kind of
             value system there as well- the get-out ticket but I never

been used to that at all because I was always fat … so the boys weren't interested but in the Caribbean … different kettle of fish! so yeah that was all in there, so it was kind of … I don't know cos I guess I've got a sister who kind of fits that model like my half-sister this western perception blonde and erm … I don't know I don't know I don't think I've ever got too caught up in that to be honest … yeah, I've never particularly felt I guess I've always kind of tried to focus on my own weight really

97.   I: OK … so in terms of your looks and things that's always been a more important thing for you than worrying about … sort of skin colour and things like that

98.   CR1:   yeah definitely

99.   I: I've gotta slightly try and move on now ….

100. CR1:   no worries!

101. I: I mean you said erm that you "anchored" yourself in the black … so as an adult is it still quite firmly so? … how do you see yourself now?

102. CR1:   It's so context based. Because I can go back- so my children I teach them cos I live now with my Dad in *[place in England]* with my kids

103. I: oh, you live with your dad now?

104. CR1:   now – yeah with my kids erm I'm on my own so I always so you know I mean *[place in England]* was a well white area but now it's more Asian I think the white folks are

going again because when I look at my daughter's school photo there ain't a lot of white kids left so I don't know where they go next, but they're leaving *[place in England]* … so now when I tell 'em you know you know you're Jamaican heritage as well I let them know that you're black kids I don't I don't if you call yourself mixed race I don't know whether I confuse them I probably do but you're a black child … yes you're mixed race, your granddad's white your grandad picks you up from school erm so I don't know whether I'm still protecting them too by telling them that they're black but if they wanna call themselves mixed race that's cool … so- see, there's something about the hair as well they have to have their hair canerowed so whereas my hair didn't necessarily have to be canerowed as a kid … well it always was because my mum couldn't canerow my hair she just grew up with black hair but my children's hair needs to be canerowed … what was the question again?

105. I: how do you see yourself … your ethnic identity now?

106. CR1: so it's context-based cos I teach my children that … our Jamaican heritage ... but when we go to Jamaica I watch my daughter tell a woman "I'm Jamaican" and the Jamaican waitress says "you're not Jamaican, you're English" so my daughter's looking at me like: "bloody 'ell, woman! What are you doing?"

I am me: the lived experience of a mixed-race identity
by Haran Rasalingam

107. I: so, when you say it's "context-based", in Jamaica you're English

108. CR1:   exactly so- but I had to talk to the waitress and had to say to her you know as black people in England you have to instil in your children their cultural identity so that's why my daughter will say she's Jamaican she's of Jamaican heritage because it's important that the kids know that … you know … and so … I mean … it depends … if I go to join a gym and, on the application, they ask … I might not even tick a box I might put human species

109. I: Really? And why would you do that?

110. CR1:   because like I feel freer … because like in the gym they're not gonna refuse me membership, but if it's an application form for work, I might tick … I don't know … I'll probably tick … mixed … Caribbean … depending on my mood … or I might tick black … depending on how I'm feeling … sometimes I might tick mixed because I might be of the view that I might because also there is that other stereotype or this myth that mixed-race people are also more likely to progress … they're more palatable, they're more acceptable to white society

111. I: so, you might have a better chance of getting the job?

112. CR1:   sometimes, maybe, yep, so I'll be mindful to tick it there which feels a little bit like … hypocritical … but I'm mindful of that often, but what does that mean?

Sometimes when you explore it you can think shit ... that sounds shit, but sometimes you know ... so it does depend on the context ... if I'm thinking about box-ticking but I think once I'm there you know ... like ... working for the probation ... so even things like having my radio ... I was conscious of which station I had it on ... I'll keep it on *[mainstream radio station]*, but really and truly, I wanna listen to some pirates ... because that's what I usually listen to ... but you know ... how well's that gonna go down?

113. I: right ... so there's a sense of – in some contexts – hiding your blackness

114. CR1:   yeah definitely which makes me feel like ... erm ... like a bit of a pussy really ... sorry ... you know ... like a bit of a ... you know ... like when is the truth self gonna stand up ... do you know what I mean?

115. I: yeah, sort of "why am I hiding? why am I hiding?"

116. CR1:   but the BBC have One Extra - I don't know if you know this - but I feel like I can play that because like- everybody comes in and they're like what's that? It's the BBC, it's One Extra, it's legal!

117. I: so, it's weird isn't it, on the council estate you had to hide the Bros music whereas in the workplace you have to hide the pirate stations

118. CR1:   yeah … I mean erm I don't know if you've heard of Colin Lago ... he's got a very good piece in "Politicising the person-centred approach" *(Politicizing the Person-centred Approach: An Agenda for Social Change. Proctor, Cooper, Sanders, Malcolm (eds))* … and he talks about what it means to be white … he says that white people … their race isn't defined, it's like they don't think that they have a race … it's like neutral … it's the default you know and he's like encouraging white people to explore- white therapists to explore their concept of race, their own race … oh wicked man, he held it as like a workshop at *[therapy training school]* and he was you know superb so I think you know it's and I discussed it with somebody and they said to me well how come you regard yourself as black? Even my friends say to me: "well you do live with your Dad and your Dad is white" I'm ever mindful of that I'm ever mindful … that … my Dad … is middle-class as well … and … that it does give me a privilege

119.   I'm now sitting at *[therapy training school]* paying God knows how much because of my Dad's position because I can live with my Dad, rent free, and then go and pay you know some people say "oh *[name of a local college]*, it's only 500 pound!", but ... I know that … it matters where you train … reputation is important, so sometimes it does

feel kind of – cos somebody else said "don't you feel guilty?"

120. I: Do you feel guilty?

121. CR1:   … I think I'm just very conscious of my privilege … yeah, I'm conscious of it … I'm conscious that, if I compare myself … you see, people always used to say to my Mum "you're kids'll be alright cos they're mixed" – but they wouldn't always say "mixed", they would say "HC" - people used to always say that to my Mum … and I always wondered really what they meant by that … that always kind of baffled me … but now if I compare myself to my counterparts on my estate … same age … probably got themselves in the same predicament with two kids on their own … I think were those people right who said that to Mum?

122.   Because now here I am and if you look on the television now, you got like Alesha Dixon, mixed race, you got the other girl on the X-factor, the black girl … see? I call her black, Leona Lewis, but then I'll call the other girl mixed race … you know there's a lot of mixed-race people … Barack Obama … you know *[person's name]* is like the Head of Psychology at the prison and she said to me – cos she encouraged me to read the book – she says she doesn't think he would have got it if it wasn't mixed race … Malcolm Gladwell … you know …

I am me: the lived experience of a mixed-race identity
by Haran Rasalingam

123. I: so, do you feel uncomfortable feeling that you've got privileges because you've got a white father? A white, middle-class father ...

124. CR1:   do I feel uncomfortable? I think I think it's given me a ... but then I'm also conscious that what would have happened if my dad wasn't a human being who would wanna help me once I had screwed up, so on the one hand I'm mindful that it's because he's middle class and white ... but then I think well if his human quality was of the kind that was like "oh boy! You got yourself with your two kids now ... you're on your own" but do I feel guilty? I think ... I'm just very mindful of it ... I'm mindful of it but it makes me also wanna give back ... still ... but I'm mindful that, ok you wanna give back but you still want somebody to give you 50 pounds to talk to you for 50 minutes ... people you might wanna give back to ain't gonna have that money ...

125. I: so, it's like you've got an allegiance with the sort of black community, but you're sort of conscious of the fact that although you got an allegiance with the black community, you're getting some of the privileges of the white community

126. CR1:   that people used to tell my Mum your children will be alright ... people have said it and people often say it! And maybe that's why I tick the mixed-race box when I'm

going for job interviews and such because you know … I think there was a programme on TV recently about whether mixed-race people have an advantage or something like that … through their genes or something like that ("Is it better to be mixed race?", Channel 4 documentary, February 2010) and erm I don't know I guess there is- I do sometimes feel like maybe through exposure to like my Dad that there is certain- I mean you know like there is things that my Dad says that makes me cringe … cos you know I think my Dad has, like I said, a flavour for black women but he still said things, not so much now but in the past, things that were a bit stereotypical and erm … I don't know …

127. I: would you find that your Mum would also do things like that?

128. CR1:   My Mum does it all the time

129. I: does that bother you as well?

130. CR1:   it does, because now she's complaining that – I think most Mums would be proud like "you've fixed up your life, you've turned it around … you're going somewhere far", but my Mum finds it a problem because she thinks I'm challenging her about some of the- she works for a Jewish company and she's always complaining like "the Jew man" this and "the Jew man" that … or white people she's

got this kind of venom now about white people as well erm so-

131. I: do you have any venom towards white people?

132. CR1:   it's odd like sometimes at work you know you're working in a- I've grown up at grass roots level and I think when I went to Jamaica as well, it was grass roots, you know, you had to carry water and stuff, bathe in a little bowl so I think there's certain things that I've been exposed to and I think it's not text book for me, I don't have to read about certain experiences and you kind of look at your white counterparts ... a little thing that happened the other day

133.   I do a little ceremony at work when people finish groups and the prisoners were told to bring CDs in – they forgot, so I put on the radio station it was a pirate ... white colleague's sitting next to me, they was playing Shaggy, "You're My Angel", so they was playing away and she was sitting there singing "... you're my angel ..." and swaying and she said: "oh I haven't heard this song in ages" and then later on a kind of dance hall song came on that she never knew, so the men now were like "Zoob! Zoob! Zoob! Zoob!" waving their hands in the air and she looked up and said to me: "oh! Is that pirate radio? Oh! I don't think we're allowed those! I don't think we're allowed those!" and me and the prisoners looked at each other and my other two colleagues, they're black women,

it was just one of those moments that's like *(rolls her eyes)* what shall I do? Put it on *[mainstream radio station]*? No. So, she went and changed it

134. I:　　there was some sort of understanding between the rest of you that didn't need to be said

135. CR1:　it didn't need to be said … because it was all good when you thought it was Shaggy, swaying along, "haven't heard this one for a long time", but once it was like you know and the boys were "Zoob! Zoob! Zoob! Zoob!" you know … it was a problem then … so … yeah it's difficult … it's difficult when you can identify with the boys … erm … you know you can really identify with their experiences … you don't feel like some of your colleagues really … you know- and I can understand you know why somebody might feel intimidated by some of the group members as well … but I think, culturally, there's something about- you kind of have a way of communicating with each other … you kind of know about so when I see them I don't feel intimidated by that or-

136. I:　　right so there was something cultural about that which made it comfortable for you, but uncomfortable for this white lady … what do you think that was?

137. CR1:　well … I don't know what it was I don't know …

138. I:　　you said it was like intimidating maybe … for her

139. CR1:   probably intimidating … and it was a spiritually uplifting song and I think prisoners are very drawn to those songs especially prison and I guess the way that that person responded to it – you know like this is sort of like a gun salute sort of thing – was intimidating for her

140. I: so, she maybe saw it as aggressive in some way

141. CR1:   yeah … I guess it was an animated response which she wasn't au fait with that made her question the radio … and when we came out of there she comes over to me and says: "I knew you put it on a bloody pirate radio station, I knew you had!"

142. I: it almost makes me think something like maybe she thought it was "uncivilised" or something

143. CR1:   something like that, but like I said it was so odd because the singer that came on was Garnett Silk, this Jamaican singer and he died in a fire, so he's really highly regarded, because he's a bit like a Bob Marley, cos he's been taken away, a bit of a legend, but it was like, the Shaggy, who's been on like *Top of the Pops*, number one, so he was OK, because she was swaying to him .. and I guess it's just one of those erm ….

144. I: was that a moment where you where you felt black?

145. CR1:   no. I think I think the prisoners were- it's always with me, no, I'm always black, I'm always me, that's who I am, do you know what I mean? You know I have to present

myself in a particular way at particular times which maybe people are like: "I'm clueless ... clueless ... about what side of the fence is she on"

146. I: ah, it comes back to that again ...

147. CR1: yeah, but then there might be something that they say like checking and they ask me "are you street, miss? Are you street? You're street, innit? I knew you was from road, miss! I knew you was from road!" so there's something about the way that I might say something to them that something might click-

148. I: which means that you're-

149. CR1: - I know what's going on ... yeah so, it's odd even the dialogue around it it's odd-

150. I: and it's like you're able to switch in and out of that and then people will start talking about the fence and where are you ... it sounds like you know where you are, but other people may not know where you are

151. CR1: yeah, I guess so ... the thing is black culture is so kind of popular you know like "baby mother" was something that I heard Jamaican boys used to say "baby mother" ... now the white dudes is talking about "my baby muvver", "yeah, miss, I'm gonna invite my baby muvver" so you know in the black community now which I shift away from that – what do you mean "baby mother"? That's your woman, no? Or is she just a vehicle for bringing you

children? That's your woman! They're wearing their pants low now they're doing what black boys are doing they got the whole black music now, it's like pop music now … so … it's becoming so kind of … I don't know … it's becoming mainstream it really is …

152. I: I'm gonna move on slightly

153. CR1:   No worries

154. I: Have you ever felt like an outsider?

155. CR1:   I think … I always anchor myself … see there's an old mixed-race woman in my counselling group and there's a black woman in the group and she's a judge and she spoke to her and she said: "I've always had negative experiences from black women" and I thought about that and I thought you see I think I've always been nurtured by black women … erm … maybe that's because my Mum is a black woman obviously and my Mum's twin and then since I started to – well I hit rock bottom and then I started to look at myself

156.   I think I regard myself as a bit of an 'Educating Rita' and erm when I volunteered at the prison I volunteered there before I got the job there and I did my degree and the Head of Psychology, *[person's name]*, she's a black woman, and I was just in awe of her because she talked about the strategies how you gotta get there, you gotta be focused, you know like networking, you know I'd never heard of it

all before, she just kind of introduced me to all of that …
so have I ever felt like an outsider? … yeah … when I've
been more so with white people … yeah … definitely …
never in relation to black people … there might be the odd
black person who might …. I don't know, I've never really
felt pushed out … no … but you know I am always
mindful to sometimes you know to hold down my
sometimes I'll hold things down I know education can be
intimidating for people sometimes …

157. I: so how do you mean you "hold things down"?

158. CR1:   so maybe like in certain situations I'll observe more I try
to observe more but I've got you know some of my friends
I'll let them talk so sometimes my friends might say things
that I disagree with like last year I went to a club with my
black friends most of my friends are black I don't have
any white friends not through choice I just don't have any
not consciously who knows? But erm we was in a club in
[place in city] and there was kind of like a funky kind of
neo-soul kind of black folk with afro hair and erm I don't
know like the Erica Badous you know the differences?

159.   So anyway there was some white folks there … you know
white folks are more freer they just get up and dance and
do their thing so the girls I was with were kind of laughing
at the white girl the way she was moving herself and I
think part of me years ago would probably have joined in

with that … but the more I thought about it I thought you know what? This woman paid to come in here … she's having a good time! This is her Friday night. She's not come here to stand and stare at people … I just wonder sometimes: who's the fool here? You know, this woman is so anchored like she probably knows you lot talk about her she probably don't care! She might not even process you and realise … so who's the fool here?

160. I: you said she was "so anchored" - what does that mean?

161. CR1: I don't know, I rate that like to be able to get up and just be free and just start dancing you know I don't know if she was in time but she was just doing her own thing like … regardless of everybody else in the room … but then she becomes a focal point for my group and they're kind of laughing at her but I was in a reflective mood that day and I just thought to myself: here we are … but we're not dancing! We're not enjoying ourselves! But then the person who does get up and decide to dance, we're then kind of hee-heeing her. Is that because … in our group we have we don't do the neo-soul thing we're supposed to do the hip-hop, the ragga … I don't know it perplexed me

162. I: so, you found yourself questioning stereotypes it sounds like cos earlier on you were saying …

163. CR1: mmm, within my group I thought you know what? I'm gonna go and dance and so I think they began to think that

I was a bit odd because I was the one who thought you know what? Let's just do our thing

164. I: so, was that an example of you being a bit of outsider?

165. CR1: well then it made me feel like they looked at me and then it makes me think that they might think *(whispers)* "it's cos she mixed"

166. I: right … and how does that make you feel?

167. CR1: well … that's another thought process. But then that makes makes me just think well I don't I don't know … if I hold that thought and if I focus on the fact that it makes me feel like I'm being more free rather than being rigid rather than going with the group and colluding with that behaviour … it helps me to feel freer … then if I explore the fact that they probably think *(whispers)* "it's cos she mixed" … … … … *(speculative)* they could be right I don't know … I don't know, maybe it's what their narrow definition of what black is, that might be the problem … it keeps them where they say … you know … so it's a point for debate

168. I: that's so interesting because, in a way, it's kind of says to me that you can say that "I'm black" but it doesn't mean "I'm a black stereotype" … it means … it's much more fluid than that

169. CR1: yeah … or you know … I did erm I did anthropology at uni and the woman said - I remember this … there's the

Iraq war on - "there's either millions of races or there's one race" ... well flippin' 'ell! Well that makes it all ... well what am I talking about, then? The human race and done! Which is what I put on the application when I go to the gym – human race! What's wrong with that? I wouldn't put it on a job application because *(laughs)* I wouldn't get the job! But I can do that at the gym

170. I: so, it sounds like then – just to go on to a slightly different question – that because of racism and things that you ... on applications, you're kind of wary of what you put because of, basically, prejudices ... I mean have you sort of suffered racism? And what kind of racism might you have suffered?

171. CR1:   I don't know, I guess ... I guess what happens to me is like my Mum ... what my Mum's experience it's something that I never forget because I watch my Mum struggle to find an identity and even now as narrow as she is with all her stereotypes no matter what my Mum is I always make excuses for her because of how she grew up you know ... so no matter what and I'm always mindful of that I think historically I'm mindful that my mother's mother left- I always think about the black side of my family I don't even know about my Dad's but I'm always mindful that my Mum's Mum left the Caribbean, sold up shop, left her children and come here, cleaned ... and did

all that stuff … for better … so I think … I don't know I can't say like …

172.   I guess racism might have come in terms of things like "the kids'll always be alright" that's the sort of thing … or where do I find myself, where do I fit myself? But I never ever felt like … well I guess … like … at work recently, they failed me on a training … I had to train for five days to be a facilitator and erm I was training in *[city in England]*, but I had to come off of that training because I had a family incident … so, basically the feedback from the facilitator was that I would have passed, I was fine … but, when I went to *[place in England]* … they failed me … now from day one the people there they never liked me

173.   Now … I explore that because I know that sounds really defensive … but there's something in the prison, right, you have prison staff also doing programmes with people, so prison officers come from a historical kind of background which is like … they don't always have the kind of … I don't know … "I believe in jail" and all this, but there was a kind of altercation which let me know … I guess maybe people don't quite realise that I'm as articulate as I am … they might have a you know … a kind of perception of me … and when you start …

174.   I think some people didn't like the contributions I was making in the group and kind of made reference to that,

and erm from that point I kind of just chose to keep myself to myself ... and at the end of the week they failed me and when I digested the feedback that they gave me ... it didn't sit right with me ... it didn't sit right ... and the more I analyse it the more I looked at it I thought it don't sit right ... and I got a colleague in my office and she said "tha's racism, man!" and ... sometimes I don't wanna play the race card ... I really don't ... it's like the last one you wanna do ... but the more I chop it up and the more I look at it ... like how come the person in *[city in England]* who wrote the manual said I would have passed and then I go somewhere else and I'm failed ... and when I look at the reasons ... they kind of just don't sit right with me ... so ... yeah I guess I do ... but it's more covert ... far more covert...

175. I: do you mean it's not obvious?

176. CR1:   it's never overt, it's never in my face

177. I: it's kind of very subtle ...

178. CR1:   yeah ... definitely ... mmm

179. I: you've never had outrageous, kind of straight to your face kind of ...

180. CR1:   well, there's things like, you know, somebody calling you the HC word

181. I: have you ever had that?

182. CR1:   oh yes!

I am me: the lived experience of a mixed-race identity
by Haran Rasalingam

183. I: as an adult? Or ... in childhood?

184. CR1:   yeah, well, when I was in the prison, there was a boy who lives upstairs from me, one of my neighbours, he was in there, last year he was in there ... and he said that word. And I said to him "what does that word mean?" ... and erm I don't remember his response ... I don't think he had a response ... but I never heard anybody call themselves "full-caste"

185.   So ... you know ... or you hear some people saying "three-quarter" ... three-quarter what? What does that mean? I don't know ... and what does half mean? Half of what? I mean you're either whole or you're dead, no? I thought you had to be whole

186. I: so, these things about halves and mixed and three-quarters ... I mean even the term 'mixed race' how do you feel about that?

187. CR1:   I work with 'mixed', even if somebody says something like 'half', it seems to do something to me, something about the word, you know you hear people saying: "well I'm half Indian and I'm half-" what is 'half'? How can you be half of something? Do I learn half of my Mum's Jamaican culture? Half of my Dad's English? I don't know, it seems more like an integration, really

I am me: the lived experience of a mixed-race identity
by Haran Rasalingam

188. I: so, do you use the word 'mixed', cos I mean on this research, I'm using the term 'mixed race', right? How do you feel about that?

189. CR1:   Well, I was OK with- because I started to call myself 'mixed race' a little while ago, and then my friend *[name of friend]* says to me: "how come your calling yourself mixed race?" I couldn't remember why, but she just left me with a thought to ponder and I think I took it to my therapist as well but she was saying that she thought I would have read up about it and I hadn't heard of the issues around the word 'mixed race' and I think my Auntie isn't I don't know if my Auntie has a problem with it … she has a problem with the word 'ethnic minority' and I like her rationale behind that … so I don't know, what are the issues with the word 'mixed race'?

190. I: well, I don't know, some people don't like it, some people think that like using the word mixed is like you're mixed up or there's something negative about it like you were saying in a similar way I suppose to half, how can you be a half, you're integrated whereas mixed sounds worse than integrated, maybe?

191. CR1:   isn't it 'dual heritage' now?

192. I: yeah, a few people say that now

193. CR1:   a new word, yeah, yeah … I don't know … I just think you know what? In the 90s I remember like the first

Somalian in my school and that wasn't something I was au fait with and then I thought what if this Somalian has kids with this person or that person, you gonna have to keep making up names! D'you know what I mean it's just getting silly, so I mean it's like 20% mixed race now do we have to keep redefining things or is it just back to that human race thing?

194. I: I heard that Tiger Woods jokingly called himself 'Cablinasian' because he's got a real mix of everything and everyone was going "what do you mean calling yourself Cablinasian!?"

195. CR1:   Where do you anchor yourself? You know? Mmm... controversial I think I heard him say that he wasn't a race or something like that and then I heard people saying that he doesn't have black identity

196. I: and do you think it's important that you should have black identity?

197. CR1:   well, I do believe it's important, but I know it's very context-based ... maybe if I lived ... I don't know out somewhere else ... it wouldn't be so important ... but I just can't believe that though ... I don't know ... in the Caribbean would it matter so much? I don't know ... for me, the racism out there is like classism, they have the whole classism thing there, which is still here, but I do believe it's important I just do

198. I: We haven't got on to psychotherapy yet, so I'm gonna ask in that area … so in what way was your initial engagement with psychotherapy connected with your mixed-race identity or your black identity?

199. CR1:   erm … I kind of did the whole erm … stereotype thing … got myself pregnant … in a kind of domestic violence relationship as well and then I read my first self-help book through Oprah … I remember she has this woman on there preaching about this book so I bought the book and then I bought another book and that was like really looking at yourself … that'd never happened before, but my Auntie was always a therapist well she used to be a social worker then … she was always one of them ones … planting them questions onto you that just make you start crying … so erm … I think she always gave me little books over the years, but I never read them … so then I did the whole … I think I always wanted to become a counsellor, but then there was nowhere to go like for careers advice, so I just did an access course, then did psychology and then, I think the more I kind of you know I kind of had the idea that when I finished that that'd be it, I'd be there … but then the more you look into it you think "well hold on, what areas can I go in to?" … and therapy was always something that I wanted to do, so I finished my degree and then [person's name] the Head of Psychology, she told me

that I should go back to college and carry on and I thought for God's sake can't I just do a little course in the evening?

200.   So I went to my local adult ed and I decided to do a ... integrative counselling course ... so I started that and erm it was 300 pounds and I put it straight on my CV because I was looking for work at the time and that was helping me to get more interviews ... and erm so I was there, it was in *[place in England]*, it's like where my Dad lives, leafy suburbs, and they asked us to erm talk about our experience of stereotypes and there was two black women in the group, a black man, and it was like in a circle, so they started like with the two black women, they spoke about theirs, the first one was talking about because she was well-spoken people presumed that she went out with a white man, the next black woman said that people was surprised that she owned her own property and then there was these white ladies, one of them was like erm *(impersonates posh, sheltered voice)*: "People think I'm really organised at home and erm if only they knew ... my office is a total mess!" and then another one couldn't think of anything *(laughs mockingly)* another thought that she'd been stereotyped because she was really smiley *(impersonates posh, sheltered voice)*: "Oh people think that I'm so smiley all the time!" and then they got round to the black boy he was next to me and he spoke about

people crossing the road because they thought he was a mugger, which angers the group no end and I'm sitting there fuming I'm vexed! And then they came to me and I spoke about being at my Dad's house and erm a health visitor coming and thinking that it was flats and she kind of wanted to know *(impersonates)*: "do you do you have a flat upstairs? Is it flats?"

201. I: right, you couldn't possibly be part of the same household

202. CR1:   yeah ... it was kind of like "how are you in this house? It's got to be flats, that must be the only reason why you'd be in this fat house, detached ..." you know and erm and I spoke about that and when I finished – and I was really careful about this – but I said that black people's experience of stereotypes seems to be quite negative, but what! Couldn't believe it! Pure venom come back at me! Pure venom! Pure venom come! Pure venom! "What are you talking about?" "That's a load of rubbish!" and I thought to myself ... "is it me?" and I think I think my words just failed me then ... and then the black woman sitting over there come in and says: "what she's trying to say is de-de-de-de-de-de" from that day- that's when I went to *[minority therapists org]* because I just thought ... it became a big problem ... two people never came back-

203. I: two black people?

204. CR1:   two white women never came back because they was offended by what I said, but they never spoke about anything

205. I: they felt personally offended by what you'd said?

206. CR1:   yeah they felt personally offended by what I'd said and then never come back and so I hadn't got all that counsellor training stuff going on then, so I took it on and felt all guilty ... and then erm you know *[person's name]* was patting me on the back "I'm glad somebody's mentioned race! Nobody's ever mentioned it here before, well done!" but there was me thinking that I was just making an observation ... I thought it was quite neutral!

207. I: yeah, you didn't feel that you were saying anything out of the ordinary

208. CR1:   yeah, I thought flippin' 'ell! You know what I think I was so baffled by it and it just seemed to go on and on in the group for ages and people weren't too sure what to make of me because I was quite a friendly open person but that maybe some people thought I was trouble and I thought you know what? ... plus, I finished my degree erm I think that they felt that I was using my academic stuff on the like course which you know like "that's the stuff that you learnt at university, that's not really for here" and I thought am I being penalised like for having a degree? Erm and I think you know some of the other people were

there because floristry was full. Floristry was full! And I'm there thinking hold on this is like my life's calling here!

209.   So anyway, I went to *[minority therapists org]* and I thought thank God! It's not only me you know I felt such solace to know that other people experienced it as well and erm I think from that – I think because it was an integrative course as well, I kind of always liked Rogers – and I thought I need to step up my game, I'm being penalised because of my degree, I mentioned like stereotypes and I got pure problems from that and you know what I went on the BPS the first place I came to was *[therapy training school]*, it was in *[place in England]*, it was near my house, firstly, and when I was at *[minority therapists org]* I heard that it had a good reputation, I thought wicked, I'll go there then and I went on the workshop and I thought yep this place is for me … so that was my first sort of … yeah … and I kind of had faith in *[therapy training school]* as well and I really liked my first tutor and she said something that I really didn't like about a dark-skinned person kind of giving an example of somebody being fearful like: "suppose you're walking down the street and a tall dark man is walking behind you, now that's a scary thing" and she carried on and I was just like "eh?" and I thought "oh fucking hell!" you're gonna break

my spell, I was lovin' it and you've just gone and said something so negative and I looked at that other black woman in the class, me and her had that eye contact, man!

210.   And cos we both like clocked each other, that was the support I needed like we both knew and it was like in the evening it came back to me, man, so I knew it really bothered me and then the next day when we was in Process, I mentioned it, I said to her "when you said this yesterday, you know I got cousins and uncles who are tall, dark men and they're not scary" and erm … cos I trusted them I trusted them and erm … she turned to me … and she said "oh when I was twelve, I was attacked by a tall, dark-haired man and he wasn't black" she said he was like tan- I don't know like olive skin and that ironically, the only man that I ever loved was a black man and the whole room was like everyone was crying, the tutor's crying and I was crying … so … but we was talking about phenomenology that day as well so it was interesting about how we all view our own world differently, I heard "tall, dark" and somebody else will hear "tall, dark", cos I don't perceive "tall, dark" to be- I don't read Mills and Boon like … I don't know what that means "tall, dark", you know when I hear "tall, dark", I think of my family

211. I: so, it's interesting what kind of image was conjured up in everyone's mind

212. CR1:   yeah … and it kind of linked in to what we were talking about … and I think from that I kind of felt safe at *[therapy training school]* that really like helped me to feel really safe like I could go there and erm yeah I think I mean even when I kind of signed up the only black staff that was there was like admin staff and erm they were saying like "we like you here" "we need more people like you here" and so you know I just it's like it's always there you know? Always there for me … definitely

213. I: what's it been like as a client in counselling or therapy?

214. CR1:   well firstly I saw the first woman I saw cos she was really cheap and I just wanted to tick criteria because she had to be a BACP person, oh she was crap though … she just kept going on about her black friend this and her black friend that and you know … she couldn't help herself, but to jump in to let me know that she was cool

215. I: she was white?

216. CR1:   yeah she was a white woman and I kind of caught on quickly that she wasn't good but she met the criteria, she was cheap and BACP, but then she decided to stop anyway … and then I kind of I used to be a drug worker and we'd get supervision for free so I selected *[name of current therapist]* I think I met her at *[minority therapists org]* and there was something about her that I just liked I warmed to … and I think too on her little blog it said

something about mixed race ... something there erm and so because I started the Masters, I needed someone who was UKCP and so I knew that I'd have to change therapist anyway and so I don't know, I just feel that anchor, innit ... with *[name of current therapist]* it's just erm but I don't know, you know, I'm so focused on criteria I don't know if I would go and select a white therapist or whatever, I just feel anchored with *[name of current therapist]* you know cos I could try something different and you know but you know what? She knows how it goes and I'm still struggling you know I've got there, you know the job I've got now, but I'm still paying back my student loan, I'm in debt again for this new course ... she charges reasonably ... you know I feel like there's something cultural she kind of knows ... she knows ... really ... just feels like certain things she just knows

217. I: there's certain things she just knows

218. CR1:   yeah ... like I don't have to explain ...

219. I: do you think you could describe that?

220. CR1:   I don't know it's like talking to her about my argument with my sister ... she can challenge me about that because my sister regards herself as mixed race ... but me and my sister's mixed race isn't the same because I have a black mum and I grew up in a black area, it's two different things ... so *[name of current therapist]* will also

challenge me about my perceptions too ... so ... I don't feel like I have to break it down so much ... like like with the white lady I always felt like I had to break it down because she looked like she'd be baffled ...

221. I: was it not helpful to "break it down"? To have to "break it down"?

222. CR1:   It was but sometimes you wanna get on with the story ... cos the next thing you know you're still breaking it down and more questions are arising ... she looks more confused ... because I mean, even just talking to you there's such a- ... it's like there's so many layers in it and sometimes it's like an unspoken- like even if our experiences aren't the same, so you know you might be mixed ... Sri Lankan ... there's certain common commonalities that you kind of experience and erm I don't know if *[name of current therapist]* is mixed, I presume she's mixed, but would it be different if she was a black woman? I don't know ... I probably think not because sometimes ... I don't know ...

223. I: in a way then it sounds important that your counsellor or therapist does have some level of the unspoken understanding you know, often in therapy we're talking about not making assumptions and that sort of thing you know ask keep asking you know but it sounds like that's

OK to a point, but if you have to explain everything ... you need some connection there

224. CR1: yes, most definitely ... and I see it with the prisoners because we offer the prisoners some counselling and they're like "this therapist's never gonna understand me"? ... "...they ain't gonna get me"

225. I: so, they really feel that if it's a white counsellor ... they would just ... would miss it

226. CR1: they'd miss it, yeah

227. I: couldn't empathise

228. CR1: and I guess it's also about how you come across to ... you know ... the clothes you wear ... the way you put yourself across, how you interact with people ... it's hard to kind of like reveal what it is, you know like to peel back the layers to see like what is the workings going on behind it ... but it's just kind of like ... I don't know maybe it's like intuitive like ... but you know ... I have supervision with a white guy ... he's cool, you know I have supervision with two other black women so it's the three of us with *[person's name]* and yeah he seems "white aware" - that's the term used by Colin Lago - "white aware"

229. I: so, you mean he's thought about what it means to be white?

230. CR1: I hope so because he's like the course leader ... I mean he does seem ... that is important ... and then again I do think

that sometimes as a therapist somebody might say something and you don't quite get it but sometimes if you can just hold it down … you'll get it in the end … cos sometimes my clients say stuff and I don't know what they mean but I'll just stay with them and slowly it evolves … it becomes clear … so I am aware of that but like I said there was something about about *[name of her therapist]* that just … like that experience … the hardship, the challenge, you know trying to break free of certain stereotypes as well … I just feel like … she gets it … and I didn't get that from the other therapist

231. I: so, what about at *[therapy training school]* then generally … do you think they get it?

232. CR1:   like I said … mmm I think at this next *[minority therapists org]* there is gonna be a lecturer there from *[therapy training school]* and I don't know whether he's- I don't know, I only know the white staff there … "do they get it?" … I mean … I trust them … I trust that they- you know I'm doing a person-centred course, so from my experiences so far like for me I think it was key with *[person's name]* that *[person's name]* thing *('tall, dark' incident)* because I really think that if she didn't do it properly, it would have just torn me down, cos I left my other little 300-pound-a-year course and now I'm paying

like 2 grand to be here and if she didn't get it, it would have really just …

233. I: it was a critical moment

234. CR1:   yeah, it was and I'm in the current prospectus, so I feel like they've embraced me … I feel like they want me there, too … there's like something going on there, like I'll sign up for a workshop and some of them are full, like Mike Cooper's was full, but I still get on and other people don't get on, so …

235. I: I wonder if you've actually made an impact and made a change

236. CR1:   … they're rooting for me … and I don't know how I know and I don't know whether it's because of the way I get on with the admin staff as well … because they are they are the cogs behind it all, do you know what I mean? And like I say they're the only black staff there … so they're rooting for me in a way, they are … so I'm glad to be there, I mean I did a workshop there the other day and I was speaking to the woman next to me and basically because not all courses demand that you have therapy, so there's a woman who's training at erm some college in central *[city in England]* and she doesn't have any therapy, but she's got her issues, they told her to go to *[therapy training school]* to get cheap counselling and the woman was saying – she's a black woman – that she couldn't afford to

pay more for a therapist, so she's come to *[therapy training school]*, because it's cheap ... and the woman was just saying you know she does feel a little bit guilty about that because here she is as a trainee who can afford to train at *[therapy training school]*, who can afford to pay for the therapy and now she's seeing a black woman who can't afford to train at *[therapy training school]*, who can't afford therapy with a qualified therapist because of the cost and she was just talking about what that brought up for her ... you that feeling ... like ... I feel it sometimes, I feel guilty, I feel privileged to be there ... because ... it's damned expensive and ... there's not too many black people there ... put it that way ... not too many at all.

237.   So, I do feel privileged to be there like, I am waving a banner ... and there is something about them asking me to be in the prospectus that I kind of do feel kind of ... chuffed about you know? I think the cost of training there does exclude people

238. I: yeah, I think it's the same at *[therapy training school]* as well

239. CR1:   exactly ... exactly what *[name of her therapist]* said about her training there too ... erm my Auntie's a Gestalt therapist ... so you know ... mmmm

240. I: do you think erm therapy or counselling has affected your sense of identity?

241. CR1:   ... flippin' 'ell, there's no stone it don't unturn, is there!? You know ... it gets into every nook and cranny in your whole ... your whole life ... yeah most definitely ... like my Mum now ... I have to challenge her about- cos it just felt like she was constantly negative towards me about my achievements, so I've had to have an open dialogue with her about that ... which was hard which is- but I'm glad because she's started to shift ... she's started to get it ... and she's also started to realise that ... like ... at work ... as a black woman at work ... it comes to you in different shapes and forms in different guises at work ... it's ever present ... if it's your colleague not understanding about pirate radio stations or feeling like somebody's failed you on the course ... or you know trying to hold certain things down culturally about what you do ... so she's starting to realise ... you know ... you have to present yourself in a certain way to get in then once you get in, you can switch it off a little bit ... and I think things like going to *[minority therapists org]* once a year just to get that erm that anchoring just every year just to go to see what other people are seeing cos it was so comfortable for me

242. I: is it something to do with feeling that other people are sharing your ... issues maybe or ...?

243. CR1:   I guess for me, the first year was so extreme that I didn't realise I thought you know in counselling, people care about people and I didn't think you'd get all those stereotypes ... I just didn't realise ... so now it doesn't feel like such a hot topic for me like it's not so like afraid of it now, I kind of understand ... but there's still something about going there and just hearing different people's experiences that I kind of you know I just really highly value that ... it just kind of gets talked through and looked at

244. I: and does that mean then that outside of *[minority therapists org]* there are still prejudices and things or stereotypes in the psychotherapy world that you've experienced?

245. CR1:   ... I mean ... well people think that you're always trying to get into their heads ... generally I mean like in the Guardian today in the Society section they were talking about the costs and the NHS won't pay and the costs are just ridiculous ... and I guess I'm just mindful of you know ... this whole middle-class pursuit thing and, whilst I do kind of live at my Dad's, I know I've got a certain middle-class things going on now you know but is it something for people with a disposable income? It just feels ... wrong in a way sometimes ... you are kind of helping people who are better able to help themselves

through finance ... and some of the people down ... who might need the help more ... who are less inclined ... yeah can't even go there ... so anyway ... I brought up raise in my current MSc group, so now this is a new group, this is my second year, I brought it up, I had this this Mike Cooper, he asked us to talk about what draws us to people and what takes us away from people and so we did that in fours and erm there's a woman on my course, black woman, African woman ... she's a judge in court ... it's an immigration court and I am in awe of her, I just look up to her and you know so what draws me to you? You're a black woman, you're in a powerful position, I could learn a lot from you ... and so when I said that to her I was thinking cos we worked with two other white people I wondered I wonder how they felt about that and I said that and I thought how would I have felt if they had said that to each other? You know "I really look up to you you're a white guy" ... how would that have been? Hmmm, so I mentioned it in Process time and, so there's 18 of us, four black people in there ... mixed/black ... and erm mentioned it like: "I wonder how that was for you hearing me saying that" and he was like "oh well, I kind of ... I understood" he was cool about it, so I don't know, I think in my current group people wanna mention it, cos like the other two black women in there were like "well done for mentioning it!" it was like something they really wanted to say, thank you for bringing it to the table! Because it's not been mentioned, and I thought "oh ... OK ... I hear you" but I don't know, I don't know whether they feel that I've opened up the flood gates I don't know, but then I'm thinking ... "was there something you wanted to say about race that you haven't said?" Do you know what I mean like?

246. I: it sounds like on more than one occasion you've been like the instigator, the one who sort of trailblazed ...

247. CR1:   *(pondering)* yeah, but I don't know what it was that- she wanted to thank me ... I don't know ... we work in supervision together as well ... so ... and I don't know if some of the dynamics there are related to ... she's already a counsellor she's already done an MSc ... I don't know ... so I do the MSc on the Friday and then I do the diploma at the same time, and on the diploma, the judge is still there with me and we still have a dialogue about black issues and so we had that dialogue together when nobody else was there, but in Process I've mentioned that I'm of Jamaican descent and that I feel that I still hold certain negative views about African people ... if you kind of know a little bit about that ... and so like to dispel that myth, I'll have to go to Africa, and she's offered to take me, so I mentioned that in Process time as well, so maybe

there is something about me that kind of ... but I do feel

safe there at *[therapy training school]*, I do ... thus far

248. I: mmm .... fantastic ... we're gonna have to stop!

249. CR1:   did you get all your questions answered?

250. I: well, you said lots, ... I didn't need to ask everything

[End of interview]

INTERVIEW: Small-town racism

"Well, it doesn't really matter what other people want to label me. I'm me."

About Co-Researcher #2

Co-Researcher #2 (CR2) is a psychotherapist in her early forties. She grew up in a small town in England with her white mother. Her father is black from *[country in Africa]*. CR2's parents separated when CR2 was very young after which she had almost no contact with her father. CR2 describes herself as being of dual heritage. Visually, one can see CR2's black heritage and it is possible to speculate that she is mixed race on account of her being quite fair skinned and the curls in her hair are quite loose.

Research interview with Co-Researcher #2

[I = Interviewer; CR2 = Co-Researcher #2]

1. I: So, I've just got some questions here, which I'll ask around in a semi-structured way.

2. CR2: Okay.

3. I: Great. So, the first question I'm going to ask is how would you describe your family history, or family roots?

4. CR2: Well, my Dad being from *[country in Africa]*, my Mum being English. I don't know a lot about the roots of my

family. I know more about my African side now. I don't
know how to describe it, though. I don't know what you
really are looking for, when you say, "Describe it."

5.   I: Well, anything that you could tell me about your family
             background, I suppose.

6.   CR2:   Okay. Well my Mum's grew up with her family in *[small
             English town]*. My Dad is… I think he came from a larger
             family from *[country in Africa]*. My Dad comes from the
             [name of a tribe], which is the one of the tribes in *[country
             in Africa]*. There are several tribes there. My Dad actually
             went to *[place in England]* to study. And then stayed and
             met my Mum.

7.   I: So, they met in *[place in England]*?

8.   CR2:   Yes! My Mum was a bit of a wild child and her and her
             friend used to drive over to *[place in England]* to party at
             the weekends. And my Dad, by all accounts, was quite a
             reserved, shy young man. He was… I think he was about
             maybe about three years younger than my Mum. And they
             met. It's funny, my Mum tells me a story of when she was
             a little girl, very young, maybe about seven or eight, going
             down to the town, the main street, with her Mum, my
             grandma…

9.   I: And that was in…?

10. CR2:   In *[small English town]*. And there was a black couple
             passing. And my Mum had never seen black people

before, so this was her first ever contact with black people. And she said this memory stayed with her for the whole of her life.

11.   She said she looked at them both and thought they were absolutely beautiful. She said they looked really regal and just beautiful, she said. Which I always think kind of steered my Mummy in the direction of black men. So, when she saw my Dad, I imagine, her eyes completely lit up. He was a very, very handsome young man.

12.   So, apparently, then he moved to *[town in the UK]*, but my Mum found out she was pregnant. So, she followed him and, being a decent boy, he came back to *[small town in England]* and they got married. Back in the 60s – well, bearing in mind this was a small town – my Dad's black, my Mum's white, and it turned out that this was a problem for a lot of people. She'd married out of her race.

13.   So, it was kind of, I guess, I would say doomed to fail from the beginning.

14.   I: Overall, just because of the environment?

15.   CR2:   Yeah. They moved to *[city in England]*, but my Mum was homesick, and she actually got a lot of abuse, there, for having a mixed baby.

16.   I: So, she got that in the city?

17.   CR2:   Yeah. And my Mum never suffered any… obviously, being a white woman from a white country, she never

suffered any abuse, and she couldn't cope with it, and she wanted to go back to her hometown.

18.   So, my Dad brought her home. But then he got a lot of racism and he couldn't cope, and I think it took its toll on their marriage and it began to fall apart.

19.   He moved to *[another country]* when I was young, and that was it.

20. I: So, you never saw him again?

21. CR2: I never saw him, from when I was three, throughout my childhood. And I found him when I was grown up.

22. I: You tracked him down?

23. CR2: Yeah, yeah. I tracked him down to *[city in another country]*. I tracked him down because, you know, I grew up with this empty void. There was always a piece of me that never felt whole, never felt … I always wondered who this man was that I looked like. Because I don't look like my Mum.

24.   And I used to look at my Mum and I used to not identify with my Mum.

25. I: You didn't identify with her?

26. CR2: No.

27. I: Right…

28. CR2: And I think it was probably hard for my Mum, too, you know? She didn't really know what to do with … you know … what to do with my hair, what to do with my skin.

I am me: the lived experience of a mixed-race identity
by Haran Rasalingam

It wasn't the sort of cultural knowledge she had. And if I came home and said, "Somebody called me a nigger", she didn't know how to deal with it.

29.   I: She was kind of in unknown territory?

30.   CR2:   Well, I told her once, "Mummy, somebody called me a nigger."

31.   And my Mummy said to me, "Well, listen, I don't know really how to deal with that, and I won't always be with you, so you're going to have to find a way to deal with it yourself."

32.   And so, if somebody had spat on me or called me names or threw stones at me, I came home, and I just walked into the house and sat down like nothing had happened.

33.   I: So, you just kind of left it?

34.   CR2:   Yeah. And you just had to sit there feeling like shit but not really knowing what to do with it.

35.   I: So, the issue, then, of your cultural heritage, your background, wasn't really spoken about?

36.   CR2:   Not really.

37.   I: Not really?

38.   CR2:   I mean, I tried to speak to my Mummy once about my Dad, and it took so much courage, and I was so young and I didn't know how to just directly come out and say it, because it was a difficult subject. He had left her after all.

39.   And my Mum was a very good artist and she'd sketched portraits, and there were sketches on the wall, and his sketch was still there. And I remember it really clearly; my Mum was hoovering, and I remember standing there, looking at the sketch, thinking, "She'll see me looking at this sketch and maybe she'll say something." But she didn't.

40.   So, when she turned the Hoover off, I said to her, "Mummy, that sketch of that man, is that my Daddy?" And my Mum just looked at me, and she looked so sad and hurt, then just turned around and walked off. I think she did the sketch for me so that she didn't have to talk about it.

41.   And I just felt oh, I've really upset her. And, actually, I just felt bad. And so, it was never brought up again.

42. I: It was like a big taboo really.

43. CR2: Yeah. I had a toy he sent me, but it was never kind of like, "These are from your Daddy. Write back and say thank you." So, they were kind of just given to me; "Here are some clothes."

44.   I always knew, you know, they were from Dad, but it was, "What is Dad?" you know?

45. I: Did he ever write to you or anything?

46. CR2: Yeah. But I only ever saw one letter, and it was on my tenth birthday and he had sent me £10.00, which was a lot

of money back then. And because he was so abstract in my head, it was kind of this letter from this man and I was more interested in the £10.00.

47. I: Less abstract!

48. CR2:   Yeah. It was right in front of me and I could go and spend it. Mummy didn't give me the letter. She read me the letter and gave me the £10.00. And then I was really excited because I had ten pounds. But she couldn't say, "Write back and thank your Daddy." I think that was too painful.

49.   And to bring it up would have just been massive. So, I had ten pounds, I remember I bought this cuddly toy, and you pulled this string and it spoke and, for some reason, my Mum was raging that I had wasted £10.00 on this cuddly toy that spoke. And I never spoke up for myself, but I remember hearing her at home saying, "You think she could have bought something better with that money." and actually going into the room and saying to her, "It's my money and I'll buy whatever I want."

50.   And I never spoke back. So, there was something in me that "This is from my Daddy. It's mine, and you can't take that away."

51. I: It's not her business, kind of thing.

52. CR2:   Yeah, yeah. And, after that, there was nothing. No letters.

53. I: No more letters after that?

54. CR2:   No more letters after that. If there were, I didn't get them.

55. I: Yes, because she read them to you. So, what was it like growing up in *[small English town]*?

56. CR2:   It was just outside *[name of city]* and they built all these new houses. It kind of became a 'nothing' spot.

57.   They just kind of dumped people.

58. I: So, what is your experience, growing up where you did?

59. CR2:   A lot of my childhood, I realise now, I was quite dissociated from. I kind of was just 'there'. I guess the kind of pivotal points I remember very much, when realisations would hit me, and I was about seven. And I remember where I was and this kid called me a nigger and I didn't really know what it was.

60.   And it was like, at that moment – because before then I didn't actually know I was different…

61. I: It was like the first time you were made aware of it.

62. CR2:   Right. And it was explained to me, "Yeah, you're a nigger. You're black. You're less than us", you know. And it was at that moment that I remember kind of just waking up and looking around me and seeing white kids and then me. And it was like, at that moment, that I kind of shut down.

63. I: Somebody had made a distinction between you and everybody else.

64. CR2:   Yeah. And it wasn't a good distinction. And it was then I kind of became more aware of my surroundings and being in the world and not being accepted. And it was then I kind

I am me: the lived experience of a mixed-race identity
by Haran Rasalingam

of saw people and the way they looked at me and the way I was treated. It all became clearer.

65.   And not in a great way. So, what I learned was I wasn't good. I was shite, actually. I was the bottom of the heap. We weren't well off, by any means, but there was a family that was... I guess people are given labels, and this family was labelled the 'smelly family'. They were really poor, and they smelled very badly.

66.   And I stuck up for every underdog. And this family, they all had really big lips, and people used to call them 'rubber lips', and I used to think it was really horrible. And I remember sticking up for this girl, one time, and saying, "Stop calling her that." And she turned right to me and she said, "I may smell, but at least I'm not a nigger."

67.   So that was it. Okay. I am seriously at the bottom of the pile.

68.   So, a lot of my life I just used to go tuning out. Just tuned out to a level where I wasn't really, really present, you know, but aware. But just not feeling it on a certain level. And a lot of my life, I feel like in my childhood I walked around in a bubble.

69.   That's what I used to call it; like a bubble. Where it took a long time to get through to hurt. But it always got through, and it always hurt. So I was a very insecure child and, whenever my Mum used to go with me and maybe

one of my friends into *[name of city]*, I used to say, "Mummy, Mummy!" really loudly, you know, so people would go, "Oh, that's her Mummy. Not the white girl's Mummy".

70.   And my Mum didn't realise, and she'd go, "Why are you always saying my name really loudly? Will you calm down!" What I wanted was people to say, "She actually has a Mummy. She's not adopted. She belongs."

71. I: So, you were consciously trying to affect people's perceptions.

72. CR2: Yeah. It didn't work, you know, because that would confuse them even more. They'd be, "Oh, that's her Mum. Oh."

73.   But I became very, very aware and very hyper vigilant of everybody around me. I used to scan the crowd, from very young; scan the people on the bus, scan the people on the street, and become very good at picking out who was going to call me names, who was going to give me the strange looks.

74. I: You could suss them out?

75. CR2: Yeah. You could see it in their eyes. And so, I spent my life being on survival mode, on edge. Waiting for it. And then just holding it in, when it happened, because not knowing how to deal with it, until I reached my late teens, maybe about 16. And then I discovered sarcasm.

I am me: the lived experience of a mixed-race identity
by Haran Rasalingam

76.   I read a lot, so I was very eloquent at speaking. Books were my escape throughout my childhood. And so, I used to just cut people to ribbons with my tongue. And that became my main defence, and I used to sometimes pre-empt people. Just cut them to ribbons before they even got there.

77.   And it used to make me feel like I was standing up for myself. And I always used to justify it to myself by saying, "Well, I'm not telling them anything that they aren't." You know, "I'm not making it up. They're calling me a nigger, I'm going to call them a red neck racist. So, I'm not being bad to them." You know, that's how I dealt with it.

78.   I: It was kind of fighting a label with a label, in a way. Hitting them back – they too can be labelled.

79.   CR2: Yeah. And I hated labels, you know. I hated being labelled and put in a box, because I've been labelled and put in a box from so early. I kind of knew there was a piece of me that was always fighting being labelled.

80.   I: So, you had a feeling of being put in a box.

81.   CR2: Yeah. And I never considered myself white, but I grew up surrounded completely by white people. But I never considered myself black because I had no understanding of my black heritage. But I identified more with black people.

82. I: Why do you think that is?

83. CR2:   Well I remember we watched *Roots (an American TV miniseries drama recounting the true story of a Mandinka boy kidnapped in Gambia and sold into slavery in America)* back in the 70s. We avidly watched *Roots*. I think that was one way my Mum tried to help educate me about my background.

84. I: Sort of indirectly.

85. CR2:   Yeah, yeah. So, we'd sit down and watch *Roots*. And I remember it used to break my heart. And I was young; I was born in the 70s...

86. I: And 'Roots' came out at that time.

87. CR2:   yes ... and I was young, but it struck something so deep in me that I remember watching it and sometimes crying and sometimes being really, really, really angry. And then being even more angry, because you'd go to school on the Monday and people would call you 'Kunta Kinte' or 'Kizzy' *(names of main characters in Roots).*

88.   And being really angry, because it had just given them more fuel, and they'd missed the whole point of it. But identifying with these black people because we got called nigger all the time and we were treated as less, so I identified with being black and being 'less'.

89. I: Yes. Being the one being treated as an inferior.

90. CR2:   Yeah, yeah.

91. I: You've kind of answered, in a way; you said you never saw yourself as white. You never really saw yourself as black, either, although you identified more with, say, a black world maybe.

92. CR2:   Mm. Mm.

93. I: How would you describe yourself, in those sorts of terms? If you would at all, in fact.

94. CR2:   Well, I mean, I don't know if I've ever been able to give myself a category. I guess I kind of was very shocked when I first came to *[city in UK]* and I realised that something... there was a piece in me that felt more 'white' than I actually realised. Or maybe it was the socialisation of the white culture.

95.   When I came to live in *[city in UK]*, I saw this black man drive past in a BMW and my first thought was, "Oh! He stole that!" And I was shocked and so ashamed that...

96. I: That that thought had come into your mind?

97. CR2:   ...I had thought that. That I realised, "You really have been surrounded completely by white people all your life". So, I guess it was the white socialisation that really came to the fore. And there was a piece of me then, when I was there – that I began to feel... I just felt at home around black people.

98. I: You felt at home.

I am me: the lived experience of a mixed-race identity
by Haran Rasalingam

99. CR2: Yeah. There is a different vibe from black people. And I eased into that really quickly. And so, for a while, I felt I was black. Yeah, "I'm black, I'm black, I'm black".

100. But then I realised that, "Well, hold on a minute. I don't actually feel like I fit here either, because they're telling me I don't fit." Because I had black people saying to me – black Africans, who I worked with – saying to me, "Oh, you're sitting in the sun because you want to be black like us." And I'm thinking, "No, it's just a lovely day. I was just eating my lunch on the bench, in the sun."

101. And then black men, African men; I had an African boyfriend, he was actually *[from country in Africa]*, and him saying to me, "I would like to take you back to *[country in Africa]* because you'd be treated like a queen because you're lighter skinned, and your hair is loose. And then it was like, "Oh man. These black people are just treating me like the white people treated me, like different. Only this time, I'm a commodity to black men. And to women I seem to be a bit of a threat, because it would be like, "Mm, hmm. She's got her own hair" or, "Who does she think she is?"

102. So, I kind of, then, got quite confused, and I felt quite hurt when I first came. And it was like, "Well black people don't want me, white people don't want me. I don't know what I am." And then, somewhere in there, I kind of found

that, "Well, it doesn't really matter what other people want to label me. I'm me. I don't say I'm black or I'm white. I will say I'm mixed heritage, if I have to say anything."

103. I: If you have to say anything at all.

104. CR2:   Yeah. And what I will normally say is, "I'm actually English / [African – name of country]."

105. I: That's what I was going to ask. If somebody says, "Where are you from?", what would you say?

106. CR2:   I'd say I'm from England.

107. I: You say you're from England?

108. CR2:   Yeah. You know, that's actually where I'm physically from.

109. I: If you say that to people, what is their reaction?

110. CR2:   Shocked. They're shocked. And people from [the area CR2 is from] can be quite shocked when they hear my accent, and they look at me. They can be quite shocked. For them, it doesn't really go with what I look like.

111.   And, since then, I've met a few other people. I realise that, actually, culturally, I'm very [from the area CR2 was born]. I guess there's good and bad in every culture.

112.   And so, there's a piece of me that feels very torn.

113.   So, there's good and there's bad in all of it. I guess I kind of jump, you know. I can jump into my [side of CR2 picked up from the area she grew up in] and, when I met my first cousin from [country in Africa], I felt like I'd

114. known her all my life. And I guess maybe that was the other part of me, kind of being stirred, stimulated, evoked. She evoked something in me that my English side doesn't. And I love her to bits and I just feel completely at home with her and, when I first met her and when I first met my Dad, I realised that some of my mannerisms are quite African, but I'd never met them before.

115. I: So, you're wondering: how do you pick them up, kind of thing?

116. CR2: Exactly ... is this in my genes? Or, what is it? Because I am a mixed – well I guess we all are, of our socialisation and our genetic ... and she kind of brings out an African feel in me, and my English family and friends bring out kind of an English feel in me. And I like them both.

117. I: Yeah. They're all part of you.

118. CR2: Yeah, yeah. Evoked by the people, I guess.

119. I: And so, I suppose, in different situations, different things are evoked, really.

120. CR2: Yeah. Very much so. I mean, I spoke to my cousin *[from Africa]* a couple of days ago and she... my *[African]* family bring this warmth out in me, that is very expressive. But my English family bring out that kind of stoic working-class thing!

121. I: You said that you didn't think of yourself as white or black, when you were younger; so is it the case, now, that

I am me: the lived experience of a mixed-race identity
by Haran Rasalingam

you just see yourself as 'me'. You don't have any tension there or anything?

122. CR2: No, I don't actually have any tension there at all. I think other people have tension.

123. I: Other people?

124. CR2: Yeah. But, you know, I think, from the moment that I realised I was different, it was like a search began in me, you know? "Ok, what's different? Why is it different? What's wrong with it? Is there nothing right? Well, why, does there have to be something wrong with it? So, who does that mean I am, then?"

125. And I've searched for something beyond the physical all my life. So, I would call myself... there's more to me than my physical body so, when I think of me, I think of more than this physicalness. This physicalness is what I exhibit. It's what is seen.

126. But, when I think of me, it's very hard to say I'm this or I'm that or I'm the other, because it's fluid. I'm fluid. I consider myself fluid.

127. I: Yes, I hear what you're saying. So, it's almost like, if you are trying to categorise yourself, it's for the benefit of the understanding of other people in a way. You're trying to help them to get it.

128. CR2: Yeah. I don't really feel like I need to get it anymore because, as soon as I've got it, I'm something else.

129. I: It's like there isn't anything to get.

130. CR2:   Right. I am what I am.

131. I: Do you find now – perhaps in the 70s it was probably worse than now – but do you find that people struggle with the idea of your 'heritage'? Do they struggle with that idea?

132. CR2:   I think people do, but maybe in a more politically correct, nicer way. You know, they kind of go, "Ooh, gosh, that's really interesting ..." or, "Gosh, I've never met anybody your colour with that accent!" Whereas, in the old days, they would just call you nigger and be done with it!

133. I: So, in a way, it was the same confusion manifested differently?

134. CR2:   Yeah, yeah. And I'm not in [area of England] anymore, and where I live now is much more multicultural, and there are a lot of mixed-heritage children running around now. Still, though, because I do have an accent, people still raise their eyebrows. Maybe if I had a more standard English accent, they wouldn't...

135. I: They would cope with it better, somehow.

136. CR2:   Yes.

137. I: As if, somehow, a local accent is unacceptable with your appearance.

138. CR2:   It's not meant to be.

139. I: Right.

I am me: the lived experience of a mixed-race identity
by Haran Rasalingam

140. CR2: Well, it's kind of, you know, "What?" Every other person with that accent is white.

141. I: That's interesting, it's not an issue for you, it's others that struggle.

142. CR2: Yeah. It never was an issue for me until people told me it was an issue for me. Until they made it an issue for me.

143. I: And, in fact, the first time you noticed it at six or seven, was because somebody said, "you are different to everybody else."

144. CR2: Yeah. And I don't think I'd ever had an issue. Other people's prejudices, other people's fears or misunderstandings or reasons, or whatever, they seemed, back then, to think they had a right to voice it in really verbally abusive and sometimes physically violent ways. And so, they made it an issue.

145.   And so, I struggled in my life where I grew up, thinking, "Can somebody just actually tell me what it is that's wrong with me that offends you so deeply? Because I'm not getting it. I actually think I'm quite a decent, good person. But I seem to offend you by just walking down the street".

146.   And so, I just never got it, as a child. And so, what I did then was I kind of turned it in on myself and looked for the bad. Because I thought "Well, if I can find the bad and fix it, then they won't treat me like that." And then,

somewhere along the line, I realised "Do you what? It wouldn't matter what I did. It's actually that they just don't like the colour of my skin." I mean, like, it's so simple and so irrelevant, but so damaging.

147. I: That's the crazy thing; so irrelevant, and yet so relevant.

148. CR2:   Yeah, yeah.

149. I: Did that ever make you wish that you were different?

150. CR2:   Yes. When I was really young, I used to watch Doris Day musicals, and Doris Day was the girl to be. And I used to pray, before I went to bed, that I'd wake up in the morning with blond hair and blue eyes, like Doris Day. And then my life would be fine. It would be alright, everything would be great. Well, of course, it never was going to happen. But then what that did was reinforce how wrong I was, because I'd wake up and look at myself in the mirror, in the morning, and there I'd be, with my little natty afro and my brown skin. And so, I'd be disappointed in myself. So, I punished myself. Then, I did what the way people did to me then, which was punish myself.

151. I: Yeah. you saw something you didn't want to see, basically. What you looked like was unpleasant.

152. CR2:   Yeah. I think I saw myself through their eyes.

153. I: Presumably, you don't now.

154. CR2:   No. Not at all.

155. I: Do you remember that changing? Do you remember when that changed?

156. CR2: It was always a conflict, through my early teens it was always a conflict. I'd be like "I don't actually think there's something wrong with the colour of my skin." But, but, but, but, but, but... and then it started to change whenever, I guess, in the late eighties, when I was kind of in my late teens, and I was more mouthy and I was more "Fuck you all!". And I started to maybe grow a bit more comfortable with myself. I think there was a growing acceptance that it wouldn't matter what I did, I can't change the colour of my skin. So, somewhere along the line, I had to accept it. And I would say, my early twenties. I think there was a piece of me that always wanted to... it was always inside me, but I never knew how to bring that out. And so, I did that young searching thing of trying some drugs, and asking lots of questions ... drugs weren't really for me but I did get a different perspective, and I realised that actually, there's more to life than the colour of your skin, and what other people think. And that opened me up more to the me that was inside. The soul, if you want to call it, or the spirit, or the spiritual side. And I began to... I don't know if it's that I began to accept the colour of my skin or is it that I began to accept the inner self. The self-hatred wasn't so massive.

I am me: the lived experience of a mixed-race identity
by Haran Rasalingam

157. I: It's almost like you sort of transcended the problem. You kind of saw beyond it.

158. CR2:   Yeah, there's more to life, there's more to being than... I mean, I never was a person who was about clothes or about fitting in with the group, or had to have the latest this, that or the other. There always seemed to me there was more to life than that, and I never really understood what it was. And I remember I used to say to my friends "Do you ever just want to be?" and they'd look at me like "What are you talking about?" and I would go on "But do you not just ever want to be?

159.   And I guess what I was trying to say was "Without all the shit, without all the drama, without all the crapness, the issues of the colour of your skin, or your hair, or your this, or your dress, or your trousers, do you not just ever want to be?" because there was a real pining in me just to be allowed to be. Because I think that's something I was not allowed, as a child: just to be allowed to be a child.

160. I: You probably noticed it more acutely than the others you grew up with.

161. CR2:   Yeah, yeah. And I think that's been my mission, is just to find me and be. Just be. And, yeah, I would say that it's still a struggle sometimes: just to be. Without the history.

162. I: Yeah.

163. CR2:   Yeah. I think that, once I found that … that was kind of like my food, when I realized that it's not about their side. Everybody else it seems to be, but… And I remember looking people in the eye, as a child, and thinking "If you could just see me, you wouldn't hit me. You wouldn't call me names. You're not seeing me."

164. I: Yeah. I think I know what you mean. Because, if somebody looks at you and calls you 'nigger' or whatever, they're not seeing you. They're seeing something, they're not seeing you.

165. CR2:   Yeah. and I wanted to be just seen for who I was, not for what they thought I was, not for the colour of my skin, not for the label. Just for being a little girl. That's all I wanted. And I think that's something I deeply remember pining for that, as a child. And so, what I did to sooth myself was I said "Well, God sees me." I was never religious, I never went to church, I never went to chapel, I never went to any of that. I didn't see God in there, because even the minister of the church used to look at me and not see me. So, I used to think "Well, God isn't in here, and I'm not coming."

166.   So that's where I kind of found my solace, as a child I used to sit and look out of the window and think "Well, you may all hate me, but I know that God loves me, because God sees me." I never realised then, but I kind of realise now that that was a defence, to protect. That's what I

needed from me, as a child. And that God, for me, doesn't really exist, because I invented that God to protect me. But it allowed me to think that "Well, something loves me. Something sees me."

167. I: There are some more questions. I'm trying to be structured! Trying very hard. I'll ask a bit about psychotherapy; to what extent was your initial engagement with psychotherapy connected with your mixed heritage?

168. CR2:   Well, because I was studying to be a counsellor, I needed to have personal therapy. I've always been interested in 'underneath'. What's going on behind that? What's going on behind you?

169. I: I guess your childhood made that inevitable.

170. CR2:   Yeah. I think so. And I particularly chose a counsellor who was trans-personal, because that's the underneath, for me.

171. I: Trans-personal, okay.

172. CR2:   Yes. And I particularly made sure I went to a multicultural counselling centre, because I know every issue that I have is because of my history. Every issue that I have ever had has been because of my history in *[hometown]* and of being of mixed parentage. And what I wanted, when I went to see my counsellor, was a witness. I wanted my life to be witnessed, because it wasn't witnessed in *[hometown]*, it was acted upon.

173.   So, I wanted someone to actually witness that child and what she carried. I didn't want my counsellor to interpret or… I wanted my counsellor just to be there, and let that child, that couldn't have a voice at home, in the house, and that couldn't have a voice at school, or in the street or anywhere else' – I wanted my counsellor to sit and look me in the eye and witness that child.

174. I: And how was it?

175. CR2: Well, it was a very intense experience and, when I look back at it now, what I've gone through, partially since I finished my counselling, has been even more intense, because I think I held a piece, I wasn't 100% trusting of this counsellor. I actually let the full ferocity of the depth of the emotions and the feelings that I stored up, because I just suppressed them and suppressed them and suppressed them.

176. I: What was this therapist's ethnicity?

177. CR2: She was actually mixed heritage herself. I think she was Spanish, white, she didn't look black. But I didn't realise, because I've kind of worked on myself, I've always been my own therapist and I held me together, because I was a very depressed child, there were many times I could have just let go. Quite a few times I did think about just letting go and not being here. I used to think about going home and, to me, 'going home' was going home to where I

really belonged, which was with God, or with the universe, or with the 'presence', the 'being' that is everything.

178.   So, what I was thinking about was suicide. I used to pine to go home, because then I would just be. It took me a long time to understand that I could just 'be' here. I think I held a lot of that back from my counsellor because, in part, I was on a counselling course, and I didn't want her to go "This woman is seriously disturbed, and she's on a counselling course.", but there was also the relational aspect; I never trusted anybody, because I had people, that I considered friends, at some stage, when the pressure got too much, then turned on me and called me a 'nigger'.

179.   So, it has always been very hard for me to trust, and then I had issues of being abandoned by my Dad, so you give yourself to somebody for 50 minutes and leave, it was very hard for me to do. However, I guess I gave as much as I could at that time, and she held me very well. But it's funny, it's only these past four or five months, when the real after-effects of my personal counselling have hit me, where I have actually really allowed myself to plunder my depths.

180. I: And is that without the counsellor being involved? This is on your own.

181. CR2:   This is on my own. I have really plundered my depths of despair, because I used to despair, as a child and as a young teenager, because I used to think there was nothing I can do. Every day you wake up and there's nothing you can do to make these people like you, to make these people leave you alone. And some of it was quite torturous because, when I was at high school and I had to take this route home, to get to the bus to get home and, every Wednesday, they were filling the coal lorry, to deliver the coal. And, every Wednesday, these coal men would fire coal at me and call me a nigger and laugh at me. And this happened every Wednesday, from a few years. But they always made sure the coal never hit me.

182.   So, every Wednesday, I'd walk with my head down, feeling really shamed, while they laughed at me and threw coal at me, waiting for the coal to hit. The one day one piece of coal was going to hit, and it was really shaming. I never told anybody that, and you just carry it, and you just carry it, and you just carry it. And you just suppress and suppress and suppress it. And I kind of let it out a bit in my personal therapy, but even I wasn't aware of the depths of despair, because no one could stop that. And I had to go to school, and I had to take that route home, because that was the only place the buses went from. So,

I am me: the lived experience of a mixed-race identity
by Haran Rasalingam

there was helplessness and there was shame and there was despair; you just get on with it, I just got on with it.

183. I: And, I guess, there was never anyone around thinking anything was wrong with it.

184. CR2: Yeah, and you can't go home and say "Mummy, those men did this.", you know, "Would you go and talk to the people who own the coal yard." So, I guess I am layered, there are layers to me. There's layers of my history, and I think that this moment in my life I've reached layers in my history that I didn't even know existed. And made me realise how disturbing it was to grow up as a mixed heritage child in *[hometown]*. A disturbing, disturbing experience.

185. I: So, over the whole course of your training, it's kind of loosened this stuff up and you've found it on your own, in the end.

186. CR2: I think I always knew I would find it on my own. I had my witness for when I needed my witness, and I have always left the door open, that I will go back. Maybe to the same counsellor, maybe not, but I think that the depths of where I... I don't think I was ever going to go there with anybody but myself.

187. I: I wonder, then, how helpful or unhelpful therapy has been for you, or training has been for you, on this kind of stuff.

188. CR2:   Yeah. I don't think training has been helpful for me, really, on this kind of stuff. I think what I did was help myself in my training. Because I am a searcher, because I know that there's so much and because my searching has been just 'to be' – well, just 'to be' then you have to work hard, just 'to be', to get rid of the layers, to find the 'just being'. Then I helped myself, I took what I learned and found myself in it or applied it to myself. It was never tailored to being mixed heritage in any way. I think we might have had one lecture.

189. I: And how was that?

190. CR2:   And, in fact, I might even be lying, we might not have had one lecture. Maybe that was wishful thinking! I placed myself in the middle of my training and made sure that I got the best that I could out of it. My personal counselling, I don't know, it wasn't tailored – I don't what I was looking for, other than a witness.

191. I: And I suppose you were going in there for yourself, as a person, not specifically for mixed whatever. It's just 'me', I'm going in here to...

192. CR2:   Well, I was aware that, when I was going, that I am mixed heritage and that it was a multicultural centre that I made sure that I went to, you know, hoping that they would have an understanding of what it's like. But it was, ultimately, about me, about me.

I am me: the lived experience of a mixed-race identity
by Haran Rasalingam

193. I: But did you feel there was an understanding?

194. CR2:   I don't think it was an understanding of what it's like to be multicultural, mixed heritage. I think, maybe, what my counsellor was trying to understand me as me. As much as she could. But I don't know if me, as me – if she was always aware of that dimension. Does that make sense?

195. I: Yeah.

196. CR2:   I don't know how she could have done that. I was the one that constantly referred to being mixed heritage.

197. I: You explored, she didn't. Did she challenge that in any way? Did she seek to gain a better understanding of that sort of dimension?

198. CR2:   She didn't challenge it. No, she didn't challenge it in any way. Maybe she was overly accepting of it, I don't know. I think she sought to understand my experience and the effect that it had on me.

199. I: So, you didn't find, at any point, that she was dismissive of it.

200. CR2:   No. No, but then I brought it every week. It is me, you know. It's who I am. I know I was quite… sometimes I use to worry about whether she could contain me. She always did, you know, and I'd come away thinking "Well maybe that's just you thinking that you're more than you are." But sometimes I used to see her, in the session, she would be physically perspiring and get quite flushed in the

I am me: the lived experience of a mixed-race identity
by Haran Rasalingam

face, and so, then, I think I would rein myself in, thinking "Am I too much?", "Is this too heavy?"

201. I: That's interesting. This was part of the holding back. Could she take it, basically?

202. CR2:   Yeah. Well, maybe that came from when my Mummy couldn't take it, so how am I supposed to believe that this stranger can take it? Maybe it was partly that.

203. I: You couldn't dump it on your Mum.

204. CR2:   Not at all, no. It's funny though, since I got older, I guess, in some ways, I've dumped it on my Mum, because I got to the stage where I thought "Well, you know what? You're my Mum, so you need to hear this one."

205. I: That's another point, as well, I suppose in adult life have you had more chance to actually raise these issues with your Mum?

206. CR2:   Yeah, yeah.

207. I: And how has it been?

208. CR2:   Well, it was uncomfortable for my Mum, in the beginning. I think guilt. And then, I guess I badgered her that much that, one day, we got down to the nitty gritty, which was my Mum saying to me "Yeah, I didn't speak out against these people because I didn't know how to, I didn't want to believe that people we knew would do that".

209.   And this really cut me. Really, really cut me at the time, but it gave me a deeper understanding of my Mum. I didn't

hate her. I love my Mummy, I really love my Mum. And I know there was truth in it. But it was conflicted as well, because I see, at times, how she is so proud of me, you know "This is my daughter, this is my daughter".

210. I: It kind of feels like she felt that her loyalties were torn?

211. CR2:   Yeah. Once when we went shopping, in *[hometown]*, and we were walking down the main street, and I saw this man coming – I think I might have been about ten – I just saw him in the crowd, and I just knew. And I guess my Mum saw. And it was like slow motion, he just veered towards us in the crowd and lifted his hands like he was going to slap me across the face. My Mum just pulled me completely out of the way, never broke stride, and we just walked on. She just never mentioned it. That was the end of it. It was like we went into a shock then.

212. I: But that's the sort of incident where she's witnessed.

213. CR2:   Yeah. I guess she was more alert than she ever wanted to make out. I think my Mummy thought if you keep it all under wraps, it will go away. Keep it away and we won't have to have that uncomfortable conversation. Once, she did go down and shouted at these guys. Once. And I remember…

214. I: Which guys, the coal guys?

215. CR2:   When I was 11, I had my front tooth broken by some 19-year olds. I came home screaming and crying, blood

I am me: the lived experience of a mixed-race identity
by Haran Rasalingam

coming out of my mouth. My Mum just got out and went down, and I was going "They're down there, they're down there." My Mum's small, and these guys were really tall; and my Mum's just standing there, yelling at them.

216. I: How old were you?

217. CR2:   I was just turned 11.

218. I: How had they broken your teeth?

219. CR2:   I'd been on the roundabout with my friends, and they'd come along, and they were "Look at the little nigger, look at the little darkie.", every name. So, they spun it really, really, really fast, and they were laughing. I couldn't hold on, and I banged my head on the metal footplate, and then kind of spun out, and banged my head on the concrete and I was out for a couple of minutes. When I woke up, I was just lying on the ground and they were laughing.

220.   And my friends were just sitting on the roundabout crying. I got up and there was just blood and I just started screaming. But that's the one time I remember my Mum actually really making a stand. I had to go and get my head X-rayed, and it was a really big thing, and the neighbours... because you could hear me coming for miles, just screaming. And I was really proud of her, I felt kind of protected, for once.

221. I: It's so brutal, isn't it? It's just so brutal.

I am me: the lived experience of a mixed-race identity
by Haran Rasalingam

222. CR2: Yeah, really brutal. For some reason they just couldn't cope with the difference, but it affected them in such an extreme way.

223.   I remember, when I visited a friend of mine who lived in the country, and we called down to see a friend of hers, and her granddad was there, and he actually thought I was going to eat him. That's kind of how ridiculous the mentality would get, at some stages. And I looked at this man, I just laughed; he was in his late eighties, he had never been out of the village in his life, he'd never seen anybody that didn't look like him or sound like him. So, he thought, first of all, that I didn't speak English, so he talked about me like I wasn't in the room, and said "Them darkies, they eat you." I just laughed.

224. I: Maybe he was a bit too long in the tooth to be converted.

225. CR2: Yeah. Well, you know, even I can't be offended at that. That's just ridiculous.

226. I: I've just got a couple of questions that I want to ask. I think we covered loads of stuff here, without me even asking the questions. Last two questions: what makes you most happy about other people's attitudes to your identity?

227. CR2: Just accepting me for me. I don't want anybody to accept me because they feel they have to, because it's politically correct. I'm me, that's it.

228. I: That's all you ask for.

I am me: the lived experience of a mixed-race identity
by Haran Rasalingam

229. CR2:   Yeah. You either take me for me, or you don't. And, if you don't, then it's not my issue, it's yours. If you want to deal with it, then deal with it; if you don't want to deal with it, then don't. Then go away. It's alright. I don't think I ask for much in life, just to be allowed to be and accepted for who I am.

230. I: What frustrates you most about other people's attitudes to you?

231. CR2:   When they try to put me in a box, you know. Like when I had that [African] boyfriend saying "Oh, you would be treated as a princess, because you've got pale skin." I don't want to be treated as an anything! Or black women – they don't do this much now, but they used to kiss their teeth at me in the street. Another black woman saying, "She thinks she's all that, because she's got her own hair" It's only hair. And that is actually your issue, and you don't know me to say that I think I'm anything.

232. I: They think you're kind of shoving it under their noses, your hair.

233. CR2:   Well, there is the whole… then you get into the whole black thing of 'shades of blackness'. And, apparently, back in the day, the lighter skinned you were, the better opportunities you had. Yes, black people have their hang ups as well, but they're not mine. So, you're now going to label me, because of the colour of my skin. So, you now

want to put me in a box and say that I now think I'm better than you. I don't think I'm anything more than you; I'm just me. So, it frustrates me when somebody wants to put me in category, and then they want to give me characteristics to go with it? You don't even know my name! That frustrates me.

234. I: The whole thing about labelling, I think I can sort of identify with that. What is it with this labelling business? Why are people constantly trying to stamp everything?

235. CR2:   Well, it's all about them feeling better, isn't it? They have got something to work with then: "You're a 'this', you're a 'that'."

236. I: There's a formula.

237. CR2:   Yeah. And so, they know where they are. But you're not dealing with me on a real level.

238. I: And does that run through your life generally, this? Not just in terms of race or whatever. That kind of resistance to labelling, do you get that generally in life?

239. CR2:   Yeah. I have a real resistance to putting labels on people and being labelled by people. And I also had to learn to chit-chat, because I also then had a real resistance to kind of relating to people on a shallow level. The persona that people present, or "Well, you're wearing black trousers, so you must be one of those depressos, goth..." You

know, putting a person in a category and treating them like that. And so, all you relate to is what you see.

240.   To me that's really false. I want to relate to you as a human being and also as a human being who may have a spurt or an energy about you. So, I used to find it very hard just to chat about the weather and things like that. I guess people, maybe, used to think of me as quite intense, because I never did superficial chat. No, no. So yes, throughout my life, there is a real resistance to labels. I won't label my kids, or…

241. I: Yeah. And what about in terms of therapy? Your approach to therapy.

242. CR2:   Yeah. I don't want to label anybody.

243. I: But what about the label of your approach? You know, some people like to say, "I'm psychodynamic.", or…

244. CR2:   That's why I started integratively.

245. I: Is it almost natural to work towards integration, do you think?

246. CR2:   Well, everybody is an individual. And I don't believe you can relate to everybody in one way. And, at the end of the day, they're called theories for a reason. Because they're theories. And, as well as knowing your theories, know yourself. Bring yourself, as a therapist, into the room. And, when you bring yourself, then you can go beyond the theory. Yes, the theory's there, and the theory is good to

know – I don't take anything away from the theory – but the theory is not going to do anything for you, unless you know yourself.

247.   And I became a counsellor because I like to relate to people, to the realness of people, whether that is their pain, or whether that is their joy. Whatever that is. Bring what you bring, be what you are, and that's what got me into being a counsellor, because you go underneath the daily persona façade, the look, the hair, whatever. And, when you get under there, I don't feel I have any right to label it, because then you make that person small.

248. I: That is so well put. I think that is a really good place to stop.

[End of interview]

INTERVIEW: Where are you really from?

"Looking in the mirror …
what I feel like and who I am
inside aren't always the same
thing."

About Co-Researcher #3

Co-Researcher #3 (CR3) is a trainee psychotherapist in his late thirties. CR3 never knew his biological father with whom his mother had had a one-night stand. He describes his mother as white English, but he does not know the cultural, ethnic or racial background of his father and speculates that he might be Mediterranean, Middle Eastern or north Indian. CR3 describes himself as culturally white mixed race. CR3 says he was darker skinned as a child and now he has slightly tanned skin which leads people to speculate that he might not be English.

Research interview with Co-Researcher #3

[I = Interviewer; CR3 = Co-Researcher #3]

1. I: I'm going to ask you first to describe your family background, your roots, however you want to put it.

2. CR3:   That's an interesting one, I think, as it is quite current for me as a theme. I define myself as mixed race. Half my

family are English – white English – and I grew up with them. So that is very much part of my identity.

3.   My mother had a... I'm the product of a single parent relationship, because she had a one-night stand with someone of another ethnicity. And, whenever I talk to her, she's quite vague about... well, she doesn't know where my father was from.

4.   And, when I talk to her about this, I ask, "Did he look Middle Eastern, or did he look more this, or that?" And she's very kind of, "Oh, I don't really know, I'm not sure." Because it really was, as far as I can tell, a kind of one-off. It's a kind of unknown factor, but I grew up in a white English family.

5.   I: An unknown factor for you, I guess, when you say an unknown factor. Something that you don't know anything about.

6.   CR3:   Absolutely. Apart from the fact that I don't look like any of my white English family. You know, I've got olive skin, black hair and big brown eyes. Things that no one else in my family has. So, I obviously took a lot of the looks and colour from my dad. So, there's always that kind of being part of the family, but then there's being a bit of a black sheep, in a way, as well.

I am me: the lived experience of a mixed-race identity
by Haran Rasalingam

7.   I: Right. Although your mum may not have been able to say, "Oh, Middle East" or this or that, has she been able to give a description of your dad, in any way?

8.   CR3:   Well, it was a while ago now and, obviously, we didn't really talk about it when I was a kid. And I think, for her, there was quite a lot of stigma and shame around being a single parent. You know, early 70s…

9.   I: What year were you born?

10.   CR3:   73. So it was kind of… yeah, I think there was a lot of stigma and shame. Probably initially just about being a teenager and getting pregnant and sort of saying, "I don't know who the father is". But then also having a mixed-race child from it. So, I think there was added stigma.

11.   I: So, your mum was a teenager at the time?

12.   CR3:   Yes, she was about 18. So, there was a big… her parents supported her and me, and I kind of grew up, really, more with my grandparents than with her, in a way. My grandmother was more of a mother figure to me, anyway.

13.   I: Because your mum was so young.

14.   CR3:   Yeah, and she went back to work quite soon, anyway. So, when I've talked to my mother about this, she can tend to say, "His first name was *[English-sounding name]*, but I don't know if that was short for something…" because most people choose Anglicised names.

15.   I: Perhaps a contraction of a more exotic name?

I am me: the lived experience of a mixed-race identity
by Haran Rasalingam

16. CR3: Yeah, yeah, exactly. And she said to me that he was a student, she thinks, living over here. And she could say, yes, we had similar colouring, but she really can't be more... When I said, "Was he Indian, Asian, Pakistani, something like that? Or was he Middle Eastern or was he more North African, for example?", she could never really pin it down. And I've talked to her about it more in recent years and she really can't pin it down.

17. And I get responses from people all the time of... which range from people not even recognising that I'm not white, to people presuming, you know, if I go to Italy, everyone thinks I'm Italian. I was in a restaurant, the other day, and a waitress was saying to me, "Do I know you?" and my friend had just said to me, "She could be your sister." And we talked, and she was from Algeria. So, I get a lot of people saying, you could be half Kurdish, or Middle Eastern, Asian. I really get everything.

18. I: People pick up on the fact that you somehow look different in some way or another?

19. CR3: Yes. Although some people don't. Actually, I said to my therapist, Mike, "Oh yeah, blah, blah, blah, I'm mixed race." And he said, "Oh really? I hadn't registered that at all. I didn't realise you were black.", were his words. Which really wound me up. I got really angry then,

I am me: the lived experience of a mixed-race identity
by Haran Rasalingam

because I said, "I didn't say I'm black, I just said I'm mixed race. You've made that assumption.

20. I: Or you've used that term just to describe someone. Grabbed it out of the air from somewhere.

21. CR3: Yeah. But I have had people say to me, "Oh, I didn't realise you weren't white, I just thought you'd just been on holiday and had a bit of a suntan.", to "Oh, are you Jamaican?", or something else. A real mixture.

22. I: So, people do see you in various different ways?

23. CR3: Yeah, absolutely. Absolutely.

24. I: I just wanted to ask a little bit more; it sounds like, during your childhood, it was something that wasn't really spoken about?

25. CR3: Not very much, no. From my mum's point of view, there was shame about being pregnant. She didn't tell her parents until she had to. I think she was trying to avoid it or pretend it wasn't happening.

26.   So, no, it wasn't really something that was talked about very much at all. One of the few things that I remember – because I lived with my grandparents, and my hair is black, and I had longer hair – and I remember playing with it, one day, and I was piling it on top of my head, and my grandfather saying to me, "Don't do that. You look like a Sikh if you do that."

I am me: the lived experience of a mixed-race identity
by Haran Rasalingam

27.   So that was the only comment I can remember about, was a kind of: "Don't do that, avoid it." Avoid looking like that.

28.   I: Avoid looking different. So that's all you remember, in all that time? Your mother or your grandparents touched on it?

29.   CR3: Yeah, to be honest. Yeah. It was something we didn't talk about. There was maybe talk about not knowing who my dad was. There was probably a bit more of that. There's one of those stories in the family where I think I said to my mum, when I was about four or five, and she said to me, "What do you want for Christmas?" And I said, "I want my dad."

30.   So, I think there was that kind of… there was maybe more recognition of the whole not knowing who my dad was, the stuff about ethnicity. And yeah, I probably had said to my mum at certain points, "Where was he from?" But I can't really remember the conversation. I was very careful around her feelings, often not to ask difficult questions around her, because I grew up with the impression that she didn't want to talk about it. Don't talk about.

31.   I: So, in a way, you were protecting her by picking up on her discomfort.

32.   CR3: Yeah. Absolutely. Absolutely. A few comments at school; a bit of Mickey taking.

I am me: the lived experience of a mixed-race identity
by Haran Rasalingam

33. I: I was going to ask about that; what was it like growing up
            at school? What kind of Mickey taking?

34. CR3:   A bit of racism… you know, mainly in secondary school.
            And it wasn't anything major, a few 'Paki' type
            comments. Which to me… I was confused. "What are you
            talking about?" I'm not what you would normally describe
            as a Paki anyway. It was just generic, ignorant, racist
            response. But it wasn't very common or very prevalent. It
            was pretty minimal.

35.   I wouldn't say I felt ostracised or isolated or anything like
            that because of it. I went to a very white secondary school.
            There were a couple of black kids in my year and maybe
            a couple of Asian kids, but it was like 95% white.

36. I: Did people at school generally see you as like one of
            them?

37. CR3:   Yeah, yeah. I think so. And I think I did as well. I'd always
            had this thing of looking in the mirror and, sometimes,
            what I feel like and who I am inside aren't always the same
            thing. Or they haven't always been, at various points in
            my history.

38.   But I think I was quite a cute kid, actually, and quite
            charming and I think the parents of other kids always
            really liked me because I was quite well behaved and quite
            polite. And it was always, "Oh, isn't he charming?" which

was always the case of what other mothers would say to my mum.

39. I: So, you were charming, you looked nice, other people thought you looked nice.

40. CR3: Yeah, yeah.

41. I: You didn't look weird to them, in some way.

42. CR3: No, I was quite a cute kid, I think. I kind of knew there was a difference, but it was hard to. The only other thing I can think of, that relates to this, is being maybe at infant school and the teacher saying, "Alright everyone, imagine what animal you would be, if you were going to be an animal." You know, a giraffe or an elephant or whatever, and the teacher saying to me, "Oh, I think you'd be a bush baby." Only because I had big, brown eyes.

43.   And so, there was something about my colouring, I suppose, about the eyes. I had these big, brown eyes and this little face, you know. It didn't feel felt like it was hostile or threatening, so there was, I guess, an awareness that I was different, but I didn't encounter a lot of racism, or anything like that.

44. I: Were you aware that you were different because you knew that your father was from somewhere else?

45. CR3: Yes.

46. I: Do you remember how old you were, when you became aware of that?

47.   CR3:   I think I always felt a bit different. I think it was actually something that came from birth, in some ways. Actually, I've just thought of another thing I did. I must have been very aware of this when I was at primary school, so I guess around seven or eight. I had this whole thing where I went through a phase of telling lies; kind of making up who my dad was, to explain to people. And there was a whole kind of, "Oh yeah, he's a Red Indian" and things like that.

48.   I had all these stories, and then I would make up, "Yeah and I've got these other middle names." and I would just make up names. And I was quite an imaginative child and I would make up these little stories about, "Yeah, I'm also this, this and this." and I guess that was my wanting to fill a gap, a mystery, that I couldn't.... so, I'd make up a story.

49.   I: So, the sense of difference was prominent enough in your childhood for you to want to make stories about it. So, you could sense some sort of difference, but couldn't quite put your finger on it?

50.   CR3:   Yes. And I wasn't maybe conscious of it, I would be carrying it with me. I've done a fair amount of work on it since! So, I can see I was probably carrying it with me, but not necessarily consciously. Because I've always really carried a sense of difference with me.

51.   I: You always have done?

52.   CR3:   Yeah, absolutely. And I think a lot of my own personal therapy has been around that. My current therapist has been great about exploring that with me and how that's affected how I mix with people in different social situations, whether it's work or relationships. And he suggested to me – quite recently, actually – that all these different situations where I might say I felt some trepidation or lack of confidence in myself, sometimes – and yet be quite a confident person at other times – he suggested to me that maybe this comes from a sense of ambivalence or hostility to your existence from birth.

53.   Which has been really useful, to explore that idea, because, single parent, teenage pregnancy kind of thing, there was that kind of 'unwelcomeness' there and then the… my mixed race has added a layer that goes with that.

54.   I: If somebody asks you where you're from, for example, how do you answer that?

55.   CR3:   I hate that question so much! I hate it, I hate it, I hate it. There was a really good article in The Guardian the other day about this very issue. I don't know if you read it. This woman who I think was half Iranian and half American, but she looks Iranian.

56.   I: I haven't read it.

57.   CR3:   Okay. It's a really good, really short article. It may not be racist, but it was the gist of her article. And when people

would say, "Where are you from?" She'd say, "Oh, I'm from [area of city]" or wherever she lives in [name of city]. And they'd say, "No, but where are you really from?" And it's that question that I hate.

58. I: It's a very loaded question, then?

59. CR3:   Really loaded, yeah. I will either answer, "I grew up in [area of city]", or, "I'm from [area of city]", because that's where I grew up, or I've always lived in [name of city], so "I'm from [name of city]". But I know that's not what they mean.

60. I: You get this sense that they're waiting for more!

61. CR3:   Yeah. What they're saying is, "You're not white. Where are you from in the world, because you're obviously not from here." That's what they're saying. And I've had so many different strategies with this; I used to lie, I used to say I'm Italian. If it will shut you up, because they don't want to say it.

62.   But then I have people say, "Oh, *I'm* from Italy. I think you look more Spanish. I'm... Oh god, don't go there! So then, sometimes, I'll say, "I'm mixed race, but I'm half English." The problem is if I then say I'm mixed race and I have to explain when they ask, "Where's the other half from?" I have to say, "I don't know". "Why don't you know?" And actually, to somebody I don't know very

I am me: the lived experience of a mixed-race identity
by Haran Rasalingam

well, I have to say, "Well, I don't know my dad... mum was a single parent...", it's quite a personal story.

63.　I:　　So, you suddenly have to open up a lot more than you felt prepared to.

64.　CR3:　Yes. I felt like saying "I'm from *[name of random town]*", or wherever. So, I hate the question.

65.　I:　　Is it fair to say it's quite an intrusive question?

66.　CR3:　Yes. I mean, with some people who are close to me I will discuss the ins and outs of it in great, great detail, you know? With other people, they ask it... it depends where it is, who it is. There are people I kind of know, when I meet them, how important they are going to be in my life. If it's someone in a shop and they ask "Where are you from?" – it doesn't happen very often, but I'm thinking of an example of someone who I don't think is about to become my best friend or a partner, or a colleague I'm going to work with every day, just some random acquaintance, who I'm probably only going to meet once – I might lie about it or keep to the short and simple answer.

67.　　　　If it's someone I know, who I meet regularly, I would be very honest about it, because I have to tell the story.

68.　I:　　Yes, that makes sense. If somebody asks your nationality?

69.　CR3:　British.

70.　I:　　That's the easy one.

71.   CR3:   That is really easy. The difficult one is when you get the Equal Opportunity forms with the 'tick your ethnicity' box, that's the difficult one. Because, if there's a box that says: 'mixed race' or 'other', I will normally tick one of those. And then they, sometimes, have the space for 'explain in more detail', or 'explain what the two races you are mixed between are'.

72.   So, if it just says 'mixed race' and there's no other information given, I will tick that. Or if it just says 'other' and nothing else, I will tick that. If it doesn't have a 'mixed race' box but it does have an 'other' box, I will tick 'other', and then write, mixed race, if I was to write anything.

73.   And sometimes, if I can't be bothered, I will tick 'White British', because half of me is and, as far as I'm concerned, on some level, all of me is, you know, and, on some level, only half of me is.

74.   I: It depends on what way you're talking about it, I suppose.

75.   CR3:   Yeah. And, if I want to define myself in that way, who has the right to tell me I shouldn't?

76.   I: There's a lot of assumptions around these forms!

77.   CR3:   That's very true.

78.   I: I notice you've used the term 'mixed race'. I wasn't sure whether to use that terminology on this research; some

people don't like it. So, for you, that would be an acceptable term?

79.　CR3:　Yeah, I think it's fine. When I grew up, my god, you were called 'half-caste' and that was the term that was used. I remember people saying to me and about me, you're a half-caste. Or *me* saying I'm half-caste, because I was told that's the language you used. Whereas I would never dream of using that now because of all the connotations it has.

80.　　　　Mixed race, I think, is fine because, to me, anyway, it doesn't carry negative connotations. I think it's quite nice that so many people are mixed race – certainly in London – that it's a very common thing, actually. So yeah, I'm fine, in that case.

81.　I:　So, what would you say are the negative connotations of half-caste?

82.　CR3:　Well, I think a) the fact that you use the word caste as in relating to the caste system. So, it's very much relating to a kind of Indian, Asian caste system. So, if you're half Japanese and half Turkish, you're not connected to that caste system at that time.

83.　　　　So, because I don't know where my dad is from, it's labelling me as being Indian, or something like that. Which I don't know that I am that, or whatever else I may be. So, it was labelling, in terms of what the other half of me might be, and also because cast is related to a class system as well. There's all those connotations I don't like. But mixed race is not.

84. I: So, what does the word 'race' mean to you?

85. CR3:   Hmm, that's an interesting one. A race, I suppose, is a group of people from a particular place. If I say I'm British, it's because... or, actually, I would probably say my white English family, or I might say my white British family. They are English. They are British, they are white. So, it's about skin colour, and about cultural and national identity as well.

86. I: Skin colour. Cultural identity. National identity?

87. CR3:   Yeah. And about where they live. My family lived in England for a fair while. I don't know how many generations back, but my grandparents were both English. Their parents were English. I don't know further back than that. So yeah, I suppose it's about those things, to me.

88. I: I don't know if it was your current therapist or another therapist that said, "Oh, I didn't realise you were black." and you took offense to that.

89. CR3:   Yeah.

90. I: How would you feel if somebody said you were white, I didn't realise you were white?

91. CR3:   I can't imagine anyone saying the sentence in quite that way, "I didn't realise you were white." Some people do

presume I am white, totally. That's fine. I have no problem with people seeing me as white because, in many ways, I see myself, on some level, as white. Because I grew up in a white family and because I don't have any cultural connections with whatever race my dad was.

92.　　I only have the culture of England. That's my cultural identity. So being mistaken as being fully white I wouldn't have any problem with. And lots of people, I think, if they do see me as being half something else, and maybe this is what I am, it could be something Mediterranean. So, it's still kind of European, which a lot of Italian or Spanish people have a similar complexion to me, and people regard them as white, but they're a lot more olive skinned and dark haired than, say, a lot of English people.

93.　I:　So, they would certainly call themselves white.

94.　CR3:　Yeah, absolutely. Yeah.

95.　I:　You sound, then, that you're quite comfortable with the idea of being called white.

96.　CR3:　Yeah.

97.　I:　And do you think it's because you're quite fair, you're olive skinned. Do you think, if you had been a bit darker, it may have been more of an issue? A slightly leading question!

98.　CR3:　No, no, I understand the question. It's interesting; if I look at photos of me when I was a baby and very young, I looked a lot more ethnic, for want of a better word. My hair was black, my skin was brown, and the shape of my face and my eyes just looked a bit more Asian. And I'd say I looked pretty Western European now but, as a kid, I think… sometimes I can look at those photos and I looked more, for want of a better word, ethnic than I do now. Yes. I think I looked more ethnical, possibly darker, then. It was more obvious. And if it was more obvious that I was mixed race, then yes, I think I probably would have issues. I probably wouldn't be labelled as white and I would probably have more issues around my ethnicity, I suspect.

99.   I: Do you every get tired of people saying, "No, you're not.", whatever you say that you are?

100. CR3:   Yeah. There's times that I really remember; I must have been about 16, going to… I can't remember exactly what it was, it was like some kind of local council type festival that a parent of one of my friends at school was involved in organising, and it was supposed to be like an international festival of different nations.

101.   And some of us went, and someone said to me, "Where are you from?" and I said, "I'm from here.". And I think they said, "No you're not." or "Well, you're obviously from somewhere else, aren't you?" And I remember feeling really challenged by that. I thought, "Oh god, I

don't know how I'm supposed to answer this. I've grown up in *[name of city]* all my life. I *am* from here."

102.   And I knew what they meant was, "You're a bit brown, where are you actually from?" So, it's happened a few times. My favourite story of this is, maybe about five or six years ago I was with one of my best friends who is white, English. I was at university with her and her boyfriend at the time. They're both white and her partner is Irish descent.

103.   His mother is a bit of a racist, and I was at Maria's house and Tim was out and his mother was there. I'd never met her before, and we shook hands and said hello. Then she said to me, "You're very brown." That was literally the first thing she said to me. And I really didn't know what to say to that, and I didn't know whether it was, "Ooh, you've got a tan!" because it was summer, and I didn't know if it meant, "Oh, you tan nicely." or whether it meant; "You're obviously not white. You're obviously not from here.", which I think was what she was actually saying. It was just ignorance.

104.   And I've thought of another example, actually, and it actually seems to come up in therapy situations a lot more; I applied – quite a few years ago, now – to one training school, when I was initially looking to train … it was like the introductory certificate level course, and I was

interviewed by a white, plummy, middle-aged woman who, in the interview, said to me – somehow it came up that I was mixed race – and she said "Oh, you must have loads of issues about being half black." And I was so shocked that she was kind of telling me a) that I was half black – her words, not mine, I'd said mixed race – and b) that I must have loads of issues about it. Needless to say, I didn't go and study there!

105. I: Maybe *she* had loads of issues about it.

106. CR3:   I think maybe she was trying to stir a reaction up in me, or – what I really think – she was very, very ignorant in her use of language around race. And I really thought "Well, I'm not paying to come and study somewhere with people who are that thick and rude, actually. Someone said to me "Oh, you should have given them some feedback on that" but I never did, because I was so angry about it. But I thought, "Wow".

107. I: Do you find, then, that other people struggle with the concept, have problems with who you are, or who they think you are or where they think you're from, what colour you are? Do you ever get that much?

108. CR3:   No.

109. I: It doesn't happen.

110. CR3:   No. I think, in *[name of city]*, there are so many different shades of every colour. Not really. The only times I can

remember it happening was, my aunt lives in *[name of county]*. This is what I remember when I was about 16, going up to visit her. She lives in a small town in *[name of county]*, and people are literally staring at me on the street, because I wasn't white. And they were so unfamiliar with seeing anyone who wasn't white. Horrible. And I remember going back to *[name of city]* and just suddenly appreciating, for the first time, that *[name of city]* was this great place where everybody was really different, and nobody looked twice or cared. And I'd never really thought about it or realised it, up to that point.

111. I: I suppose, because you'd grown up in *[name of city]* all the time, it was what you've known.

112. CR3:   Yeah, absolutely.

113. I: Yeah. So, stepping out of *[name of city]* must have been the only time it happened, basically.

114. CR3:   Yeah, absolutely. And I didn't like the place particularly, anyway, but it really was like "god, I really do not like this place where people stare at you." And it took me a moment to realise why they were staring at me.

115. I: Have you noticed any other such stares, say, in another country?

116. CR3:   No. I haven't, actually. The only place I can think of where I became a bit conscious of it was... when I was about 17,

I went Interrailing around Europe and, when I was in Germany and Austria, I don't know if it was my sensitivity to the history there – you know, the whole thing about being Aryan, whether I was being sensitive to that or whether there was a feel there – but I did get this sense – no one said anything or did anything – but I did get this sense that there was a bit of awareness or hostility to me not being white. And I didn't feel it in France, or Holland, or other countries I went to. And I've travelled a fair bit in Europe and I've never been confronted or had any problem anywhere, but in those two countries, Germany and Austria, I did feel something because, I think, they are very large countries, and...

117. I: They probably are suspicious even if you've got olive skin, maybe.

118. CR3:   Possibly.

119. I: Too Mediterranean for them, or whatever.

120. CR3:   Although now, I think, things are very different, actually. And I travel there fairly often. I've got friends who live in Berlin... Berlin, obviously, is a big city and, again, there is a big mixture of people there. And they have a big Turkish population, in Germany, so I've not encountered any problems. I was in Vienna, a couple of years ago.

121. I: Do you think they would have taken you for Turkish, in those places? At a glance?

122. CR3: Not particularly. But I probably could pass for it. But I really don't know what people think, if anything at all.

123. I: I suppose that's a sign of the fact that people aren't staring at you. It isn't an issue.

124. CR3: Yeah. I've certainly not felt it to be an issue. And, you know, people recently have said to me things like "I was on holiday in Spain, recently, and a lot of people really look like you. You really could be Spanish.", or, you know, and I said, "When I go to Italy, and I used to have longer hair – my hair is kind of shaven now, and receding – but, when I had longer hair, it was quite curly, and I actually had it quite long and, in Italy, with longer hair, I did look very Italian. The number of people who would come up and say something to me in Italian, and I'd have to say, in Italian, "I'm sorry, I can only speak English." And they'd really go "What are you talking about? You're obviously Italian." And I would go "I'm sorry, I'm English. I know I look Italian, but…"

125. I: Yeah. That's an interesting one, like when you said that somebody said you could be Spanish. What does that mean, actually?

126. CR3: Well, it's a friend who knows my history, and so was kind of, I guess, curious about where that other half of me is. "Your dad could have been Spanish." Was what he was

saying. But that was a close friend, it was kind of said in a nice, friendly way.

127. I: These days, do you often feel like an outsider? Do you often feel different?

128. CR3:   Yes, probably. But also no. So sometimes yes and sometimes no, it depends who I'm with and where I am, in what company. I'm gay, as well, which probably adds to a level of difference and... so, you know, with my friends, no, I don't feel like an outsider. If I'm with a group of people I'm socialising with, and who I'm very close to, or maybe not close to, but just comfortable with, I feel fine. And it's more often issues around sexuality than ethnicity, where I may feel like an outsider.

129. I: Oh, really? I guess it's more of the sexual side than...

130. CR3:   Yeah, yeah. I'd say where I work is quite a straight environment, so I have more issues about being a gay man in that environment than ....

131. I: Do they know that you're gay?

132. CR3:   Yes. Actually, it's the first place I've worked, for a long time, where I'm out, but I'm not that openly acknowledging it, really.

133. I: Right.

134. CR3:   Whereas, no one has even asked about my ethnicity there. And that, I don't feel would be an issue, but other stuff might be.

135.　I:　　I wonder if this might mean that you're fairly comfortable with being different.

136.　CR3:　Yeah. I think I'm pretty sensitive to difference, because I feel like I have a lot of different 'differences' about myself. So, I've never felt like I'm the mainstream, or the norm. I'm not kind of white, middle class, middle aged, male, authority, establishment figure.

137.　I:　　I suppose you've come to just accept that…

138.　CR3:　Yeah, absolutely.

139.　I:　　…as part of who you are.

140.　CR3:　and so, I think I'm quite good at accepting difference in other people.

141.　I:　　I wonder what you feel about this being comfortable with difference? Does that give you certain strengths and qualities?

142.　CR3:　Yeah. I'd say it's part of what… it comes with this; I'm very sensitive. And I think that, from having a sensitivity about myself, and growing up with that, I think it means it's made me a very sensitive person, so I can be sensitive to other people. And, probably, it does allow me to have empathy for other people, and things like that, because I've got experience of feeling different. I think I have a pretty good idea of how other people feel about feeling different.

I am me: the lived experience of a mixed-race identity
by Haran Rasalingam

143. I: Yes, I see what you mean. You're kind of sympathetic to others and they feel on the fringe, or whatever it might be, or just left out.

144. CR3:   Yeah. And maybe it's not to do with being mixed race, I don't know, maybe I'm just a sensitive person and would have been regardless.

145. I: Do you ever have a yearning to be less different, to fit in more?

146. CR3:   Yeah.

147. I: You do?

148. CR3:   Yeah. Hugely. I often can rail with myself. And it's not about my colouring, because I think I actually get a lot of attention, a lot of interest *because* of my colour. A lot of people find me attractive, so I don't feel like it's a bad thing in that sense. If things aren't going my way, in some way, I can often be like "Oh, why do I make things difficult?" Especially around relationships, actually, thinking about the relationships I've known, there's something about me, and I do internalise a lot, like "It's my fault. There's something wrong with me." When I'm having a problem with a relationship, or I can't meet the right person, I really blame myself for it.

149. I: Do you blame yourself because you're different, do you think?

150. CR3: I'm not saying it's because I'm different. It's because being like me has caused these problems. That's kind of my rationale, when I'm not thinking very rationally.

151. I: Okay. So, it's sort of 'being like you' meaning the sort of things that you think about or worry about.

152. CR3: Yeah. And being... I almost don't know what the qualities are. I don't know what it is, but there's something about me that has caused this problem. And other people can sense something about me that I can't sense about myself or can't control giving out or not giving out. So, I can be very punitive. It's part of my personality, the whole and I never allow myself to really fully appreciate my accomplishments. I'm always kind of pushing on to the next thing. My friends are always saying to me "Dave, you've done so much. You've done this, you've done that." and I don't allow myself to appreciate it. I'm always striving for the next thing.

153. I: There is something interesting to pick up on, because you say that you're gay, and that's fixed. You're straight or gay, one or the other. And, in the same way, we might say 'black or white', but you're not in that...

154. CR3: Not at all, I'm 100%...

155. I: So, is it easier then, in terms of identity, let's say, to say "I'm gay" than your ethnicity that's certain?

I am me: the lived experience of a mixed-race identity
by Haran Rasalingam

156. CR3:   Yeah, yeah, yeah. Because it is very definite. I've never had any confusion about my sexuality and I don't have any problems with my sexuality. I don't. I'm very happy with who I am, as far as my sexuality goes. But I did grow up in England, in the 70s and 80s, where it's not easy to be gay. Every sign in life was saying it's wrong to be gay, in a very homophobic society. Which it still is, in many aspects so, although I don't have a problem with being gay, I guess I have a defensive side around it. I don't need to use it very often, because, in most situations I meet, it's not a problem. And I do, I suppose, have a sense of identity around having other friends who are gay men, or lesbians. Wanting to be around gay people. I've got straight friends too, but there is something... I feel quite secure.

157. I: A sense of belonging. There's a kind of community there.

158. CR3:   Absolutely.

159. I: So, in terms of ethnicity, do you feel that you have a community?

160. CR3:   No. Because I don't know where my dad's from. It's not like I can go to the local Turkish shop, or Greek shop, or Middle Eastern, or whatever I might be, and share in that food or in the traditions, in whatever that cultural identity might be, to go with that race. I don't have any knowledge

or part of that. Whereas I know I'm gay and I can be part of the gay community.

161. I: So there is, like you said at the beginning, an unknown. Not only do you not know who your father is, but you can't even place him, really. You can't say "At least I know he was from Greece."

162. CR3:   Exactly. I remember going to a Greek baker's on Green Lane once, years ago, and buying something. And I was asking about "What's in there?", and the woman in the bakery was like "Are you Greek?, and I really want to say "Yes.", because she obviously thought I probably was, and then she was going to explain to me in Greek. And I would have loved to say "Yes, I am" I can't share in that, because I don't know what that is.

163. I: You mentioned a little bit about the difficulties that you had, and you wished it were easier, wished you knew something about 'me'. But do you really wish you were different? Do you really wish that you weren't how you were?

164. CR3:   That's a really hard question to answer, you know, over a cup of coffee! It's like trying to imagine yourself as something different. I think sometimes I wish I was different, but maybe not in terms of ethnicity or being gay or any of those things. I wish… you know, it's more kind of qualities; I wish I was more confident or more self-

assured, things like that. And some of the negative qualities of those things, may have come from experiences. I talked about the kind of ambivalence, or hostility, in a way, that's come from my birth, and then I carry an expectation of that from people in some situations.

165.   And maybe I wish I was different in the sense that I wish I'd been born in a more confident way, if that makes sense. With more confident circumstances, of really knowing both sides of my family. Having a stronger sense of my identity from that, and maybe family who were more kind of nurturing, like "Oh yeah, go into the family business." or really cared about what I went and studied at university, or anything like that. And really guided me. So, I think that, when I wish I was different, it's often about feeling a lack of those things.

166. I: Do you ever wonder if part of it is a wish that the perception of others, or attitude of others was somehow more welcoming of you.

167. CR3: Okay. I can take things really, really personally. If I'm dating, for example, and if something doesn't work out, I can feel really, really rejected. And it could be – and people have pointed out to me – it could just be that it wasn't the right time, the right place, it wasn't the right chemistry. But I really internalise it as "There's something

wrong with *me*. There's something about *me* that caused that problem." Rather than… rationally, I can understand that it just didn't work out, or it just wasn't right; how disappointing. But I kind of twist it into "There's something that's my fault. There was something about me that caused that to happen." That could be my coming out, that does that.

168. I: When you say, "It's about me.", do you think that stems from this idea that you are different, in some way?

169. CR3: Absolutely.

170. I: "I'm different; it must be my fault."

171. CR3: Yes, yes. I can't hide that difference.

172. I: I'd better ask some more about psychotherapy. To what extent has your engagement with psychotherapy been connected with your racial, ethnic identity?

173. CR3: I've never gone into therapy specifically to talk about this and, choosing to train myself, I was never particularly driven by this. I think, being mixed race has formed me in some ways, and what I was saying about being more sensitive to myself and to other people, and developing a sense of empathy, because I think I am a naturally sensitive person. And I am also a people person, I like people and I like working with people, so I think I was driven by those things. And I think my sense of difference,

probably, has driven or allowed my sensitivity to develop, in some way.

174. I: Perhaps it made you reflect a lot more.

175. CR3:   Yeah. Absolutely. I'd never gone into therapy to take this. Particularly as it has more been about stuff like not knowing who my dad was. That's had more of an impact on the whole kind of who are male role models for me, in my life, and all that kind of stuff. And what was my relationship with my mother, all that kind of stuff is big for me. And choosing to train, I suppose I feel like I have something to say that other people may not, who are white, for example, because I have this experience of being mixed race.

176.   One of my tutors, last term, handed me a handout from an organisation for black and Asian therapists. I think it was black, Asian and African therapists. She was really friendly, she said "Oh, let me give you this. you might be interested in that.", and I just looked at it and thought "Why would I be interested in this. I don't identify as any of these groups." And I felt really, really … I don't think she did anything wrong by giving it to me, but I really felt very labelled by a counselling tutor who – and she was very, very sensitive around these issues so I know she didn't mean anything by it, but she was, in some way,

saying to me "You would identify with a group of black, Asian or African therapists. You're one of those."

177.   And she didn't mean it in that way. And she probably wants to be one of those herself! She was very sensitive. I really felt like: what would I have to say? Because it was all about: is your cultural identity an effective way...? I thought "Well, I don't have that cultural identity, of being black, or Asian, or African, so it doesn't mean anything to me. So why would I want to go?" Just because I might share a skin tone with someone who is there?

178. I: You mentioned the word 'labelled', do you find that you get labelled sometimes? And what's your attitude to being labelled?

179. CR3: No. I don't think I get labelled, actually. Certainly not regarding racial identity. I will comment on the fact that I'm mixed race, if it's appropriate, but it's not the first and foremost thing about me. I probably get labelled more as a gay man than...

180. I: Is that a label? Would you call that a label?

181. CR3: It's an identity I think, actually, and it's one I choose.

182. I: So, you're perfectly comfortable with that label.

183. CR3: Yeah. And within the world of counselling and therapy, I think it's pretty easy to be a gay man, you know. There's a lot of straight women and a lot of gay men there. So, it's a very easy group to get on with. There are a couple of

straight men on my course as well, there's two straight men and two gay men, so it's quite evenly balanced. And 16 straight women.

184.   Do I get labelled? No, I don't think so.

185. I: So, you don't have any particular reaction to the labelling, or you haven't really experienced it. Someone saying, "You are this, or that."

186. CR3: The times when I've had it, you know, like the interview with WPF, or when my tutor gave me forms, I do have strong reactions when I feel I'm being labelled and pigeon-holed. It's fine for someone to label me as being mixed race, it's like "We don't really know much more about your racial identity, other than you're half white." That's fine.

187.   But to then give me a form saying "You must want to go and meet with other black, Asian and African therapists, that's when I feel labelled. I do have a strong reaction to that. Or someone saying to me "Oh, you're black. I didn't realise that.", or "You must have lots of issues about being black." I have a very strong reaction to that, because that's someone misunderstanding me. And I feel that I have to correct that and, with my therapist, I did correct it. I think it was like that, he said that in my first session. I came back in the second session and said "Actually, I felt really

uncomfortable when you said to me 'I didn't realise you were black.' I'm not black. I'm mixed race."

188. I: How did the therapist respond?

189. CR3: Yeah. he took it. I challenge him quite a lot, actually.

190. I: Have you had the same therapist throughout?

191. CR3: I've been seeing him for a year. I've seen other therapists in the past, but I've had this guy for a year, and he took the challenge. I've had to challenge him several times on some issues, where I felt that he hadn't got me, or quite understood me, in some way.

192. I: Do you often find that therapists struggle to understand you?

193. CR3: Mm, that's interesting. Yes, sometimes I have. I have felt very misunderstood by some – not by my current therapist, I think he's great, actually. I think he *really* understands me – but I've had a few who've got it very wrong.

194. I: In what way?

195. CR3: My last therapist, prior to my current one, I didn't really realise that at the time, until seeing my current therapist, how much she was missing. I'm not sure what her model was. Quite humanistic I would imagine, and she was quite interested in this family relational kind of stuff. And she would make notes during our session. She would sit there making notes, which was very alienating. And she would

I am me: the lived experience of a mixed-race identity
by Haran Rasalingam

look up at me and talk to me, but she was making notes whilst… and I couldn't really say what it was, maybe it was that we just didn't quite click. I thought, at the time, that I was getting somewhere with her but, when I look back on it now, I think, god, that there was a huge distance. And actually, I think a big part of that was that she was a lesbian, but I think I should have gone to see a man.

196.   And several, several years ago, I'd seen a therapist, whose model I don't know at all, but I'm guessing that she was either pretty psychodynamic or, possibly, even moving more towards the analytical side, and she was doing a lot of long silences, or leaving me to kind of say random stuff and then really being – you know, the first thing she said to me was "Draw a picture of how you feel." – that was the very first thing we did – and then told me she wanted to do a lot of work on my dreams.

197.   And I felt very hostile towards all of that. I was just "What is this namby pamby load of crap?" I really didn't like her, and I started talking to her about someone at work who I really wasn't getting on with, and she loved it, she'd absolutely love it. You could just tell she loved this. "Oh, this says so much about you." And I was like, what I wanted was someone to empathise with me and be like "Yeah, that person does sound really annoying. I totally understand why you're finding him…" and she wasn't

that at all. She was "I'm sure there's loads of unconscious process kind of stuff." Which, you know, I'm open to that, but it has to be handled in a way where there's a very strong working alliance.

198. I: Yeah. A sensitive way.

199. CR3: Yeah. Absolutely. And I felt more a subject in the laboratory, with her, you know. There was no personal rapport between us.

200. I: You're still training?

201. CR3: I'm training, currently, yeah.

202. I: Do you see clients?

203. CR3: I'm just about to start working with clients.

204. I: Do you have a sort of an idea of what your modality, or your approach is, or will be?

205. CR3: The model I'm training in is integrative. It's Clarkson Therapies in Relationship. That's my model. In terms of clients, I've just started at my placement, and they're doing a lot of training with us, before they'll let us work with their clients, but it's been very interesting to work with people from different places with very... you know, there's person-centred, there's integrative, there's psychodynamic people there, the whole range of styles. And personal styles as well. I'd say my personal style is a mixture of... obviously, I'm working within my model, but my personal style is... I'm quite warm, I'm quite open,

I'm quite congruent and, I think, accepting of people. And, you know, that's a hugely important thing, that I've really realised this, like I'm being able to... I am being able to hold people who are very angry, or very upset, you know, with strong feelings. And I think part of me has been scared at some of those feelings, and I've worked on that ability to face up to them.

206. I: Do you think that your ability to do that is very much connected with who you are?

207. CR3: I think, yeah, you know, what I was saying about the same amount of sensitivity to diversity and difference. I think, certainly, when I started training, I was really worried about 'How am I going to handle people's anger, or grief, or strong feelings? How am I going to be strong enough, or is it going to knock me over?', and I've learned, from experience that I *have* been able to handle them, and hold them completely, and people have actually said to me "Oh, you have a very calm presence, and you really are able to cope with those strong feelings." Which I think is great. Sometimes, when I encounter strong feelings, I feel incredibly challenged by them. And inside I'm thinking, "Oh my god! What do I do now?" which is really frightening, it's quite frightening, this person's anger. But, apparently, I'm able to not show that and, actually, to contain that.

208. I:　　　So, what do you think, then, drew you to integrative approach?

209. CR3:　When I'd done my foundation level, I'd been on the person-centred course, and I had no problems with that. And it was taught by people who weren't solely person-centred themselves so, whilst they were teaching a humanistic perspective, they weren't necessarily complete proponents of it themselves.

210.　　　I've been very, very wary of psychodynamic models, feeling that they were a bit too cold and analytical. And I've actually come to review that, and I'm actually getting warmer, because the model I am working in has a transferential strand in the relationship, it also has a trans-personal strand, and it's working with some things that really aren't person-centred at all. And I actually think, "Thank god!" now, because I'd met and seen work a few people who were coming from a very strict person-centred approach, and I think they're very limited, actually.

211.　　　I think there's too much following the client and not enough challenging the client, and I feel very comfortable being able to challenge and question, as well as follow my client. And I think that's really important, I think I can really see the value of understanding the client, I think it has to be quite a long way down the road of having really built a rapport, before you can use that. so, I think the integrative model is great because it's a whole toolbox.

212. I: I guess we're going to try and finish up, now. A couple more questions. What makes you most happy about the way others perceive you?

213. CR3: I suppose when they accept me for who I am, and don't really care about the differences. Or they can acknowledge them, so it's not pretending they're not there; it's recognising they're there, but just treating me like a person, regardless of what my skin colour is, or what my sexuality is, or any of those things.

214. I: And so, by contrast, what is it that frustrates you most about other people's perception of you?

215. CR3: Being pre-judged. Having people make assumptions about me. Those kind of "Oh you must be…", "Oh, you must have felt like this, because of…" I hate that. Don't tell me how I feel; it really annoys me. So, anyone who makes assumptions or presumptions. That's a big problem.

216. I: Fantastic. I could go on asking, but… I've certainly got one I think I really should ask. One last question: in terms of feeling mixed race, are there ever times when you feel more, when you notice that more? And other times when you don't?

217. CR3: Yes, definitely. If I'm travelling, and I've got my passport, you know, those kind of things, depending on what

country I'm coming from or going to, I am – and especially since what happened on September 11th and all that kind of… because I've got that paranoid thing – I am very, very attentive to my appearance when I go through customs and passport control, and those kind of things, I groom my beard, so it's very trimmed, very closely cropped. I don't like leaving looking straggly, or anything that could let someone think "He looks like a terrorist." I'm pretty paranoid about that, actually.

218. I: So that sort of context makes you very aware of it.

219. CR3:   Yes, absolutely. Am I dressed… I generally tend to dress very casually, but I will often err towards being a bit preppy as opposed to…

220. I: In what… again, in the airport context?

221. CR3:   Yes, absolutely, yeah. If I feel that people are making judgements about what you look like, you know you're being monitored in some room, you know they're deciding "Who are we going to pull out." to go through their luggage, or whatever. And especially if I'm travelling on my own, I think, because I feel, as a man travelling by myself, I look more suspicious than if I'm travelling with another friend.

222.   And actually, I went to Canada, last summer, with my ex, who is Canadian white, Canadian looks, really white European looking, and we were walking through and a

customs woman, in Canada, stopped me, because he walked on, and it wasn't obvious that we were together. She went "Excuse me, where are you going? Why are you here? When are you coming back?", and I went "I'm with him.", and she said "Oh, that's fine." And I said to him, I was really annoyed, and I said "Look like we're together, we do not want to look like two men travelling by themselves. They will be a lot more suspicious of us. But if we're travelling together, they won't be."

223.   Anyhow, we had all the customs questions "Where are you staying? How long are you here for? Why are you here?" We were staying with his parents. For a holiday. All fine. It makes it a lot easier. If I was by myself "Who is this mixed-race unknown, who may have a British passport, but…?"

224. I: Actually, that does remind me of one more question. To what extent does ethnicity play a part in who you date?

225. CR3:   That's a good one. Quite a bit, I guess, but in an odd way. I tend to only go for white men, and I tend to be quite attracted to white, Celtic looks, things like that. I suppose a very British, Celtic, northern European; other white Europeans.

226. I: Do you think it's an aesthetic thing, or is it political, or social…?

227. CR3: I would say it's an aesthetic thing, really. And I actually find the contrast of someone who is quite pale, and maybe has red or blond hair... the contrast of that look, with me, I find that attractive and appealing. The idea that, as a couple, we might have that look ... I find really attractive.

228. I: Okay. So, you're thinking of the aesthetic of the couple as well.

229. CR3: Oh, yeah, yeah. Absolutely, and it's also what I find sexually appealing in someone else. It's not a political thing. I would date any ethnicity, actually, who I find sexually attractive. That would be, usually, Caucasian. And I really... occasionally, I've dated Mediterranean guys, who have more similar colouring to me. That's fine. I don't go for black or Asian guys, there's no attraction. And that's purely an aesthetic thing.

230. I: We have to leave it there. Thank you so much for participating.

[End of interview]

INTERVIEW: Feeling Ashkenazi, looking Sephardi

"I have one thing that
embodies all of it, which
is that both my parents
are Jewish"

About Co-Researcher #4

Co-Researcher #4 (CR4) is a trainee psychotherapist in her late thirties. She describes her father as a Sephardi Jew of Persian-Indian origin and her mother as an Ashkenazi Jew of East European-Swedish origin. CR4's parents separated while she was in her teens after which she spent most time with her mother. CR4 feels a much closer affinity to the Ashkenazi side of her heritage and she describes herself first and foremost as Jewish. Visually, CR4 says she was darker skinned when younger and now considers herself 'white, but only just'.

Research interview with Co-Researcher #4

[I = Interviewer; CR4 = Co-Researcher #4]

1. I: The first thing I'll ask is: how would you describe your family background, your family history?

2. CR4: Very mixed. I think the fact that both my parents are Jewish, that's the main identity. My family are from quite, quite different cultures, though. Although I was born here,

my mum was born in Sweden, so there's the Swedish culture, and she's also... within the Jewish religion there's two identities: Ashkenazi, which is very Eastern European, basically, and then Sephardi, which is more Middle Eastern and Spanish, Morocco etcetera. And my dad was born in India. He's actually of Iranian... well, Persian – I like to say Persian! – of Persian descent. And then he came to England.

3.   But he comes from a very Middle Eastern culture that's kind of seeped into the Jewish identity there, so it's quite different.

4.   I: Different to...?

5.   CR4:   The Ashkenazi. It's a different mentality. It's a different way of seeing, I think, the roles.

6.   I: Could you sort of give a rough outline of examples of differences?

7.   CR4:   It's quite, I would say, chauvinistic. More chauvinistic, in that sense. The man is very much more dominant and food has to be on the table when you get home, dinner... that kind of mentality. Men are definitely more significant and more important than women.

8.   And sons are very lauded. And I can even see now how that is, how it plays out with my children. Say, with my dad.

9.   I: And so, can you distinguish, then, between traditions: which are Sephardi or Ashkenazi versus Jewish tradition, versus Indian or Persian or Swedish?

10. CR4: Um, yeah. I think I would be able to. I think I'd probably get a little bit mixed about the… for me, I think the Middle Eastern mentality is very much a blanket description of what I would put on how the role of the woman in the family, etcetera. And I don't think it makes a difference whether you're Jewish or not.

11. I: And that's kind of a clear distinction between a Sephardi Jew and an Ashkenazi Jew, would you say?

12. CR4: Yeah. It might not necessarily be *that* different, but it's certainly not under the carpet, it's quite evident, I would say. I don't tend to mix in those circles. I've really manoeuvred myself far away from the Sephardi part of the family.

13. I: So, you're quite detached from that side of things?

14. CR4: I've intentionally detached myself, to an extent, yeah.

15. I: So, you just don't like that side?

16. CR4: No, I don't like it. I find it a little bit too caveman-ish! It's a bit too caveman mentality for me.

17. I: And, on the Ashkenazi side, do you feel comfortable with that side of things?

18. CR4: I do feel comfortable with some of my Sephardi side, and the Ashkenazi side I do. I find it very much… I think the

I am me: the lived experience of a mixed-race identity
by Haran Rasalingam

Swedish culture is very different to the English culture. So, I think that makes a difference as well. It seems a bit little more... well, they're kind of more Swedish in their ways of doing things, the Jews there, than they are here.

19. I: What sort of thing springs to mind?

20. CR4:   Oh, I just think the way... they are very much – a little bit more formal and I think, if you go back here 30 years, say, the 1950s and 60s, how everything was a little bit more... you know ... there were ways of doing things, or ways that you would... that formality that was there.

21.   You know, when you would sit down to tea, it would be... etiquette and things like that. And that seems to be very much, almost, that's still very much around, I think, in the Swedish society, anyway. Much more so than here.

22. I: You were born here, you say?

23. CR4:   Born here.

24. I: How would you characterise the cultural environment that you grew up in? You're in England, then you've got the Swedish side of your family, then you've got the Sephardi, Persian, Indian side.

25. CR4:   Yeah, yeah, yeah. It was very odd. I never went to India or Iran. I've never visited, I don't know anything of it. And my dad probably never really knows... I don't know how old he was when he moved from India, but he was only about eight or something.

I am me: the lived experience of a mixed-race identity
by Haran Rasalingam

26. I: So, he moved from India to England?

27. CR4:   Yeah. They moved over after the war. I can't remember when they did… so I don't have any links to that culture. Only through the community, in the Sephardi community here. But, whereas, I go to Sweden. And that, I think, makes such a difference because, that's how my understanding and how I am are very different.

28.   Say, in Sweden I'm a little different and I act a little differently there, because it's a different culture. And you kind of slot yourself in.

29. I: And you know the rules of that culture. You know where you are.

30. CR4:   Yeah. I kind of know the rules.

31. I: And do you speak Swedish?

32. CR4:   Yeah, I do.

33. I: Fluently?

34. CR4:   Fluent-ish. I can get around, definitely.

35. I: It's a good second language for you, sort of thing.

36. CR4:   Useless in any other country but, yeah! Unfortunately, really useless.

37. I: But you're perfectly comfortably on your own, communicating in Swedish?

38. CR4:   Yeah. It's a difficult language to read, but, yeah.

39. I: So, was your first language English?

40. CR4:   Yeah.

I am me: the lived experience of a mixed-race identity
by Haran Rasalingam

41. I: So, presumably, your mum and dad spoke to each other in English?

42. CR4:   Yeah, absolutely. That was their common… but my dad learnt Swedish.

43. I: Did you pick up Swedish off your mum?

44. CR4:   Yeah.

45. I: So, as a child, you learnt it?

46. CR4:   Yeah. I grew up bilingual, but I think I stopped learning it, or whatever.

47. I: And on your dad's side, is there any other language that he speaks?

48. CR4:   Yeah, he speaks quite a lot of languages, but I don't necessarily speak them. He just has an ear for languages.

49. I: But you didn't pick up any of his…?

50. CR4:   No. I don't speak any Farsi. They speak Farsi. I can say maybe three words. So, I don't speak any Farsi, I don't speak any Hebrew and I can't write in it. But my dad can. He speaks Hebrew and he speaks Farsi, and he speaks Indian, and he speaks Swedish and Spanish and English.

51. I: All sorts of things, yeah. So, at home, you had a Sephardi influence through the community, a little bit? You're kind of familiar with that world.

52. CR4:   Yeah. And I think because my mum came from Sweden into my dad's culture.

53. I: How do you mean?

54. CR4: Well, she married my dad and, therefore, his community was more the Sephardi community, so she came into the Sephardi community.

55. I: So, was she in Sweden before she married your dad? Or was she already in England when she got together with your dad?

56. CR4: She met my dad in England.

57. I: So, she was already here first?

58. CR4: She was here a little bit. I think a year or something and then she met him.

59. I: He was obviously well established here, because he came over when he was young.

60. CR4: Exactly. You know, he had all his friends and his community, and he had his own company. He was already established.

61. I: Whereas your mum came over here as an adult.

62. CR4: Yes. And, therefore, she went with *his* family and friends. Although there's a few Swedish friends that she has here – family, or whatever – it tended to veer more towards the Sephardi community, that we were with a lot.

63. I: And then what about school life? What was it like going to school? What sort of school did you go to?

64. CR4: Well, first of all, I went to a Jewish school in *[place within city]*, not far. And that was fine. I kind of fitted in. It was

very normal, because there were lots of Sephardim and Ashkenazi kids, who were also Jewish.

65. I: So, it was quite a mixed Jewish school?

66. CR4:   It was a mixed Jewish school. It was a private school, but it was a mixed Jewish private school, and that was fine. But, when we moved to *[outside city]*, which is out of the community here, definitely out of the Sephardi community and into an Ashkenazi one, that made a difference.

67. I: How old were you?

68. CR4:   I was about five or six. Although there were Jewish kids in the school – it was a lovely little State primary school – I was quite different, because I looked Iranian.

69. I: That was going to be another of my questions: when people look at you, in a Jewish environment let's say, would they pin you as a Sephardi Jew?

70. CR4:   Yeah. I will always be pinned as Sephardi and never get pinned as Swedish.

71. I: They would never think that you're Ashkenazi?

72. CR4:   Yeah, I might get seen as Ashkenazi.

73. I: So, you might get seen as Ashkenazi?

74. CR4:   Maybe, but definitely Jewish. In a Jewish community, more Sephardi.

75. I: They would make a guess at Sephardi?

76. CR4:   Yes, definitely.

I am me: the lived experience of a mixed-race identity
by Haran Rasalingam

77. I: So why would that be?

78. CR4:   Very dark. Dark, thick hair. Dark skin. Brown eyes. You know, you don't really have blue eyes. Slightly thick eyelashes, although I don't have such thick eyelashes. But, you know, it's a very Sephardi look.

79. I: And so that sounds like it's kind of a... quite a clear divider within the Jewish community. Sephardim on the one hand, Ashkenazim on the other.

80. CR4:   Yes. My parents were actually in the Jewish Chronicle as 'Mixed Marriage, Do They Work?' No, is the answer! They don't work, no. 20 years later, where are they?

81. I: Is that surprising to you that it's considered a mixed marriage? Do you see it as a mixed marriage?

82. CR4:   I think... yes, I suppose I do, if I think about it. Yes, a little bit, because of the difference... of cultural differences. But it was big in those days, obviously. I mean, I thought it was hilarious, but obviously not *that* hilarious, after they got divorced!

83. I: When you say it's hilarious, does that mean it's much more common these days, it's not such a big deal?

84. CR4:   Oh yes. It's not even a big deal. I think more in the Sephardi communities it's a big deal. They're very much more closed about that. A bit Neanderthal.

85. I: The "caveman" thing you mentioned?

86. CR4:   Yeah. I'm just being slightly nasty about it because I don't really like it that much! But I have a very ambivalent relationship with the Sephardim. I love some of the things and I *hate* loads of the things, so it's kind of a prickly relationship.

87. I: So, what do you love about it?

88. CR4:   The food, probably! Yeah, I like the food. And that's it, really.

89. I: Anything else about the temperament, the attitude? You mentioned that kind of chauvinistic thing. Is there a difference in how…?

90. CR4:   Probably warmer. Yeah, they're a little bit warmer …

91. I: It sounds like you don't really identify with the Sephardi style.

92. CR4:   I probably do a little, but I don't want to. I don't want to be pegged as a Sephardi at all.

93. I: You don't want to be?

94. CR4:   No. I had somebody walk up to me, a couple of years ago, and she said – okay, because you are different sects within that: you are Bihari or you're Mashadi, they're all different, dependent on the region of Persia you came from. It depends what kind of person you are – this woman came up to me, saying, "You're Iranian or something, aren't you?" And I went, "No, I'm not.", "Lie." And I got

really annoyed. I was just… I just thought, "I hate you!" Pegged.

95. I: And, if somebody says, "Oh, you're an Ashkenazi." Do you feel good about that?

96. CR4:   They would never say that to me. People would always say, "Oh, you've got some Sephardi in you or something." But they would never really go, "Oh, you're Ashkenazi" because I just don't really look Ashkenazi.

97. I: But if you were together with just your mum, say.

98. CR4:   Yeah, maybe. They wouldn't really say that. I think Sephardi is seen as a little bit more exotic, because we live in England and there's a bigger Ashkenazi community, so maybe it's a little bit more exotic. And different, maybe.

99. I: So, if somebody asked you, "Where are you from?", how do you answer them?

100. CR4:   I will say, "I'm English. I'm born here, but my dad was originally from Persia [or Iranian]. But he was born in India." I might add that. And I'll say, "My mum's from Sweden."

101. I: So, you'd say, "I'm English." So English is part of your identity, then.

102. CR4:   Yeah, yeah.

103. I: And you'd say, "my mum's from Sweden." You wouldn't say, "I'm half Swedish." or something like that?

104. CR4:   Or I can say, "I'm half Swedish, I'm half Iranian.", or "…half Persian."

105. I: And so, what is it about saying Iranian – your preferred term is Persian…

106. CR4:   Persian sounds more acceptable and exotic. Iranian sounds… I kind of imagine these women with their burkas on! That's what I think of as Iranian. Very negative for me.

107. I: A negative connotation. Very Muslim, maybe. Do you think of that?

108. CR4:   Maybe. But not really. I suppose maybe that's part of it. But it's that whole region and the whole mentality that goes with that, and I don't…

109. I: Persia sounds less locked down, maybe. More open.

110. CR4:   Iranian doesn't sound… I don't know, it just has a sound to it that just means oppressive.

111. I: Because Persia sounds more romantic.

112. CR4:   More romantic. There you go.

113. I: So, would you say that you are mixed, in some way? Do you say, "I'm mixed."? Is there some language that suggests that? Would you ever define yourself in that way?

114. CR4:   If I think about it, I suppose I am mixed.

115. I: But you have to think about it.

I am me: the lived experience of a mixed-race identity
by Haran Rasalingam

116. CR4:   Yes. I have to think about it. I think I went for an interview for a job – and they said about cultural background. And I said, "Oh, I can put myself into a Middle Eastern camp, I can put myself in the… "My parents are from Sweden, I have ethnic culture." or "I have a mixed identity." You know, I can tick all the boxes but, if I think I'm mixed race and a mixed cultural identity, I think that's where I… If somebody said to me, "Are you mixed race?" I would say, "No."

117. I: Okay. Let's move away from the race bit, then. Are you comfortable with the word 'race' at all?

118. CR4:   'Race' makes me feel quite uncomfortable. It does. I don't deal very well with it. I just think of mixed race as people who… I'd say, I think, someone who is mixed race is somebody who has maybe an Afro/Caribbean background and then, maybe, one parent who is white.

119. That's what I'd consider mixed race, but I wouldn't necessarily consider myself mixed race, although I probably very much am! Because I think being Jewish is a race as well. And I think that makes a difference.

120. I: So, in a sense, primarily you're Jewish. It sounds like your main identity, almost. Is that fair to say.

121. CR4:   Yeah, yeah.

122. I: "I'm Jewish." you'd say.

123. CR4:   Ultimately Jewish.

124. I: Would that come before English?

125. CR4:   Depends on who I'm talking to. Really. I get to pick and choose where I am from …

126. I: So, your identity is fluid, in a sense. Depending on context.

127. CR4:   Yes. I'm quite patriotic in being British and I like to feel I'm British, but I'm quite patriotic when it comes to Swedish things as well. I get confused when it comes to supporting England or Sweden in a match. That's very hard for me! But if it was Iran – forget it!

128. I: You wouldn't be rooting for Iran?

129. CR4:   No, I wouldn't. Absolutely not.

130. I: But Sweden, you have an affinity.

131. CR4:   I feel an infinity to, yeah.

132. I: Because you spent time there as well.

133. CR4:   Yeah. I spent loads of summers there. I kind of grew up there, a little bit.

134. I: It makes sense. So, we've just touched on the word 'race'. What does that mean to you, the word race?

135. CR4:   Well, race means almost like a division to me. It's a divider. You're in that, and you're in that, and you're in that. And, when you're mixed, it gets a bit confusing.

136. I: Confusing in what sense?

137. CR4: Well it can be, for the person who is mixed, to find what their identity is. You know, it's how you are identified and what you identify with.

138. I: So, does that mean that you think it's important that somebody can identify themselves by some single racial term. Because you said, "I'm Jewish".

139. CR4: I think it depends on the person.

140. I: For you.

141. CR4: For me, personally, yeah, ultimately, because I have one thing that embodies all of it, which is that both my parents are Jewish and I come from a very long line… both Jewish, that, ultimately, that is the thing that I can hone in on.

142. That's who I am more than anything else, because in everything else I'm kind of split

143. I: Yeah. And so, what does it mean to be Jewish for you?

144. CR4: I just think it means like you're carrying… for me, it's about carrying on the race, I suppose I would call it. And moving towards the future. So, I just see it as carrying on. You're handed the mantle.

145. I: The torch.

146. CR4: Yes, exactly. That's exactly it. You've got the torch and you'll just keep the torch going. And that's how I see it. It's like an identity.

147. **I:**   So, it's passing things on, keeping it going. So, is that a very Jewish principle?

148. **CR4:**   Yeah, I suppose it is.

149. **I:**   Keep it going. Keep it going. Pass on the torch.

150. **CR4:**   Yeah. Keep it going, passing the torch, keep the tradition. Know who you are. Have a strong identity and very much stay within that community.

151. **I:**   And so, to maintain a strong identity, then, I suppose it's important that you stay in contact with the Jewish community.

152. **CR4:**   Mm. And knowing who you are.

153. **I:**   How do you mean by, "Knowing who you are."?

154. **CR4:**   Well, who are you? Well, I'm Jewish. Well, it's a culture of people who identify with... I'm not religious enough, really. I'm very traditional, but a kind of cultural identification of this long history that goes back.

155. **I:**   Jewish is far more than just a religion, isn't it? It's the whole culture, everything. It's a heritage.

156. **CR4:**   Yeah, it's a heritage.

157. **I:**   It's not just religion, is it?

158. **CR4:**   No, because I'm not religious, and yet I'm still Jewish. And I carry on with the traditions. So, it's almost... it's a weird identity; and I think it's the same with possibly Muslim religion. I think you'd say you were Muslim. You might not be religiously Muslim, but it's who you are.

I am me: the lived experience of a mixed-race identity
by Haran Rasalingam

159. I: I suppose some people may call that an ethnicity, or something like that?

160. CR4:   Yeah. Yeah.

161. I: Or, in the olden days, they might call it race.

162. CR4:   Yeah.

163. I: Another word used, in terms of race, is 'white' – would you ever describe yourself as 'white'?

164. CR4:   I always go for 'other'. You know, when they have these boxes. I don't like to be put into the coalition of being white. I don't mind it, but I'm more than white, so I can't. I feel like I'm lying.

165. I: You feel like you're lying?

166. CR4:   Yeah. Because I'm not really white.

167. I: So, when it comes to these tick box things, what do you tick?

168. CR4:   If they don't give me the opportunity to put 'other' and explain it, then I just put white.

169. I: And if there is 'other', what do you explain?

170. CR4:   I would say Jewish, or I might say mother, father, different countries. Generally white. Ultimately, I'm white, but I'm 'Jewish white' I think, is slightly different. Don't ask me why, but it just is.

171. I: Because I suppose the word white or black, it's a colour word, but it's much more than that, isn't it?

I am me: the lived experience of a mixed-race identity
by Haran Rasalingam

172. CR4:   Yeah. But, if you looked at me, you wouldn't think I was white.

173. I: Well, I don't know. Do you consider yourself white?

174. CR4:   Just.

175. I: And would you consider your dad white?

176. CR4:   No.

177. I: So, your dad's not white?

178. CR4:   No.

179. I: What is he?

180. CR4:   He's a... my dad's quite Indian looking, actually. He's definitely very Sephardi looking, I'd say. He's got very dark colour skin. He definitely doesn't look white. My mum does. But my dad not.

181. I: And so, you said you might think of yourself as 'just' white.

182. CR4:   Just.

183. I: What does that mean, 'just' white?

184. CR4:   Well, I think, if you put me next to somebody who was, say, definitely born here and has a long line of being born here – not that that makes any difference, because you could be Irish and you could have a lot of white skin, not dark hair. I have quite a dark complexion.

185.   I have the ability to look quite Indian. I get mixed up for Indian, Italian, loads of different... never English.

186. I: Right. So, if people see you, they don't...

187. CR4:   If I was away on holiday somewhere, they would never look at me and think I was English.

188. I: What might they think?

189. CR4:   Maybe Mediterranean or Indian. More Mediterranean now I've grown up, but when I was younger, I was quite dark.

190. I: So, you were darker when you were younger?

191. CR4:   Yes. I think I was darker when I was younger.

192. I: And I wonder to what extent that might affect the way you see yourself now, even though now you're lighter?

193. CR4:   Yeah. I definitely don't feel… I think it's changed a lot, the society here, because we're much more mixed now, and I think that's made such a difference that I think it's changed it. But, growing up, I definitely felt different. I didn't feel white.

194. I: You didn't feel white?

195. CR4:   No. Not so say that I felt black! I clearly wasn't black, and I wasn't really brown. I just wasn't white, and that was it.

196. I: You just had this idea that you're non-white, in some way? Not white. There's white and there's not white.

197. CR4:   Yeah. Not white.

198. I: And how did that affect you, in your childhood?

199. CR4:   Well, I think I was definitely pegged as being different in my school, when I moved to this school in *[outside city]*.

I am me: the lived experience of a mixed-race identity
by Haran Rasalingam

200. I: Particularly there, because it was an Ashkenazi school, basically?

201. CR4:   Well, no. It wasn't a Jewish school, it was a normal school. There was no Sephardi community, so there were Jewish kids there, but they certainly weren't going to be Sephardi.

202.   And it was very much a very kind of white, English kind of village. There was an R.A.F. estate; it was very British. There were loads of kids from the R.A.F. estate there, and I looked different, definitely.

203. I: Did you feel different as well?

204. CR4:   Well, because I wasn't the only Jewish kid, I suppose I did feel different, but not *that* different, yeah.

205.   Oh yeah, I did, is some ways.

206. I: Was it awkward? Was it unpleasant, this being different?

207. CR4:   I think at times it felt unpleasant. But I think then I'd just gone and got used to it and it was fine. But I was definitely… I just have memories of doing things that I think were normal to my culture, my own personal culture, but that wasn't normal to the majorities.

208.   I remember that we used to go swimming and, coming from a family from Sweden, naked is not a big deal. I was the first to strip off naked in front of the boys, to get dressed, and why not? I mean, for goodness sake! That's normal, you know?

209.　　　In Sweden kids walk around naked. You have naked saunas with each other, as a family; it's very normal. And it's not here.

210. I:　　But not in *[outside city]*.

211. CR4:　Not in *[outside city]*. Not in England. You don't go to a sauna in England wearing no clothes. You know, you just don't. In Sweden, "Why are you wearing clothes? You look like an idiot!" You just don't do it. So.

212. I:　　So that's quite a big difference. What other differences have you experienced, as a result of you adhering to your personal culture that clashes with others? So not necessarily because of the Swedish side, but maybe Jewish, or maybe Sephardi, or maybe Ashkenazi or whatever it might be?

213. CR4:　I think, because I have such a mishmash of Sephardi and Ashkenazi ways of doing things, I just get confused. I think I get to pick and choose things that I like of each, which aren't necessarily right.

214. I:　　How do you mean?

215. CR4:　Like not religiously right, but I decide to do it. For instance, it's Passover at the moment, so I choose I'm going to have rice. Because I can. Strictly speaking, I really shouldn't, but I can, because I'm Sephardi because of my dad, therefore I can do it.

216.　　　Whereas I should only be having potato and no flour.

217. I: Because that's what the Ashkenazim do?

218. CR4:   Ashkenazim don't have rice. They don't have rice.

219. I: So, what makes you say that you should do the Ashkenazi thing, rather than the Sephardi thing?

220. CR4:   Probably because my husband's Ashkenazi.

221. I: So, there's the other element.

222. CR4:   My husband's Ashkenazi, but I think that I'm the homemaker - I cook, so I decide!

223. I: You have the final say!

224. CR4:   Mm. So little bits of that. Go back to your original question.

225. I: In a sense, you're multicultural. So, do you often have instances of your personal culture, as you said, clashing with the culture of others? For example, you may share something but, because you're multicultural, perhaps a Sephardi thing that you do may clash with an Ashkenazi, or vice versa?

226.   Or the fact that you're Jewish might clash with a non-Jewish person?

227. CR4:   Yes. I'll tell you what's quite difficult is, in the Jewish culture *here* you definitely don't eat any seafood or pork or ham products and you shouldn't have any non-kosher meat. But in Sweden it's really normal to be kosher and have seafood. But you wouldn't eat pork. But you'd eat seafood.

228.   And that does happen a little bit in other parts, but definitely not in England.

229. I: But it's a big characteristic of the Swedish-Jewish?

230. CR4:   It's quite a characteristic Swedish-Jewish. We all have the seafood, it's fine, because they love fish and have seafood.

231. I: So what do you do then?

232. CR4:   I'm allowed to eat seafood.

233. I: In Sweden only? Or when you're here as well?

234. CR4:   Well, I am now a snob about seafood, so I don't tend to do it here, because I don't really like the seafood here.

235. I: Is it only because you don't like it?

236. CR4:   Here? Yeah. It's really because I don't like it.

237. I: If you were to have seafood here, would it upset your husband, for example?

238. CR4:   No, no. He has it as well. He's absolutely fine with it. That's a normal thing to do; we wouldn't have any pork or ham, but it's okay to have seafood.

239.   I'm not saying that lots of other Jewish people in England don't have seafood, because I know that they do, but it's just something that's very particular… I know from the Swedish culture, that's very normal. And to have crayfish parties and stuff like that is very normal.

240. I: And you're perfectly comfortable with that?

241. CR4:   Yeah, yeah, yeah. My mum's horrified, but I love it!

242. I: So, your mum is horrified?

243. CR4:   Well she grew up having crayfish parties but, when she met my dad, she became more religious and decided she was not going to have anything not kosher. And she never went back to having non-kosher things again.

244. I: So, is your dad more religious than your mum?

245. CR4:   My dad is major religious, yes.

246. I: Could that be another factor in his more traditional, chauvinistic type thing?

247. CR4:   Yes, there's a very different... yeah. You shouldn't do this, you shouldn't do that. And I'm like, "I'll do what I like, sorry."

248. I: Do you think that was a consequence just of the fact that you've grown up in England? Your mum's Ashkenazi and you've been exposed to quite a...?

249. CR4:   Yes. I was exposed, in Sweden, to a different life and the ability to eat... You see, if you stay in a culture and you don't tend to go out of that, like you don't eat in other restaurants, you only stay in kosher restaurants, you don't eat in non-kosher restaurants, and you go to other people's houses who are kosher, you don't see what else is out there. You don't really watch somebody else having a steak while you're having a fish dish and thinking, "Oh, a fucking steak! That's not fair!"

250.   You know, you don't have that, and I did. I grew up going to these non-kosher restaurants and having fish and

I am me: the lived experience of a mixed-race identity
by Haran Rasalingam

watching other people have steak and meat, or going to Sweden and watching my family have seafood, but I wasn't allowed to have it. And it was really hard.

251. I: You felt excluded, in some way?

252. CR4:   I suppose, in some ways, I felt left out, yeah. And I didn't want to be left out. So, I made a conscious decision not to be.

253. I: You seem quite comfortable with your multiple, cultural background. Am I right in that, or…?

254. CR4:   No, I am quite comfortable about it. I think the Iranian part is the only part that, when you say 'Iranian', or somebody pegs me as Iranian, that I don't like!

255. I: You don't like it, no. So, are you uncomfortable about the way you look?

256. CR4:   Sometimes. Being Sephardi is quite difficult. You get very strong hairs and I don't see it as very attractive. And that's hard. You know, if I was Ashkenazi, I'd have light, blond hairs.

257. I: So, do you ever wish that you weren't half Sephardi, or however you might want to turn it?

258. CR4:   Maybe in some senses. The chances of me having blue eyes and that… wasn't going to happen. Even with our kids, they've both got brown eyes. I just know that Sephardi has really strong genes. That's what I find.

259. I: Is there a sort of status thing, between Ashkenazim and Sephardim?

260. CR4:   Yes. I think, in some ways, within the Sephardi community and depending on where you're from and how good you are, you can be seen as very lowly. Very kind of down there on the floor, as opposed to being a particular community, which is very affluent, and they have blue eyes. They're Sephardi, but they have blue eyes.

261. I: Okay. So, a blue-eyed Sephardi is a higher status?

262. CR4:   Well, no. I think it's a specific community where, for some reason, they're Sephardim with blue eyes.

263. I: And what about the status between Ashkenazim and Sephardim?

264. CR4:   I think they don't tend to mix that well. My only sense of it is that I look down a little bit on the Sephardi community. I do and I don't. I'm very suspicious of it. I'm not trusting of it. I don't necessarily trust it, but that's my own personal experience.

265. I: What do you mean, you don't trust it?

266. CR4:   Well, I don't trust the community. I think because, when my parents separated, the treatment that we got, and my mum got, was very nasty. And I think that mentality is very Sephardi. And I also think that the Ashkenazim tend to deal with it in just a little bit more British way.

I am me: the lived experience of a mixed-race identity
by Haran Rasalingam

267.   I think they're more… they just do the right thing, as opposed to doing what they want. So, I think there's something about that. And also, they're more assimilated. More assimilated into English community than the Sephardim. A little bit more.

268. I: Right. So, your parents separated. How old were you when they separated?

269. CR4:   I was nine, I think. You know, it's gone into 1980-something. I actually can't remember. I think it was around that time.

270. I: And do you keep in touch with both?

271. CR4:   Well, yes. My dad moved to America and remarried, but he's now back here.

272. I: Are you close to both of them?

273. CR4:   I'm quite close to my mother. Not close to my father at all. Well, barely.

274. I: That's another pointer towards the Ashkenazi side, isn't it?

275. CR4:   Yes. I think, because of the breakdown in the relationship I had with my father, definitely he pushed me away from the community. And my step-mum, my now ex step-mum and her ways.

276. I: Is she Sephardi as well?

277. CR4:   She was Iranian. Definitely born in Iran. She was definitely of a very different culture. It was just like lots

of inter-marrying, inter-breeding, lots of evidence of inter-breeding! She was not a very nice piece of work, and the community is a very odd community.

278. I: Odd?

279. CR4: Yeah, odd. Like, "Go away, don't even go near you." kind of. Not nice.

280. I: It sounds like maybe, within a Sephardi context, you feel a little bit out of place.

281. CR4: Yeah. I don't feel very comfortable. I don't feel like I belong.

282. I: What about within the Ashkenazi community?

283. CR4: Yeah. Okay, because I went to an Ashkenazi synagogue, so I've grown up in an Ashkenazi community.

284. I: And you feel like you belong? Or do you ever get the feeling that they see you as a little bit Sephardi?

285. CR4: No.

286. I: So, you kind of feel you belong in there?

287. CR4: Yeah. And, if I went into a Sephardi community, I would feel really horrible. I wouldn't like it, because I wouldn't know what to do. I don't really 'get it'.

288. I: You're not familiar with it.

289. CR4: I was when I was little. Not that interested.

290. I: In terms of your identity, has it ever been a problem for you, would you say, in any sense?

291. CR4:   I'll tell you what. My surname before I got married – now it's *[married name]* – used to be *[maiden name]* – that's always a giveaway! It's a very Iranian… and my surname caused me a lot of problems.

292.   When they had the bombs, the Pan Am bombs and stuff, oh, I was in the airport for hours! Hours! And I always get pulled over. I always get my shoes checked.

293. I: Really? Even now? Well, especially now, probably.

294. CR4:   Yeah, especially now. I get checked, because I look kind of Middle Eastern. I have that look.

295. I: So, you look Middle Eastern but, in terms of your identity, you're very much more on the Ashkenazi side and the European side maybe, you could say?

296. I: So have there been some issues around your identity, because of your name?

297. CR4:   Yeah. My name was a real… I *hated* my name.

298. I: And the way you look sometimes gives you some problems. Have you ever suffered racism?

299. CR4:   Yes, a little bit at school and stuff because I looked quite Iranian. And I think it was at a time something was going on – it wasn't the Iraqi war, but it was something that happened with Iraq.

300.   It was years ago, so I must have been seven or eight – and they called me 'Arab girl' or something ridiculous, and I

didn't quite understand, but I definitely felt some kind of shame around something.

301. I: So, do you often get called an Arab, or something along those lines?

302. CR4:   No. No.

303. I: It was something that happened in school.

304. CR4:   Yeah, when I was younger and some kids who knew nothing.

305. I: And to what extent do you think anything around your identity brought you to psychotherapy, you know, that kind of world? What got you into it?

306. CR4:   It was my parents' divorce, definitely. That was it. And I think, within that, I think there is this trying to understand who you are and coming from a very different set of – even with the nuance of being Jewish – the different cultures of the expectation of my role, my behaviour with my father compared to my mum, and the different expectations from that.

307.   If I'd gone my father's way, I would have been a hell of a lot more religious. Definitely.

308. I: And so, the separation of your mother and father was the driving force for you going into therapy, would you say?

309. CR4:   Yeah, yeah. When I was young, I did. My mum took me somewhere. But I think, in some ways, the split made me who I am today.

I am me: the lived experience of a mixed-race identity
by Haran Rasalingam

310. I: Can you explain that a bit more?

311. CR4:   Well, it just took me on a different path. Because you kind of suffer that kind of loss of your parents being together and at a time when you're trying to identify learning who you are. I was nine and I think there had been arguments going on for a good while. So, you're experiencing that and you're trying to find out who you are.

312.   And, actually, if I'd grown up with my parents being together, I would have been in a much more religious, tight, kind of upbringing. A lot more religious. Like a hell of a lot more religious! Like going to shul, shomer Shabbat, when you wouldn't go out; my dad was shomer Shabbat.

313.   My life would have taken a completely different route. Definitely. I would have been far more submerged into the Sephardi community.

314. I: I guess you would have had to toe the line that you dad…

315. CR4:   Very much toe the line and been a different person. And actually, because my mum divorced and…

316. I: Was that why you moved to [outside city]?

317. CR4:   No, we'd already moved anyway with my dad.

318. I: You'd already moved there when you were six.

319. CR4:   But you'd still be involved with the Sephardi community. I'd still be going to all the weddings and bar mitzvahs and

you'd hang around together and stay within that kind of community.

320.　　　Because we didn't, I think, and because I grew up slightly differently and my mum kind of let the reins go a bit and I started to eat non-kosher meat, and I just thought, "Yes! I like that!". And it's different.

321. I:　　So, in a way it was a kind of breaking free for you from… it was quite strict.

322. CR4:　Yes, I wasn't so confined, in some way. In some ways, yes, I had a strict upbringing and there was a definite, "You don't". I think within my culture you don't… going out with non-Jewish boys, you don't do that. Of course, I did. I did everything I wasn't supposed to do, because I wanted to try.

323. I:　　Yeah. You wanted to try.

324. CR4:　Yeah. Because I didn't want to be so… I just thought, "There's just more." Although I did end up marrying somebody who was Jewish.

325. I:　　So maybe tell me a bit about that journey. You wanted to try, you wanted to see outside of the Jewish world.

326. CR4:　I loved, loved going outside the Jewish world!

327. I:　　But then something made you decide to come back.

328. CR4:　Yes. I had a really… I had a very difficult relationship with a non-Jewish guy who I was quite serious with, but

was a complete… he was an alcoholic, a really difficult character.

329.   And all I remember is just… and I moved from him to having another relationship with somebody who, actually, was a good friend of mine where I lived at home, who knew the relationship. But I was all over the place from this relationship, it really affected me.

330.   And then I met my husband on a self-awareness course.

331.   I: On a self-awareness course?

332.   CR4:   A self-awareness course, yeah.

333.   I: And how old were you then?

334.   CR4:   I was 20, or 21. 21. So quite young. But I had experiences, I'd kind of been let loose, probably when I got to university, I broke up with my Jewish boyfriend then, and then just fell apart, but I'd actually got my fingers really badly burnt, I think, and got myself in a situation that I couldn't really handle very well. And I think that, because of that, it just shaped me into realising that I had to hold on to something that was secure and safe and trustworthy.

335.   I: You knew where you were.

336.   CR4:   Yeah. And I went back to that.

337.   I: So, there's something about being with a Jewish man that gives you some sense of reliability, almost. You know where you stand, a little bit.

338. CR4:   I suppose so. I think it's him in particular. I didn't intend to go out with him, I didn't intend it to be serious.

339. I: It just worked out that way.

340. CR4:   It just did, yeah.

341. I: And how long have you been together?

342. CR4:   It will be 15 years. And that was, in part, a conscious decision. It wasn't like I didn't fall in love with him, because I certainly…

343. I: What was, in part, a conscious decision?

344. CR4:   The fact that this person ticked lots of the boxes that I needed to be ticked. The 'safe', the 'secure'. Very much somebody to take care of me. I suppose that goes less away from ethnicity, and more to do with the loss of a father, and actually wanting to replace that. My husband was eight years older than me, so he very much became the dad.

345. I: I see what you mean. Because you were still quite young at that time.

346. CR4:   Yeah. I was 23 when I got married. Really young.

347. I: In terms of therapy, training and stuff like that, could you tell me a bit about that? When you started training, and what sort of training…

348. CR4:   I started my training three years ago. I started three years ago, and I only did the certificate, but I'd already been in therapy for a good year or so before that. And a friend of

mine had done this course and my therapist actually does one of the modules on it. And I knew somebody else who was a tutor there, so I knew that what I was going on to was a really good course. I was very happy to do it. And I wanted to see if I could do it. I wasn't quite sure…

349. I: The certificate was a one-year thing, was it?

350. CR4:   Year's certificate

351. I: A taster, in a sense.

352. CR4:   Just to see "Can I do this?" "Yeah."

353. I: So, you did that and then you continued straight on?

354. CR4:   Yeah, I continued straight on, and then I took a six-month break before I did the Advanced.

355. I: Where are you at now?

356. CR4:   I'm coming to the end of my last… clinging to my last period of the Advanced.

357. I: So, you're pretty much there.

358. CR4:   Yeah. I'm pretty much there.

359. I: And do you think the issues of your identity have come up much in your training?

360. CR4:   Only from others.

361. I: How do you mean?

362. CR4:   I struggled with my ethnicity with others because – first of all, one of my supervisors was Iranian. Really not good. I'm not very good with people who are Iranian. There was

a lot of countertransference, transference going on. And she just didn't like me at all.

363. I: She didn't like you.

364. CR4:   No, no. She's Iranian, definitely not Jewish, and I saw myself as her, viewing me. And I felt treated like a spoilt little rich Jewish girl. That's how I felt with her. So yeah, culturally, I think that makes a difference.

365. I: And what about others? Was it just her?

366. CR4:   I had a clash – not a clash, I was very aware that there was a girl on my course who was Turkish, and this was the second year, and she spotted me as being Jewish. And I never realised that people could see me, I might be naïve, but I don't think I look Jewish. And she said "You must be Jewish. Because you look like all the people" where she lives". I thought "Fucking cheek." I was shocked, I really didn't think I looked Jewish.

367. I: What, what, I mean…

368. CR4:   I don't know, I have no idea. I just have a look that looks very Jewish. The clothes that I was wearing, all those sort… almost like maybe it's a uniform or something. I don't know. I was shocked by that.

369. I: Was it that upsetting to be labelled like that?

370. CR4:   I was shocked; I never thought that I looked Jewish. What did I think? It kind of pissed me off a little bit, I felt boxed in. That's what it felt like. And I just thought "Oh, I didn't

know I was boxed in now. I didn't know I was 'Jewish'"
I can sound Jewish, but to actually be seen as Jewish!

371. I: To be boxed in. That's a good word for it.

372. CR4:   So that's how I felt. I think I possibly struggle the most
            because, if I'm Jewish, what do people think of me when
            the whole Israel thing comes up? And then, with the
            Muslim-Israel, Palestinian thing, that's quite hard. That's
            when I feel very sensitive and aware, I think. So,
            culturally, that comes in.

373. I: Sort of uncomfortable and…

374. CR4:   Yeah, clearly uncomfortable.

375. I: Do you think people have it in for you, or something like
            that?

376. CR4:   No. I'm just hyper-vigilant about it. Not wanting to say
            anything. I'm being very… maybe not wanting people to
            know that I'm maybe Jewish. I don't know. I'm generally
            genuinely quite open about being Jewish. I think it's one
            of the first things that'll come out of my mouth, when I'm
            talking to somebody. And I'm Jewish, but actually, when
            the whole 9/11 and the whole thing about Palestine, and
            there was a war going on, then you're not so open.

377.   I mean, my cousin would walk around, she would happily
            walk around with the Magen David, which is the Star of
            David, on her chest, and wear something that says openly
            'Jewish'. I would never walk around openly Jewish,

although my kids do go to a Jewish school, my son wears a yarmulke, a kippah on his head, and wears Tzitzis, these special... I'm more okay with it. My husband's really funny about it: "Take it off. Take it off."

378. I: So, he wants to hide it more.

379. CR4:   Yeah. But there is something about being... assimilation, wanting to be assimilated and not wanting to be noticed as being different. But, at the same, time cherishing that difference. It's very odd, it's just so odd.

380. I: Where do you stand with that dilemma?

381. CR4:   I think I'm always very aware of when and where I feel comfortable, or it's comfortable to do it. To be Jewish and not to be Jewish, whether to look Jewish, so to speak. But I would never, ever, ever walk around with a Star of David on.

382. I: You think that's kind of too open, too...

383. CR4:   I'd be worried I'd leave myself open to abuse.

384. I: So, it's abuse that you'd be worried about, not that...

385. CR4:   No, no, I'm not worried about people knowing I'm Jewish. I don't want to get the abuse and, if that's what I feel I could get...

386. I: Have you ever had abuse, being Jewish?

387. CR4:   Yeah, I have. I was driving to shul one day... no, walking, I wasn't actually driving, I was walking to shul, and some racist comment about Hitler and the Nazis, or some stupid

I am me: the lived experience of a mixed-race identity
by Haran Rasalingam

comment... anyway it was something... You grow up with this sense of – more so since I've had children, I'm quite aware of what's going on...

388. I: You're sensitive to it, I suppose.

389. CR4:   Quite sensitive. They have high security at my kids school. That makes me quite sad, that they have to have security.

390. I: I guess it just makes you aware of it all the time, I imagine.

391. CR4:   Yeah, because you're sitting, then you're going in, there's security people at the gates. And there are security people there and there's security down the road, and there's security up the road, and you walk into the school and it's a gated school, you can't just walk in. I don't think you can walk into any school, but that sense that there's security. And, whenever there's a war on, or something's happened in Israel, security goes up much higher, and you have to do things: you've got to be very careful when you leave, you mustn't congregate round the front – you know, when you normally chat around the front?

392. I: Yeah. There are certain things that you have to be aware of the whole time. Do you feel that any of these issues about your Jewishness, or your Sephardi, Ashkenazi heritage; is that ever something that you feel comfortable talking about in therapy, in the kind of... in training, with the other members of the group?

393. CR4:   I do a little bit. When we talk, there was this thing that came up about cultural, and there was something about not feeling… one of the girls felt that she was being attacked. Something about her feeling different, because she's from Trinidad – or her family is – and, in the news, they were always talking about black youths, and black kids causing trouble, and how she feels aware about that. And I said "Well, I can understand how you feel, because, whenever there's anything on the thing about Israel, I feel like that. Because part of me feels put down. Or that I'm put out to dry, a little bit, just because I'm Jewish." I don't discuss the Israeli-Palestinian conflict, or anything like that, with my therapist, because he mentioned it once, and he said it in such a way. And I thought "I can't actually discuss this with you." I can't remember what he said, his idea of the conflict. He made it into a bigger picture. It was before I started my training, but I remember I just thought to myself "It's too political. I can't have this discussion with you. Because my political beliefs would be quite different to yours. I can't have this discussion with you."

394. I: You didn't feel that he'd be open to hear you?

395. CR4:   Yeah. It would go into a political discussion. I think that would have taken it away from the therapy a bit. And it was, I felt, a difficult… you know when you feel the hairs on the back of your neck stand up, a bit hackled.

I am me: the lived experience of a mixed-race identity
by Haran Rasalingam

396. I: Yeah, that you would definitely clash.

397. CR4:   I would definitely clash with him on that. I didn't want to have a clash with him. "You're my therapist, I have to like you, not hate you."

398. I: Your choice of therapist, did the cultural background of your therapist come into it, when you chose your therapist?

399. CR4:   Yeah. Two things: I decided – my friend recommended this guy, he's male – I decided to go for a male, and someone who wasn't Jewish. My last therapist was Jewish. My third therapist, she was Egyptian. When I was younger, I had a woman, and she was a Jewish psychotherapist. And she was a person who I always wanted to be because of what she did. Eventually found somebody, and she was Egyptian, I tried so hard, really hard. But "No, you've got to stay with her, it will help you" and I couldn't talk about my dad, I found it so difficult, because I couldn't talk about how much I hated the whole Sephardi mentality, and that Iranian mentality. I couldn't do it. I really couldn't do it. And it was a huge part of the therapy and I couldn't. It was just too big an issue, for me to be able to manage it with somebody who was Middle Eastern.

400. I: You felt that you'd be insulting her at the same time.

401. CR4: Yeah, yeah. And I tried to work with it, and I said, "Obviously it's not about you." But it's not going to work, it's just rubbish. And then I found a Jewish counsellor, who was brilliant because there' just this innate understanding. You don't have to explain anything. But, in that, you lose a lot of things.

402. I: What do you lose?

403. CR4: Well, my understanding, my personal understanding of something is, maybe, as a Sephardi, not just an Ashkenazi. And, actually, when you explain, having to explain everything makes it a lot clearer.

404. I: Almost having to spell it out helps you clarify it?

405. CR4: Yeah, yeah. Absolutely. Like talking to you here makes me think about it more, and makes me…

406. I: Yes, because I'm asking all the idiot questions!

407. CR4: No, not idiot questions! Certainly not idiot questions. But yeah. And then I can explain. But, choosing a male as well was very important for that kind of idea of not colluding.

408. I: In a way, then, you've purposefully gone for as different as possible: male, non-Jewish.

409. CR4: He was white. I didn't go for a black therapist. And I don't know if that would have made a difference. I don't know if I would have gone for a black therapist.

410. I: And why is that?

411. CR4: Because, in some ways, I need to identify. And I didn't know how much... well, I don't know, it was never recommended, on the one hand, on the other hand, would I be able to identify with somebody who comes from a completely different culture to me? Maybe, in some ways, that would be good.

412. I: In a way, that sounds like that kind of balance between assimilation and difference again. You know, that sort of trying to get that balance in there.

413. CR4: Yeah. Definitely, I wouldn't be able to go have a Muslim counsellor.

414. I: You wouldn't be able to...

415. CR4: No. I really wouldn't. I'd find that very difficult.

416. I: Could you say why?

417. CR4: Because I'd feel very sensitive about the whole Israel situation. That's the thing that causes me the most problems. And it's not necessarily that I think that what's happening in Israel is right, that it's not necessarily... my understanding of Israel, it comes from a difference base. And I think the problem is that Israelis are seen as Jewish, and therefore it becomes a Semitic thing, as opposed to, you know, about a country behaving in a way. And so, because it's all twisted and kind of fused, it causes me difficulties, and I wouldn't be able to have a discussion. It's like I would never have a... if I ever had any help, I

would never have an au-pair who had a Muslim background, because I wouldn't be able to watch the news about Israel, or anything, and have a discussion with my husband without being sensitive about it.

418. I: You're worried about prejudices, in a way.

419. CR4: Yes, or offending somebody else, or me feeling I have to watch what I feel and how I speak. There's something very different about that as well; being Jewish here is very different to, say, going to America, or being in Israel. Where you don't have to be careful about who you are. And I'm very aware of who I am in a restaurant, of not wanting to be seen as 'those Jews', you know.

420. I: Here as well?

421. CR4: Yeah, here as well. Being very respectful and very nice and stuff, but you can't... you wouldn't talk about things that are happening in Israel, you wouldn't have a political discussion, you wouldn't talk about certain things.

422. I: So, here you're constantly having to watch that.

423. CR4: Yeah. But you don't really think about it consciously. But, subconsciously, you hold back a bit, you're not very... whereas, if I was in – I noticed this when I went to America – to be Jewish was nothing. You didn't have to be ashamed, or embarrassed about it, whereas here it's slightly hidden.

424. I: Yes, here there's more… maybe it's sort of a minority status that it has here, whereas it's got the status of a *majority* in America.

425. CR4:   Yeah, maybe. You don't feel the…

426. I: It's sort of more celebrated.

427. CR4:   Yes, as opposed to shhh….

428. I: Yeah. 'We're the weirdoes here' kind of thing.

429. CR4:   'That funny sect over there'. So that's what it's like here. And so, going to Israel is different as well. And that makes a difference, so yeah. So, it's all those little…

430. I: So, it's these sorts of things that make you conscious of that identity, I suppose.

431. CR4:   Yeah. Very conscious of who I am, and what I put out, and what others see, and what I let others see.

432. I: Did you save you have been to Israel?

433. CR4:   Mm.

434. I: Yeah. And so, in Israel, do you feel that you can let your guard down a bit?

435. CR4:   Yeah. in some ways we can. And it's more comfortable. But, in other ways, it's like, oh, you know, that Israeli mentality, it drives me insane.

436. I: What is that Israeli mentality?

437. CR4:   They're very kind of black and white, so intolerant and quite rude. Very much.

438. I: You mentioned also the whole thing about being assimilated in Britain. I guess that goes along with tolerance and…

439. CR4:   Respect, kind of respect. I like the respect.

440. I: Compromise, and that sort of thing.

441. CR4:   I'm very aware that I live in a Christian country, a British Christian country, and being respectful and aware of that. And I like that, you know, the Queen is my Queen. She's not *their* Queen, she's mine as well. Which is kind of odd, I can't explain it.

442. I: Do you feel that this is a Christian country?

443. CR4:   Yeah. Because I grew up when it was very much a Christian country. I went to a kind of a C of E school. And that's fine and I love that. And I celebrate the fact that they're able to… and it upsets me when they have to hush up their identity, who they are. In other words, the British Christian community, who doesn't want to do the Christmas carols because they're scared of offending other people, pisses me off. Because, actually, it's your country and you should be able to… and it's up to others. That's tough shit on them.

444. I: I suppose that's something that you've had to live with a lot. You've got to be able to follow your own traditions and not be ashamed of them, and not have to hide them.

445. CR4: Well, we kind of hide them, but it's your country. We've settled in your country, respectfully, respectful of the Christian identity, that I kind of find synonymous with Britain.

446. I: You say, "We've settled in your country." ...

447. CR4: The Jewish community has settled...

448. I: ...but what is *your* country?

449. CR4: It's very difficult to say. I don't really, necessarily, have a country. I'd say I'm British, definitely.

450. I: But you wouldn't necessarily say you 'have' this country.

451. CR4: No. I think, you know, the Jewish community is quite a nomadic existence, in that sense. You know, my parents, although my mum's Swedish, she's second generation, but she wasn't... you know, they came from Russia, originally. We've all moved around. There are very few communities that can go back...

452. I: There's something about... You're quite comfortable with that, from a Jewish... Jewish culture has learnt to live with that, almost.

453. CR4: I think so. And I think that who I am, what's your identity, I suppose, ultimately, it's Jewish. But what's the country that I... you know, I'm British, but I'm a British Jew. And I think the difference is... I'm very much – if I went into another country, if I went to live in another country, I

would be very much... I'd definitely be very much an expat.

454. I: An expat of England.

455. CR4: Yeah. Definitely. I would not be an expat of Sweden, because I've never really lived there, and it's not strong enough. I didn't grow up there, but this is, you know...

456. I: We've got to finish up, really. But I've got just two last questions I'm going to ask you; what makes you most happy about attitudes towards your identity?

457. CR4: I think a positive affinity towards people "Oh I've got friends who are Jewish." To have that understanding. That want, like a positive want to understand it, as opposed to "Oh... okay..." Different.

458. I: Different. And what frustrates you most about attitudes towards your identity?

459. CR4: I suppose the point that I have... some of it that you just have to kind of keep hidden, you can't just be you, or be comfortable to talk about certain things. You just don't. So, the part that you have to keep hidden. But I don't necessarily think it's different for anyone, in that sense; we all have to keep bits hidden, because that's life. But yeah, that's the thing that frustrates me the most: not being able to kind of speak out, have a discussion. Having to watch my words. That's what I find... that's what frustrates me the most. Or ignorance, definitely.

I am me: the lived experience of a mixed-race identity
by Haran Rasalingam

460. I: What kind of ignorance?

461. CR4:   Ignorance around the Jewish faith. Or being spotted as an Iranian, that annoys me as well. Definitely. Yeah, that really annoys me. So, yeah, that would be it.

462. I: Well, thank you very much, I'd keep carrying on, but I have to time-box it, otherwise I would never finish.

[End of interview]

INTERVIEW: It's never going to be boring

"It is just so unthinkable for me to choose, because I am mixed. There is no other way I could describe myself or explain myself."

About Co-Researcher #5

Co-Researcher #5 (CR5) is a psychotherapist in her early thirties. She grew up in Spain with her white Spanish mother and her black Nigerian father. Her parents separated while she was in her teens. Culturally, CR5 feels far more European than African. Visually, CR5 is fair skinned with frizzy light-brown hair and she points out that both her hair and her skin have fluctuated in colour over the years. She is generally considered to look unusual.

Research interview with Co-Researcher #5

[I = Interviewer; CR5 = Co-Researcher #5]

1. I: Are you okay to start?

2. CR5:   Sure.

3. I: So, it's kind of open-ended. I mean, I don't have a particular agenda in the research. It's kind of, you know, what comes up I will try and find the themes, and so on.

4. CR5:   See the patterns, yeah.

5. I: Yeah, things like that.

6.   CR5:   Go ahead.

7.   I: So, I might start off with just a question: if somebody asks you where you're from, how do you answer that?

8.   CR5:   Well, sometimes I'll answer, "You mean ethnically or culturally?" Sometimes I'll just tell them where I come from. I'll say I'm Spanish, I'm English and Nigerian. But, most times, when they ask me, they want to know what's the mix or what am I

9.   I: "What are you?" they ask?

10.   CR5:   Yes. Yeah. But, obviously, you know, maybe you have the same experience. You become very, you know, skilled at answering that. Yeah, I would say culturally, ethnically.

11.   I: So, you usually have to give quite a bit of a complex answer. You don't normally just come out with a single…

12.   CR5:   No, it depends. If it's people I am meeting, like new friends and all that, I'll tell them a bit of the background. If it's people in general, I just say, "I come from Spain." and then they just say, "Oh, good!" Yeah. Check. I'm dark and, you know, Spaniards are dark, so there we go.

13.   I: So that 'check'. Do you notice people actually saying, kind of mentally checking that off if it sort of makes sense or…?

14.   CR5:   Yeah, because you can see that they are happy with the answer.

I am me: the lived experience of a mixed-race identity
by Haran Rasalingam

15. I: Right. But are there ever times when they're not happy with the answer?

16. CR5:   Sometimes, yes. If it's another Spaniard. You know, they'll go, "Yeah, but you know…"

17. I: "Yeah, but…". There's a sort of a 'but'.

18. CR5:   Yes. They call it the authenticity testing. They want to know exactly. They can't really…

19. I: Authenticity, yeah, right.

20. CR5:   You know, pinpoint exactly where I'm from.

21. I: So, does that mean that, when people usually ask you that, they are usually thinking about… you said ethnicity. Do you think that's what they're after?

22. CR5:   Not all the time, but a big part. I could say 80% but, because of my life experience, I'll say 60% of the time, especially if their eyes are looking very curiously. You know, sometimes I can't really tell.

23. I: Yeah. So how do you describe yourself, in those sort of terms?

24. CR5:   Mixed race.

25. I: You would use the term 'mixed race'?

26. CR5:   Yes. In Spain, when I was growing up, that's their term… no, actually, that's not the term we use. We use 'mulatos'.

27. I: 'Mulatos', yeah.

28. CR5: They didn't have a lot of mixed race. Now they have more but, at the time, in the 80s, early 80s, 90s, they didn't have a lot of mixed-race people. So, I would be *mulata*, because I was half-black, half-white, and I was happy with that.

29. I: Right, right.

30. CR5: Now I've been living in the UK for six years. Before that I was living in Canada and, before that, France. And, since France, I would say 'mixed race'. So…

31. I: Okay. So, the *mulato* thing you kind of left behind.

32. CR5: Yeah. Now I even say 'biracial', but in Spain, I have to come up with a word, because they still don't have a word.

33. I: *(in Spanish) Birracial.*

34. CR5: *(in Spanish) Sí, birracial,* something like that!

35. I: Yeah! Okay.

36. CR5: So, mixed race, when I read about it, I thought, "Yeah, this is me." I'm very comfortable with that.

37. I: And that's another important question, that you are very comfortable with it. It doesn't… it's not an awkward description for you?

38. CR5: No, no, I am both races and both heritages.

39. I: Yeah.

40. CR5: I have been doing a lot of research on this topic in the UK, from the UK literature and also American literature. And I've come across 'half-caste'.

I am me: the lived experience of a mixed-race identity
by Haran Rasalingam

41.   I: Half-caste.

42.   CR5:   I don't know that I like that.

43.   I: Okay.

44.   CR5:   It just sounds 'half'. So mixed race, it's just a concoction. And so that's what I am.

45.   I: Okay. So, there is something about 'half' you don't like.

46.   CR5:   Yeah. I mean, I haven't been called that in my face. So, if someone says 'half-caste', I think that's a bit outdated. It just sounds so weird. I wouldn't be insulted, but I would correct them.

47.   I: So, you would say half Nigerian or half...

48.   CR5:   Yeah. I would say I'm mixed race and then I would say quickly "I am half Nigerian and half Spanish. Culturally I am Spanish-English and a bit Nigerian."

49.   I: Oh, okay, I see. So ethnically you say you're Spanish and Nigerian, then culturally English as well. Is that through living here for…

50.   CR5:   I was born in England, lived here until I was seven, and then I was sent home for summers and studied here in '99, so, yeah...

51.   I: Right, so, culturally, you've got more culture…

52.   CR5:   Culturally, Spanish. Yeah, I've got two cultures. That third culture

53. I: Oh, fantastic. Okay. So, really, it sounds like you're quite comfortable with the whole… with who you are and how you can describe yourself to people.

54. CR5: Yes, yes.

55. I: Even though, sometimes, people need to probe a little bit and say "Mmm, are you really…?"

56. CR5: I say "Yup. My, it's clear to me but, the more I've investigated this topic in the last two years, the more I see that it's other people. I knew it when I was growing up, that other people had question marks and they were confused, but…

57. I: Other people?

58. CR5: Just some other people would be… not everybody.

59. I: Mixed-race people?

60. CR5: I haven't heard it expressed by people in the UK, but people who are from one race, sometimes I find…

61. I: They find it…

62. CR5: Mixed race, yeah …that you have to be one thing or the other.

63. I: Yeah. So, it's not a problem for you, but it might be confusing for others.

64. CR5: Yes, and actually, even till this year, I am surprised when I talk about it with people I've known for a bit, and they just tell me they forgot I was half-half.

65. I: They forgot?

66. CR5:   Yes. They forgot my white family or things like that. Yeah.

67. I: So, they forgot your white family, so they are thinking of you as black, or something like that?

68. CR5:   Yes, yes. Or light black.

69. I: And does that bother you at all?

70. CR5:   Sometimes it does. Yeah. Sometimes I get very angry if it's forced upon me, but it's not been many times I've tackled some rude people who tell you what you are.

71. I: Right, right, right.

72. CR5:   That is very rude.

73. I: People telling you that you're black, for example.

74. CR5:   Yes. Yes. Or that I am Spaniard or that I don't have other cultures. So, I've had it with those people.

75. I: You don't have a culture?

76. CR5:   Other cultures.

77. I: Oh, other cultures. Right

78. CR5:   Yeah. I must say, when I found the insistence from other people to tell me, "You have to choose one side", I just think it is just so unthinkable for me to choose, because I am mixed. There is no other way I could describe myself or explain myself.

79. I: Yeah. So, some people think you have to choose?

80. CR5: Yeah, unfortunately. It's every now and then, you know.

81. I: Every now and then? Yeah, but it happens?

82. CR5: It happens. When I was little, it happened even more, because...

83. I: Really?

84. CR5: Yeah.

85. I: Was that in Spain more or...?

86. CR5: In Spain, in Nigeria, in England. I mean, it happens.

87. I: Did you get a different type of reaction in Nigeria, to Spain, to England?

88. CR5: Mm, no, similar. Good reactions, confused reactions. I've never had a very bad reaction. I have only had confused reactions, or reactions that were like, "Oh, interesting!"

89. I: Yeah. I think you said that it's here that people tend to sometimes forget your white heritage.

90. CR5: Well, I mean, when I'm with minority groups, for example, or groups that are particularly from minorities, they do forget the white part. I understand *why* it happens.

91. I: Why does it happen?

92. CR5: Well, politically, it happens because we're very... because it's minorities, that's the label; and, psychologically or psychically, I can see they forget it because I'm... I don't look Caucasian.

93. I: Right. So, you are either Caucasian or not, in their eyes.

94. CR5: So far, people who haven't met... I don't know, people who are used to being from one race, even if they have friends from different races, but people who are from one race, they do – what was I saying now? – they do forget that part, you know. It's interesting and it's happened because of the minority part. Because we all talk about the minority thing and the history that we share and the discrimination and all those things. It's very easy to forget I'm not.

95. I: Right. Yes, I could see that you may share those common issues that ethnic minorities might suffer.

96. CR5: And, as you say, psychologically, they forget. Sometimes I do get people who forget the black part, so it's not only, you know...

97. I: Do they tend to be white people or black people, in Nigeria, or...?

98. CR5: I've had it both, white and black people. White and black people forget that I have the black side, yeah.

99. I: Alright. So, you've had it from all angles, really! Every angle.

100. CR5: I have had it from all angles, yeah, yeah.

101. I: And do you ever, kind of, forget yourself, that, "Oh well, I'm white as well." or, "I'm black as well.", or, you know, something like that?

102. CR5: Because I grew up in a town where the majority, the vast majority was white – 99.9% were white – there were just, when I was there, another inter-racial couple with kids. My mother is white, and we were very close to my mother's family, a very big family. When I was little, I did tend to forget that I was half-half. That I was mixed race. Now it happens to me because I'm more used to white environments. Sometimes I am more aware of my mixed-race-ness when I am in a place that is either very white or very black. More when I'm in black environments, I think, I am more aware of my whiteness.

103. I: Okay. Yup, yup.

104. CR5: When growing up I was… since the teenage years, when I was more aware of the colour and the difference, I just see myself. So, when I look at the mirror, I just see myself. What I forget is that there are other people who look like me, because I didn't get to know a lot of people who look like me when I was growing up, just my brother. The other mixed-race kids were very black We were very light, we were both blond when we were little.

105. I: Blond hair?

106. CR5: Yeah. My mother has green eyes.

107. I: Yeah. So, your hair has darkened?

108. CR5: Yeah, yeah.

I am me: the lived experience of a mixed-race identity
by Haran Rasalingam

109. I: Does your tonality stay pretty much the same?

110. CR5:   No, that's the interesting thing with mixed-race kids. At least, so far, I've known black and white; we change. When I was ten, nine, I was quite fair and then I got a bit darker and then I got a bit fairer, and now I think I have gotten a bit more golden.

111. I: Yeah. So, you were... me too, you know.

112. CR5:   Yeah, yeah. If you're tanned, if you have a very different colour. You have darker hair, darker skin and it did change. My mother was very aware of this in the family.

113. I: So, was it your mother that's Spanish or your father's Spanish?

114. CR5:   My mother is a Spaniard.

115. I: Right, your father is Nigerian.

116. CR5:   Yeah.

117. I: Probably, before I jump into that, I was going to talk about the family background. But, before that, when we've talked about race, what does that word mean for you?

118. CR5:   Race definitely is a social construct but, because we still don't have the words to talk about differences, I still say... I would say Caucasian race, or now I'm learning to say Hispanic race because I don't know if Hispanic is right, but Hispanic race. Well, I do say tonality, so I use it more.

119. I: Tonality. Yeah, that's an interesting word.

120. CR5:   But race is a social construct. It is the human race, so. It's only pigmentation and genotype, you know.

121. I: And is that a view that you formed recently, or is that a view you have always had?

122. CR5:   No. It's something I had to develop myself, I had to study myself because they didn't talk about that when I was growing up. My family didn't talk a lot about racial differences...

123. I: Sure, sure.

124. CR5:   ...and heritages, you know. They were very colour-blind.

125. I: They were colour-blind.

126. CR5:   That's it. That's how they were.

127. I: Do you think that was a good or a bad thing?

128. CR5:   Growing up it was good, it protected me. But there are some losses. The losses were, mm, lack of acceptance, or understanding fully my circumstances. But, wholly, it was... I was in a bubble, so that helped me develop in other ways.

129. I: In other ways.

130. CR5:   Yeah, in other ways. Socially or, you know, intellectually. But I think it comes to a lot of mixed-race people who are brought up in colour-blind families, that you have to do your work afterwards. At one point...

131. I: So, when did you start *your* work?

132. CR5:   I met this mixed-race woman, when I was studying psychology, and she had similar... she was half Nigerian, half German. And then, through her, I started talking about blackness, being a minority within black and white societies. And she was talking about Duvoir and other writers and that's when I started getting into this, and that was... how many years ago? Five years ago. Before that I just thought "I'm mixed race, it's both worlds."

133. I: Yes. So, it was more of a kind of an implicit understanding before, and now you have started to study it.

134. CR5:   It was just what I was.

135. I: Just what you were.

136. CR5:   I don't know if I could say it was an understanding. I was always, always very aware of black people's hurdles, you know, difficulties. So, I was always very interested in [charity for Africa] and civil rights, even as a child and a teenager, so I would always follow that and watch documentaries. But I never really looked at terms to describe myself or, you know, the history of terms, the picture of black and white relationships from the fifteenth century to now, what has happened in the last years.

137. I: It sounds like you had a sort of a general interest, which has become more and more detailed, kind of thing.

138. CR5: Yeah. I could say I was different from my friends, from my teachers, from my grandparents. And we didn't travel to Nigeria as often as now I think I would have liked to.

139. I: So, you have grown up feeling different?

140. CR5: Yes.

141. I: In a big way, kind of thing?

142. CR5: Yes.

143. I: Yeah. And what's that been like?

144. CR5: It is hard as a child. When you are a child, when you are below 10 or 11 it's fine, because there's not a lot of focus on difference. But then, when you are a teenager, and you just don't want to stand out, you know, that's where my difference has been very uncomfortable, because I got asked more about my race.

145. I: So, it was apparent then, to people, that you were racially different.

146. CR5: More apparent when I was in my teens.

147. I: What was it do you think, that...?

148. CR5: The hair.

149. I: The hair?

150. CR5: It's only the hair. Because the thing is that, in Spain, people are quite dark, because of the, you know the moors, and invasions.

151. I: Mixed race themselves, you could say.

152. CR5:   Yes. So, in tonality, I have friends who are darker than myself and noses like myself, you can find them every now and then. They do have broad noses, but it was the hair, the curly hair.

153. I: It's the hair that singled you out.

154. CR5:   Yes, yes. Because I've been told so many times, "If it wasn't for the hair, I wouldn't have noticed."

155. I: Right, right, right. Noticed that…?

156. CR5:   Yeah. And being a girl, you know, in the teenage years, you learn how to make the best of your assets. I didn't know what to do with my hair.

157. I: Right. So, did you feel any awkwardness about your hair? Did you kind of wish it weren't there or wish it were straight or, I don't know…?

158. CR5:   Yeah. I guess, well, you did it for you so … You could do it there, in other places. So, everybody on TV or the media, singers, everybody had straight hair. Or curly hair, because, in Spain, they have a lot of curly hair – the curls were looser. And they always said to me, my friends, "Oh, but I have curly hair." and I said "Yeah, but your curls bounce." So, I did have fantasies, I did. But I didn't have my hair straightened till I was 19.

159. I: Right.

160. CR5:   So yeah. I did wait a bit.

161. I: So, you had it straightened at 19.

162. CR5:   Yeah. Which is a record.

163. I: What happened as a result of that?

164. CR5:   Well... I wrote about this recently. I didn't notice, but I blended in more, and I guess, unconsciously, that's what I was aiming for after the teenage years, to blend in.

165. I: You wanted to be one of the gang, kind of thing.

166. CR5:   I didn't not want to be mixed race, don't get me wrong, because the moment there was any misunderstanding, I would always say that I was half-half. I would say that. But it was just that 'leave me alone now'. When you are mixed race, also I am a tall woman. In Spain, I was quite tall, much taller than the average men, even. And so, I wasn't invisible. And getting out of the teenage years, I wanted to be invisible. So yeah, unconsciously, I wanted blend in. So, I got...

167. I: So, it wasn't that you didn't want people to know you were mixed race. You just didn't want too much focus.

168. CR5:   Too much questions, like enquiring.

169. I: Too many enquiries.

170. CR5:   I bet you've had similar experiences, that people would ask questions that are very personal, maybe, too soon, inappropriately. When you don't know them that well. So, every now and then, I would have to explain, you know,

I'm not happy or comfortable with that kind of joke. Because I'm mixed race, I'm also black.

171. I: Right. Yeah.

172. CR5:   But I wasn't aware of that. I did have my hair straight for a long time. When I was 26, I started to let it be curly again.

173. I: So now you just leave it curly?

174. CR5:   Yeah. I do have it chemically processed, so my hair is…

175. I: You have to explain that to me a bit, because I don't know about that!

176. CR5:   I don't normally volunteer, but I can give it a try. This is my hair, my natural hair, and this is loosened hair. But I left it on the curly side. So, for three years I had this hair, till I was 28 or 29 and I have this hairdresser who really wanted me to have it a bit loose. So, he convinced me, because… I said, "I don't want to have straight hair!" It's this thing, I don't want to have straight hair. It's kind of like people are going again confuse me on this. Lots of emotions in there.

177. I: So, you actually really don't want to pass.

178. CR5:   You have heard this probably before; I don't want to pass.

179. I: So, in a sense, then, the hairstyle that you choose is quite crucial to your identity, really.

180. CR5: Yeah. Well hair, as you know, is crucial to women's identity. I know that, for a black or mixed-race woman, it's very crucial too. It's important.

181. I: Yeah. Wow. How interesting. I am going to just… getting to some other questions. How are you for time, incidentally?

182. CR5: I have to leave at ten past eight.

183. I: Ten past eight is when you have to go, okay. So, in terms of psychotherapy, to what extent was your engagement with psychotherapy connected with your kind of mixed-race identity?

184. CR5: Mm, I talk about it, every now and then, but it's not the main theme at all. No.

185. I: It was not what brought you to the therapy in the first place?

186. CR5: No, no way. Like I said before, the mixedness that I have, I have always known it. I'd always been aware of it. No, it wasn't that. No, it was other things. And I didn't even think about choosing a therapist who was black or Indian or… I asked my teacher for three therapists that would touch certain subjects. Then I went and they were all white. White women. And I thought, "Okay." so…

187. I: Right. So that wasn't an issue. And has your involvement in psychotherapy in any way affected the way you think about your racial identity?

188. CR5:   No. It's actually enhanced it.

189. I: It's enhanced it?

190. CR5:   Like I said before, I don't touch the subject a lot with my therapists, go in and out, but I did write a personal essay last year. It looks to have it published this year, and what it merits is a lot of change. I touched things about my teenage years, and then I was taken by surprise by this shame that I had repressed during my teenage years for all that difference.

191. I: Shame for the different-ness. Wow.

192. CR5:   Shame because, like I said before, everybody in the media, everybody in the public life was Caucasian. So, we worked on that, my therapist and I, and it enhanced it. Two weeks and a half, I think, it was total transformation.

193. I: Really? So, a transformation. In what way was it a transformation?

194. CR5:   Just to leave behind hang-ups about me not being beautiful.

195. I: Okay.

196. CR5:   So, it was more particular, it was just not feeling beautiful.

197. I: So, your belief, as you were growing up, was that you were not beautiful.

198. CR5:   No, I thought I was beautiful, but I repressed the bits of me that thought I wasn't beautiful. So that was an underlying belief, but the main belief that I had consciously made is that I thought was beautiful. Mm, other the things that we've touched; I touched, with my therapist and sometimes my class; the lack of enough material on differentness. On cultural differences or ethnic differences that can affect therapy. As you know, white, Caucasian, middle class men are the main authors of the work that we study at school ... I've talked about that with my therapist and in the class.

199. I: Yes. Did you find people understand these issues?

200. CR5:   Not 100%. Obviously, you can't get 100% understanding from, I think, anyone outside oneself. But I have been a bit disappointed with their reactions. But I have a theory that, in the UK, there's a lot of enforced political correctness. And lots of people were colour-blind. They said they had never thought about it and other people were emphasising a lot that it didn't matter. And I thought...

201. I: Right. So, they were kind of not really confronting it.

202. CR5:   It sounded like compensation, because some of the comments that they made later is like that. They say, "I'm

not racist." but they were not really making any racist comments, so there is... I did notice that there was a bit of fear. My therapist... I'm happier then with the class, but still this is not perfect. Because of my upbringing and seeing that my family didn't deal with the issues as I would have liked at the time when I, it would have been better, and because of my fears and everyone, I'm kind of used to getting a bit disappointed. Or I'm kind of used to doing my own work.

203. I: Doing your own work. So, what is it that they're missing, do you think?

204. CR5: They're missing that they're not mixed race, so they can't entirely get that you have two bits of you that sometimes can be conflicting.

205. I: Right.

206. CR5: I see that there's more weight to the black and white mixture, because of the history of slavery and all that. So, there is a lot of resentment, fear, anger, so those two bits, in mixed races, is something that... it's an interesting life, let's put it like that. I'm never going to be bored!

207. I: Are you glad of that?

208. CR5: Yeah, yeah. I've earned it, let's put it like that. It hasn't been unexpected. You have to be it to get it. I used to think too much, because I've got so many different things that I

can relate to that. But, like I said before, I do expect people not to get it 100%, so there are holes, in therapy, as a client, and holes in the academic side.

209. I: Yeah. That makes sense. Have you ever suffered racism?

210. CR5:   What's racism for you?

211. I: Well, I suppose there are lots of different types. So, anything that you would call racism, I suppose.

212. CR5:   I've been called names in school. Not a lot. I haven't been called anything really hard, and not as far as I remember. Maybe when I was much … when I lived in England. Maybe that's when I was called harder things, but I don't recall any. Like name calling would be more nicknames. They would call me Tina Turner or Olivia Keystone or Whitney. In terms of work, I think the work I have been… I've never felt that my condition as a mixed-race person was a disadvantage. I have noticed it more as a woman.

213. I: More of a disadvantage as a woman than as a mixed-race person?

214. CR5:   Yes. But I can't complain about my achieving something. Somehow, I always had the bosses on my side, because of accomplishment and hard work and all that. As a woman, I have noticed it more, kind of just subtle messages. No racism. In fact, I guess it's the name calling in school. I wasn't… they wouldn't call me that to my face, but that

was it. And then the jokes: the racist jokes on Chinese people and black people, with me having to kind of put the boundary, you know. I'm not happy with that joke.

215. I: So, you would always kind of be offended by any racially motivated joke.

216. CR5:   Yeah. I never found them funny. Even the ones about culture, where you have a French guy and a Spanish guy and an English guy in a plane and what happens. I guess, on that side, I didn't develop a sense of humour about different-ness.

217. I: And it's interesting because, in a way, they are sharing a joke with you, because they think you are with them, kind of thing.

218. CR5:   Yeah. Many weren't like that. Sometimes I wonder if, unconsciously, some of them were trying to test me or something like that and that's just something that I thought about later, because you can tell different-ness but, again, the hair was a giveaway. So, the jokes I would hear and being called Whitney, when my name's *[name of co-researcher]*.

219. I: Right.

220. CR5:   maybe someone thinking... like I went to an all-boys school when I was between 14 and 18. There was a lot of competitiveness. But, again, I think you know, with

grades, the guys wanted to check *my* grades all of the time because I was a good student. But I think it was because I was a woman, the boys expected me to be less clever because I was a woman.

221. I: Right, okay, yeah. What do you like most about other people's attitudes towards your multiple heritage?

222. CR5: Interest, curiosity. Because that's what motivates me. So, when I see that in another person, I'm intrigued.

223. I: Yeah. So, the fact that they take an interest in...

224. CR5: In the possibility that, you know, that there are other, other equations.

225. I: Right, yeah, yeah. Not always the same single race, single culture.

226. CR5: Yeah, and it is, like I said before, there still seems to be a lot of idea that we are with your race and you don't go out, honestly. Like asking girlfriends would they consider dating out of their race. Some of them were very surprised when I asked them. They had never considered it. They thought they would just go with one race.

227. I: How do you think about that question? Does race come into it, when you are thinking of dating somebody?

228. CR5: No. It's the person.

229. I: Just the person. Yeah, yeah.

230. CR5:   But, because of my own experience, I know that there's different possibilities of love or friendship. It's like I can't think differently. So, curiosity is what I'm interested in. When I was younger, I guess, as a woman, you have to say attention from men. Yeah.

231. I: So, you mean you got attention?

232. CR5:   But I'm in my thirties, I don't go for that anymore. But, yeah, when you're in your twenties or when you're a teenager, yeah, there's that interest again.

233. I: Yeah. So that was one of the... yeah, I guess, because you stood out in some way. It was good from a...

234. CR5:   It was good from one side but, from the other side, it was bad.

235. I: On the other hand, then, what is it that frustrates you most about people's attitudes towards...

236. CR5:   Narrow mindedness.

237. I: Which you would define as...?

238. CR5:   Being actually surprised that I am half-half. Actually, just that idea, honestly, is... It just frustrates me. It doesn't make me angry anymore. I just... I'm like I am so lucky that I'm mixed so I can be more open minded, because, honestly, it's really weird.

239. I: It's kind of surprising that people don't even entertain the possibility of it.

I am me: the lived experience of a mixed-race identity
by Haran Rasalingam

240. CR5:   To be fair with them, most people, inter-racial couples are not the norm. It's a minority still. So, people know and expect what they know. If I were in their shoes, I might have been surprised too.

241. I: Okay. Let's talk a little bit about your family and your kind of family history and your upbringing and so on; because it sounds quite busy. You said you spent some time in the UK. Could you tell me a little bit about your family background and then your upbringing?

242. CR5:   Family background…?

243. I: As in your parents, where they're from, how they came together and this sort of thing.

244. CR5:   Father's from Nigeria, mother's from Spain. They met at University, in the canteen, in Spain. My father was there with a scholarship. And they dated for two years and they didn't date and then they went back together, and then they married, and they lived in England, where my father was getting his specialisations. They were living in England, in different places, because my father was based, because of his work, in different places. So, they moved around a lot. I moved around a lot and I remember it, although not consciously, but that's there. And then we went to Spain. My father was working abroad, in Saudi Arabia, for two years, so we went – my brother, my

mother and I, alone – to Spain, where her family lived. So, she said "I don't want to do it alone, we have to go back to family." She's got two of her sisters there, her parents, she has tons of cousins. So, yeah, we moved to this small town. So, I was seven and I didn't notice, but yeah, I was the only one who looked different – my brother and I. Till, years later, we discovered another family. We tried to be friends but, in the end, we were not very similar, so…

245. I: Okay.

246. CR5:   We didn't force it, that's why we were similar in some ways. So, I was brought up – my mother is a very family person, her family are very close. So, we were brought up… My father is very close to his friends, and his friends were based in Spain. So, when he came back, it was all about his friends and my family, who would not talk about a trip to Nigeria. I think he had with his father. And so, I saw my grandmother twice when I was six and when I was twelve. And then, my father was not close to his family, so it wasn't encouraged that we go. My mother was pleased to go and meet with my father, and that was very difficult to see at home. You know, wanting to get to know those two bits, but it was impossible. So, I didn't see my family in Nigeria. I saw them when they visited, but I didn't go to Nigeria – and be, again, another minority,

I am me: the lived experience of a mixed-race identity
by Haran Rasalingam

because the majority is black – till I was 29. So that's 17 years.

247. I: Right.

248. CR5:   So, for many, many years, it was the white family. My father and his family were black. But most of his friends were white, actually, except two of them, very definitely Nigerian. The thing is that there were kids – his friends' kids – who were also mixed race, they were much younger than my brother and I. So, it was very weird to put us together. Six years there were, in difference. So, it was all the whiteness thing, and then that blackness. So, I was five years.

249. I: So, in terms of Nigerian culture, do you feel close to it? I mean, do you feel it's part of you?

250. CR5:   Mm… I feel close to it in temperament.

251. I: Temperament. Right.

252. CR5:   The history, I am not very familiar with it. That's something on my list of things to do. It's on my list that I haven't opened yet. So, I am very sure the moment I get there, I might grasp the history, I'll be a bit closer. But it's the temperament. It's not the culture, no. I'm very European. That's something that… It's always been very clear to me. And, with my cousins, with my uncles. Some of them live outside Nigeria, some of them don't. But the

ones who live in North America, it's easier, the contact. But the ones who live in Nigeria, the younger ones, we can connect in many things, but there are other things, that are cultural differences, they are very strong. And I'm not sure – if I had been visiting every year, it wouldn't have been so difficult, because I do struggle sometimes. Within a reasonable and healthy way, we continue, but there is lots of differences about religion and about women's roles. So that's where I just... I say no.

253. I: Yeah, yeah, it makes sense. We've still got a little bit of time. So, it sounds, from what you are saying, that, overall, you have a pretty positive view of...

254. CR5:   Mixedness, yes.

255. I: Yeah, being mixed.

256. CR5:   It really saddens me to see the negative view that there is in the UK.

257. I: Yes, do you see it?

258. CR5:   I do see it. I read about it. And, like I said, I have had encounters here with people. For example, I read about people thinking that mixed-race children or adults are confused. I read about it, and then, recently, someone did ask me – a black person asked me, "Would you recommend it? Would you like to marry a black, so your blackness comes back? I heard that mixed people are

confused". And I was so surprised that someone young asked me that. I said, "No.", but obviously you need the right environmental, you know, you need that love, and..." Yeah, yeah. But I don't know your experience...

259. I: It sounds similar to me, I think. I mean, it sounds... that ties in with what you said earlier; that, you know, it's others that seem to be confused, not you.

260. CR5:   Yeah, I told this girl, "It's others who have the problems, not me!"

261. I: And that may present frustration when people expect you to choose one side or the other or whatever it may be.

262. CR5:   Yeah, if I can be diplomatic, I try to veer away or to say "No." in a kind way, or just say "No."

263. I: Have you ever felt the need to choose one way or the other?

264. CR5:   I have. I have. Last time I noticed the pressure was in January, after Christmas this year, and then I told myself "Honestly, you have to live your life. If you choose things just because others expect you to choose them, you are just going to be miserable. You don't have integrity with yourself." So, I'll do what I want to do.

265. I: So, you felt, maybe, you should choose because of the pressure from the outside world.

266. CR5:   Yeah, and I thought, okay, granted, I did grow up with a lot of questions asked, a lot of unwanted attention and a lot of inappropriateness, you know, setting boundaries with questions and all that. Telling me what I was and insisting what I was but, at this point, that pressure is old, that was what was activated where I thought, "You know what? It's their problem. It's really not my business. It's their business."

267. I: Yeah, yeah.

268. CR5:   And I felt much lighter when I thought that, by the way.

269. I: Sorry?

270. CR5:   I felt much lighter when I made that decision; that it was their business.

271. I: Right And you mentioned the word 'integrity'.

272. CR5:   Oh yes, not being honest with myself.

273. I: But your personal integrity comes before satisfying…

274. CR5:   Yeah. And my personal taste, preferences or lifestyle choices, like music taste, movie taste.

275. I: I suppose that's the thing; with a mixed identity, do you think it's given you certain qualities that perhaps others may struggle to have?

276. CR5:   Yeah, the ability to think very creatively, to be very inspired. I even have this idea that, if it's nourished and taken care of – you know, the mixedness – a lot of

possibilities, socially, intellectually, emotionally, a lot of... Ah, yeah, one thing I realise – psychology, anthropology, sociology – being very good at reading trends, people's motivations, feelings, trends, yeah.

277. I: In a sense, you think you are more astute?

278. CR5:   No, because of my upbringing, again, all that unwanted attention and enquiry, I became very hypervigilant. So, because of that, I am very aware and so astute.

279. I: That's my word for it.

280. CR5:   No, I would find another word, but I can't find. But I have a friend who is half-Thai half-English, and we both talked about the benefits. She's also studied Psychology. She is a psychologist. Other things: I am very good at adapting to different cultures, to different people, whenever I want. And this I have written about and it's going to be published, so I don't mind saying it.

281. I: Fantastic.

282. CR5:   I can choose when I want to be whiter or blacker.

283. I: Yes.

284. CR5:   I take no sides. Well, I do take sides, sometimes. But, other times, I rely on my mixedness to choose, because there is a lot of polarity in the world, still, so I can just say "You know, I have got both sides, this is what I think."

285. I: So, do you think that runs through other areas of your life, this kind of 'both sides' – it's not just...

286. CR5:   Yeah, I can be adaptable when it's needed. I can be determined and focussed when it's needed. I can come up with other people's points of views. I can think what is going on with that person. Once I became more aware of what was appropriate or not, to trust someone when you meet them in the beginning.

287. I: More sensitive to it.

288. CR5:   Yes. Try not to do what they did to me. I find a lot of benefits. Like I said before, that concoction that I have will always be there. So, there are challenges, political challenges, sometimes, you know, in terms of just ideas between minority and majority, white majority and black minority in whatever country I am. There can be emotional challenges, but it's interesting. I'm curious.

289. I: Yeah, yeah, yeah.

290. CR5:   And much happier with it, in my thirties. I've always been happy about it, but sometimes I would rather be invisible. That happened to me at 26-27.

291. I: In a place like this, do you feel like you just blend in, it's not an issue?

292. CR5:   For me, internally, I blend in. Externally I don't blend in. People do look at me. I get stared at.

I am me: the lived experience of a mixed-race identity
by Haran Rasalingam

293. I: And you think they are staring at you because you are…?

294. CR5:   For many reasons, but I do still get stared at because they can't really tell. But you now put this idea of Brazilians, so many people think I'm Brazilian.

295. I: Right, right, right.

296. CR5:   But, internally, I do blend in. I do feel more comfortable, still, in white areas than in black areas, because of the lack of enough exposure to Nigeria. Annual trips would have helped a lot. And because I grew up in a town where everybody was white.

297. I: That is more familiar to you.

298. CR5:   More familiar. So.

299. I: But I guess, when I came in, I guessed…

300. CR5:   You guessed?

301. I: That you were *[name of co-researcher]*.

302. CR5:   I thought you would have guessed …

303. I: I just thought, "Yeah!"

304. CR5:   "It must be her."

305. I: I thought, "It must be you." Yeah. Wow. Okay. We're coming close to the end, maybe. I think you've covered so much. I mean, there's questions here that I haven't asked. Oh, you have been excellent. Okay. I think we've really… One last thing, which you've kind of touched on, but just

the whole... Have you experienced many negative attitudes towards racial mixing?

306. CR5:   Mmmm.

307. I: Not necessarily negative, really and actually, just sort of attitudes to racial mixing.

308. CR5:   Well, yeah, that is what I was thinking. There are attitudes because, as I said: the staring. My parents, walking, taking a stroll in my town and people looking, or children looking, you know, and commenting. And my father, he loves children, and so he would always, like, "Yeah, look at me, touch me!" And they would look at my mother and would be so fascinated by her. Adult stares. The thirty years of my life that I was living here I don't recall anything, right now, but because of the history of Britain, it must have been a problem for many people. It must have been. So, I bet I heard things, I bet I heard insults, you know, to my friends or to me. To date, I have dated a lot of men who are not my race, because being with someone who is my race has to be mixed race. I haven't dated mixed race people actually. No. I have dated majoritarily Mediterranean and Caucasian men, Middle Eastern. With Middle Eastern it's more... I think people were curious. I didn't find any negative attitudes myself but, with my parents, people stared, kids would make comments, but no

one insulted them, so far as I remember. But they were...
sometimes, you could notice when people were being a bit
uncomfortable, so there was more than intrigue or
puzzlement. There was some amount of "Oooh!"

309. I: Were you aware, do you think, of it, when you were a
child? Of it being an issue, that your parents – one's
Nigerian, one's Spanish, – was it...?

310. CR5:   Some of my teachers. It was a bit surprising for them.
Yeah. Friends, friends would be just getting to know my
father, getting to see him. But, like I said, I think about
them, the times in England, the first years, I bet I have
witnessed that. But, because of being so small, I fully
absorbed it, or just...

311. I: Right, right, right.

312. CR5:   Mm, in Nigeria, this last trip, when I was 29, without my
parents, just alone, some of my aunties would make
comments like, "You should marry a black, so we undo
the mistake."

313. I: Undo the mistake?

314. CR5:   And I had to say, respectfully, to one of my aunties "I am
not a mistake, I will do whatever I want to do. But I
understand what you are telling me. So, I will think about
it."

315. I: Right, Okay. Very diplomatic.

316. CR5:   Yeah, but they were telling me, who was younger, I wonder… I do wonder when we went, when I was 5 to 6 years old, to Nigeria. The next trip my mother couldn't come because she had to work, so, they haven't had enough exposure to both of them. My uncles, yes, they love my mother. But within walls, I have talked to them in Nigeria, "And they'd rather that you married black." So, I bet that they have been very nice and understanding.

317. I: And there was also… that just reminds me of one other issue – what was the attitude of your mother's parents and your father's parents about them getting together?

318. CR5:   My father, like I said, he had – still has, but he had, at the time – issues with his father. He was very determined to marry my mother. So, I have no… he wouldn't talk about this. So, I don't know what happened. But, like I said, I suspect that he stood up for himself, because I've been told things … On my mother's side, she had an auntie who was engaged to an Englishman.

319. I: Right.

320. CR5:   And the family convinced her not to marry this Englishman, because cultural differences are difficult to overcome in marriage. So that auntie had just said "No." to her fiancé. She was very much in love.

321. I: Oh goodness.

322. CR5: And she was terribly miserable. She married someone else. And my mother remembered that. So, my grandparents told her "We think he is a really nice guy, not a prospect as he has another culture and he is a man of colour. Have you thought about your children?" And my mother only thought about that auntie of hers and she thought "I can't. I need to marry this man. I can't say no. I am going to be miserable." So, what happened was that my grandparents were happy with their social coupling because they're both the same social caste and I think they overcompensated; they paid the newspaper to run an advert to announce the wedding.

323. I: Okay.

324. CR5: To make sure that the town…

325. I: To make sure nobody had any doubts that they were announcing it!

326. CR5: To make sure that the town had no doubts that they had no problems. One of my mother's aunties did tell my father that no black man should be close to a naked white woman. He never liked that auntie. I never knew this till recently, but I always noticed the bad vibes between my father and this auntie. She was a very mean auntie. Not to me directly, but I didn't like her, so I guess I picked up that, but the rest of the family adored my father. My

mother has like 40 cousins, without counting spouses. They just adore him, because he is very charming. A people's person, actually, but yeah, my parents did tell my mother that and I think they also told that my father was their preference. I don't know how they come across to say that, but they said it. And then the funny thing is that my brother and I were my grandparents' favourite grandkids. So, I don't know…

327. I: So, there you go… yeah.

328. CR5: So, there you go.

329. I: We probably have to stop there, that's all. Thank you so much.

330. CR5: You're welcome.

[End of interview]

INTERVIEW: Staying positive

"When I'm cycling, I'm thinking about cycling. When I'm cooking, I'm thinking about cooking! I'm thinking about identity issues probably most when somebody else is bringing them up."

About Co-Researcher #6

Co-Researcher #6 (CR6) is a psychotherapist in her early fifties and grew up in Malaysia. She describes her mother as white English and her father as Malay. CR6's parents divorced when she was ten, after which she grew up with her father and her half-Chinese, half-Indian-Muslim stepmother. In CR6's family, marrying people from other cultures is very common. Visually, CR6 says she was always taller than other Malaysians, but it is possible to speculate that CR6 has some East Asian or South-East Asian ancestry, due perhaps to her eyes, nose and hair.

Research interview with Co-Researcher #6

[I = Interviewer; CR6 = Co-Researcher #6]

1.   I: This is going to be like a semi-structured approach. I've got a bunch of questions, which I'll ask around those things. I certainly won't be asking all of those, and you'll

probably answer half of them in passing, anyway. So, it's just a guide for me, really.

2.   CR6:   Okay.

3.   I: So, could I ask you, first, how you would describe your family background and your family roots.

4.   CR6:   My mother is English. I come from *[county in England]*. My father is a Malay. Malaysia has three races. He is, I would say, the privileged race, because there is a bit of an apartheid there. Then my parents divorced when I was ten, so I grew up with my stepmother, who is half Chinese and half Indian Muslim.

5.   So, I would say I have a mixed ethnic background, both in terms of genetics and culture. And I grew up in Malaysia, which is…

6.   I: You grew up in Malaysia?

7.   CR6:   I left Malaysia at 18.

8.   I: Yes, I can see the mix in two ways; both genetically and culturally and where you grew up as well.

9.   CR6:   Yes.

10.   I: Great. So, if somebody asked you, "Where are you from?", how would you answer that?

11.   CR6:   Well, I would say the whole thing. I would say, "I was born in England, and I grew up in Malaysia, and I've lived in Europe, pretty much, more than half of my life."

I am me: the lived experience of a mixed-race identity
by Haran Rasalingam

12.   I: How do you feel when people ask you that, generally?

13.   CR6:   Fine. People used to ask me, "Malaysia?", because I look different from my stepmother, and people will go, "Oh, is that your mother?" And I would be saying, "No, this is not my mother.". So, the "Where are you from?" and the "Where are you origins?" I'm quite used to explaining that.

14.   And then, here, people ask, "Well, where are you from?" because I don't look typically Malaysian either. So, I explain it and that gives them the clues of how to put it together.

15.   And in Malaysia I often get, "But you're from here too, aren't you?" because they recognise something. So, on both sides of the story, I tell the story of where I'm from as I'm from here, and somewhere else too.

16.   It's obvious. Well, it's obvious to Malaysians, they can pick up the features. Here, people don't know. They just think, "Well you don't look Chinese or Indian. Where are you from?"

17.   I: It sounds like you're quite happy to recount that story, whenever anybody asks.

18.   CR6:   Yeah. Because it's something that everybody in my family recounted. My stepmother would recount that. She's half

and half, so she would recount it and all her siblings married mixed race.

19.   I have a Burmese auntie. I have an auntie from India. A Chinese auntie. I can't remember – there's so many marriages! There was a Chinese adopted by an Indian family. So, people would always look/not look like what they were, so it's fine.

20.   I: Yes, it sounds almost like it's quite a familiar scenario in your family, as a whole…

21.   CR6: Yes, in the family a lot.

22.   I: …because in the family there's quite a mix generally.

23.   CR6: Yeah, yeah. And then my mother remarried an Indian man, so my half-brothers are half Indian. Indian/English. They grew up in Australia.

24.   I: So, you grew up with your dad and your stepmother?

25.   CR6: My dad and my stepmother.

26.   I: Were you not in touch with your mother at all?

27.   CR6: No, not at all. From the age of ten.

28.   I: And still not?

29.   CR6: I am now, yes.

30.   I: From what age did you become…?

31.   CR6: I re-contacted… or she… I don't know who re-contacted. Somehow, we met again when I was 21.

32.   I: And your parents separated from the age of ten, you said?

33. CR6: Ten.

34. I: So, did either your mother or your stepmother or your
           father ever talk to you about the idea of being mixed, in
           some way, when you were growing up?

35. CR6: Yes, yes. My stepmother always said, "Oh, I hope that you
           can marry a Malay, because it's terrible to be mixed race.
           It would be good if you could get back to…" what she
           called the origin, because she felt a loss. But she came
           from another generation. I guess it was more difficult.

36.   But I think my biological father and mother both liked the
           fact that I was mixed, because my father, coming from the
           colonial period, saw having an English wife as very
           prestigious. And my mother, coming from a working-class
           English background, had always seen the exoticism, the
           tall dark stranger, going to the east.

37.   So, when I was born, they both thought that I was very
           beautiful, from another perspective. My mother thought I
           was amazing because I was exotic, and my father thought
           I was amazing because I'm so fair, compared to how dark
           skinned he was.

38.   So, I guess they did note my mixed race, but they have
           positive… they saw that as a positive thing. So, I had this
           from my father… *both* my parents thought of me as
           beautiful.

39. I: And that idea of marrying back to…?

40. CR6:   That's my stepmother's idea. Marrying back into the race.

41. I: What's your view on that?

42. CR6:   I just thought, "Oh, it's so hard for me! Because I'm very tall. Well, not very tall but, in Malaysia, I'm very tall and it was just really hard to find a boyfriend. I just said, "Yeah!" to my stepmother. "If I meet someone, that's great." But, in the end, I have, of my siblings – there are six of us – two married what I call 'back into' the race and the other four didn't.

43. I: Would you ever consider that now?

44. CR6:   I don't have children.

45. I: But are you married?

46. CR6:   Yes, I'm married. I'm in my second marriage.

47. I: Was it ever a consideration to marry 'back into' the race, as you put it?

48. CR6:   Um, no. It was never a racial thing. It was a consideration to marry someone who would let me grow and have my own interests and share interests. So, if I had met somebody who was Malay or Chinese or African, then that would have been fine; I was more interested in who that person was.

49. I: So, it doesn't sound like racial identity was a big issue for you, in that sense?

50.   CR6:   Well, it was, in the sense that there's a lot of pressure from the family to marry back into the race, so they weren't so happy that my first boyfriend was American. And then I finally married a Swiss man. So, there was lots of pressure. And my first husband... he did actually convert to Islam, so there were lots of pressures ...

51.   I: And are you religious?

52.   CR6:   No. It's a cultural religion. Religion is culture, so that everybody else can say, "How shameful that she married out." To me, I think it's a status thing, staying within your own race, so you can understand the customs, and you can do all the traditions. My husband won't be able to bury my father properly, and all sorts of traditional things. Things like that.

53.   I: Would you personally use the phrase 'mixed race'?

54.   CR6:   Yeah. Yeah.

55.   I: That's a phrase that you're comfortable with. So, what does race mean to you?

56.   CR6:   Uhmm... actually, do I say mixed race? I'm not sure if I say mixed... yeah, probably I do say mixed race, but I don't actually mean race in terms of racial characteristics. I actually might mean mixed culture. That means, when I think about the therapist I chose, I always chose therapists who would understand culture.

57.   Even though I once had a German therapist. I knew that
           he'd lived in India for a long time, so that was important
           to me, that he had lived in India more than ten years, and
           I thought, "That's good, then he understands Asian ways."
           And that was important to me. But I also lived in
           Switzerland for eight years, so I thought, "That's a good
           combination." and my husband was Swiss, so he won't
           understand *that* part of the culture.

58.   So, for me, culture is like how it is to be in those situations.

59. I: So, what does race actually mean, then, to you, if it's not
           really the word that you would use to describe…?

60. CR6: I think race is what is kind of what other people see, and
           culture is what I experience. I experience being with
           people who have Muslim traditions, or people who have a
           colonial heritage. There will be so many cultural things,
           and I experienced having a family that's working-class
           English, so I have all that.

61.   But race is what other people see. They see, "Oh, she has
           straight hair." Somehow Asian coloured skin. Maybe
           European eyes rather than Oriental eyes. So, race is kind
           of what I think other people see and try and put you into
           the racial category.

62.   So, when I say, "I'm mixed race", I'm just saying, "Well, I belong in more than one category." And actually, it's not too much more. To me.

63.   I: And would you say culturally you're in more than one category? Would you put it like that?

64.   CR6:   Yeah, but, as you come into the 21st century, even more people are. And I remember once writing a school essay – because in Malaysia there is a lot of racial tension and, "Oh, the problems will be solved when all people become mixed race. All the races, because there will be no thing as one category.", so that's my idea that…

65.   I: That would be a better world?

66.   CR6:   …that would be a better world. It's difficult, though, because I have lots of clients and their struggles. It's not easy! But I think it's richer. It's made my life richer.

67.   I: You've said quite a bit about your identity already. Have you ever experienced difficulty in gaining a sense of identity?

68.   CR6:   Yes. Always. Even right at this minute. Because it's not so clear cut; I can't just… it's like I can't wear ready-made clothes, you know. I can't just say, "Oh sure, I'm from England. This is my land. I know this landscape. I've got forefathers for 300 years." I don't share it with a lot of people, this identity, I mean, I share it with my one sister.

But then, everybody else is different combinations. But even she has moved on, because she's married a Chinese-Malaysian, and I married a Swiss man, and now an Englishman. And she lives in Canada now.

69.   So, lots of different things are happening. Actually, I've just finished with a client who is mixed race and adopted by a white family. So, she's half Turkish, half St. Lucian – this is confidential – and what she did was, she saw an advertisement for mixed-race children who are adopted. And they formed a group. And of course, they were all different combinations but, somehow, they had the shared identity of being mixed, and growing up in a white family.

70.   So that's a class in itself. Do you know what I mean?

71. I: Yes, yes.

72. CR6:   And that's what I mean. I understand that 'mixedness'. Other people would say, "Oh, that's half Chinese and half Nigerian. And that's half…" And they look very different. And maybe Nigeria and China are very different from St. Lucia and Turkey, but the experience would be somehow similar.

73. I: There is some shared experience.

74. CR6:   Mm.

75. I: And is it an experience that you share as well?

76.   CR6:   Yeah, I can share that with her. I didn't grow up in *this* country, so I have a different experience of growing up in a multi-racial country, where my whole class is filled with lots of different races, speaking different language, having different religion, which is maybe different from her experience. Or children who grew up out of the country and had a half, I don't know, West Indian, English... that had grown up way out in the middle of the country right on the border of Wales. So, her experience is completely different.

77.   So, I guess that's more... I'm lucky, because I grew up in a mixed community with mixed people. So, even though I feel I'm sort of a particular mix, the mixedness identity, or the mixedness experience is something I could share.

78.   I: And, when I asked that question, you said that you constantly have 'difficulties'. Even now, you said.

79.   CR6:   They weren't particularly difficulties, but, thoughts and questions. Yeah. Thoughts and questions.

80.   I: Yes, 'difficulties' may be a bit loaded!

81.   CR6:   Well, 'difficulties' means like it's a struggle, whereas 'thoughts and questions' is like, "I've got to put some effort into it." but it's not unwelcome effort.

82.   I: So, something that's always alive, in a way.

83.   CR6:   Sure. That's the word.

84.   I: And so, are there ever times when these thoughts about these things are not there, where you don't think about identity issues?

85.   CR6:   Yeah, of course! When I'm cycling, I'm thinking about cycling. When I'm cooking, I'm thinking about cooking! I'm thinking about identity issues probably most when somebody else is bringing them up. So, you're bringing them up, or my client is bringing them up. Or I have to fill in a form and I have to think, "Where do I go?" Or, I don't know. Or I hear about racism. So of course, it has to be something learnt. Not always. If it's not learnt...

86.   I: So, if somebody is specifically talking about it, or you'll put the question in a form, for example, then obviously it brings it up.

87.   CR6:   Yeah.

88.   I: And, talking of forms, actually, what do you do with them when they ask these sort of questions?

89.   CR6:   I tick the best possible box. And I'm always thinking, "What use is this question to anybody?" I think you're always allowed to leave it blank, so... I normally go English-Asian or something along that white mix. I always go mixed race, and then White-Asian but I don't quite like Asian, because Asian feels like the sub-continent, South East Asia.

I am me: the lived experience of a mixed-race identity
by Haran Rasalingam

90.   And there's no South-East, because there's East, which is kind of like China and all that, and Korea and Japan, and so I always think, "There's not enough categories" So I just think, "Well, somebody has to do the box. Does it matter?"

91.   I: Do you put 'white' down, as one option?

92.   CR6: Yes.

93.   I: Can you tell me a bit more about that?

94.   CR6: Well, my mother's white. There are strategic advantages of being white. This is, I would say, a white dominated world. Well, I don't want to damn my white identity, I want to honour it too, but I also sometimes think, "Oh I feel a bit sneaky, because I know I'm using a good card." What I call a good card. "You know what? I'm half white on my English side.", "Oh, she's one of us. She's one of ours."

95.   That's a political thing, and I go, like, "Well, I have to stand somewhere. But I stand in the middle." And that's a hard place to stand. But I don't deny one or the other. To say, "Oh, I'm Asian." would really be a denial that actually, I'm also half English, half European.

96.   I: And yet there was a sense, in a way, that that was some sort of privilege.

97. CR6:   Yeah. Well, if you grow up in a colonial country... I remember my father saying he always used to look at the District Officer and say, "When I grow up, I'm going to wear boots just like that." And I remember coming to this country, age 18, and being shocked to see white people sweeping in roads, cleaning up.

98.   And so, in our minds, they were people on TV. And people always tried to speak with English accents. And you'd say, "I went to England." It was like saying I've been somewhere really special. So, yes. If you grow up in a colonial country and you're educated in English and you read English literature, everything, it does seem 'up there'.

99.   And I know that my mother had a much higher status there than she did here. Because we would come back for holidays and she'd say, "Don't tell anybody what your grandparents do.", because they ran a fish and chip shop. And, somehow, in Malaysia, she was seen as middle-class white, though she was black in class white. But here we would have to hide. Her status was immediately better, just because she belonged to the whole white – I'd say race, but then there's class as well going on there.

100. I: But there's something about you using the good card, you said.

I am me: the lived experience of a mixed-race identity
by Haran Rasalingam

101. CR6:   I can use the good card when I go to Malaysia too, because then I speak Malay and I understand everything. And I can use the good card there. But it sounds like I'm a bit of a manipulator, and I suppose I am. Everybody uses what they've got but, if I meet some… I guess I can just say that I can share interests with different people. And hear things that probably I wouldn't hear, so.

102. I: How do you mean?

103. CR6:   Well people just say things that they probably wouldn't say if it was one or the other. So, if I go travelling with my husband in Malaysia, people would be speaking Malay and saying all sorts of bad things about Europeans, and I can hear that.

104.   And I remember my stepmother, because she speaks Cantonese but doesn't really look Chinese, and she would always say, "You must never let people know which language you speak." And she'd hear all these things and she would then be able to say, "Oh yeah, they're trying to cheat us with this money. But I'll get them back." You know, the prices of things.

105.   And I understand Swiss-German. And of course, Swiss-Germans maybe think I speak German, and that's like, "Ok, I don't know." And then you can hear things because you have the identity and they think, "This person won't

understand. They won't know." It's a bit like being a spy, I suppose. A double agent!

106. I: Have you ever been unhappy with your identity?

107. CR6:   Yeah. In Malaysia I was unhappy that I was so tall, that I didn't look like other girls. Well, half, half because some features I think I look better. Or other girls would say, "Oh you're so much fairer." But my unhappiness also is missing my mother and just feeling a bit like an adopted child, or the odd one out. They're a bit the unhappiness of race, but they're also just the unhappiness of being different. Looking different. Well I suppose the only way you can look different is you're of a different race.

108. I: So, overall, your recollection of growing up?

109. CR6:   Extremely unhappy, but nothing to do with race!

110. I: And how do you feel now about your identity, as it were.

111. CR6:   Maybe the different thing is, "What can do with my identity?" I think I've been talking about what I've done with my identity, so… it's always like, the feelings come from, "Oh, I can't do this." or, "I can't do that.". Or, "I can do this." and "I can do that." So, as I get older, I realise I can do more. And now I have ten nieces and nephews who are all really kind of non-diverse, because my stepbrother married a Swedish woman and they live in Germany.

112.   So, I have a niece and nephew who are all really kind of, like, "Oh where am I?" And I feel I can somehow give them tradition. Well, not tradition, some sort of stories of this mixedness. And I think that's what I do with my clients. I'm quite happy with what I can do with this, because I can be a voice that honours this mixture, and values it and respects it. Which, sure, people who are not mixed will say, "Yes, we respect you and your values." But I think it's more important when it comes to me, because it's mine, I can really mean it. It's not just a thing.

113.   Okay, let's say my parents valued my mixedness. But they valued it, the otherness, because… my father was like a "Oh, from my poor beginnings, I married a white woman. And for my mother it was like, "Oh, from my poor humble background I've met this Eastern prince!" He wasn't an Eastern prince, but you have the Hollywood idea. I know there are fantasies, where I kind of think, "I'm valued, I know something." My experience I think is real, other than…

114. I: And there's something about what you say about the mix in your family. You know, the younger generations. It's so widespread in your family.

115. CR6:   Yes, it's a virus!

116. I: I wouldn't put it like that! But there's something very comfortable about that. It's like everyone can say, "Well, we're all mixed here."

117. CR6:   Yeah, pretty much they are. Pretty much they are. Yeah. And cousins too, and extended family too.

118. I: Have you ever suffered any negative attitudes towards racial mixing?

119. CR6:   Well, I'd say it's quite negative, it's mostly people pitying. You know, the whole, "Poor thing, mixed, thing." Yes, this is my impression. Not blatant outright, but a sort of, "Oh dear.", somehow there's the fall. Like you've fallen into a kind of a mix. Have I got any negatives? I think I'm quite a positive person, so I don't pick it up too much. I'm positive about this aspect of myself, I must say.

120.   But it's an odd environment; if I had grown up in a little village in *[rural area of England]*, I don't know how good it would have been for me. So, it's a lot to do with community, too.

121. I: So, would you say that you haven't really suffered racism or anything like that?

122. CR6:   I've suffered racism, yes. Most definitely. All of my boyfriends whose parents have met me have gone like, "Oh, are you sure she's the right one. Wouldn't you rather go out with someone who's more mmh…" or whatever. I

I am me: the lived experience of a mixed-race identity
by Haran Rasalingam

think, yeah, that's racist. But, in time, you just wait, and win them over!

123. I: Challenge their prejudices. So, I'm going to move on more into the psychotherapy now. Perhaps you can tell us a bit about how you got into psychotherapy in the first place?

124. CR6:   Yeah. I was having problems. I lived in Switzerland. I was very interested in… I had just read some stuff about Jung and, of course, Jung was born in Zurich, and that's where I was living, and there's the Jungian Institute there. And I knew there was either free, or low-cost counselling for English speakers, because a lot of trainees who went there spoke English and, of course, they didn't have enough clients because most people are German speaking.

125.   And I just had a lot of problems in my marriage, so I went for some psychotherapy and that's how I started. And I saw a Japanese man for about a year, and that was great. That's how I got in.

126. I: And then you went into training?

127. CR6:   No, no. And then I read an ad, in the newspaper, about a group, and I kind of thought it was an experiential group just for people, but then it was an introductory training group for biosynthesis – I don't know if you know David Boadella.

128. I: I know the name.

129. CR6:   Well, he's English and he married a Swiss woman, and he was running this training group. And I did this weekend, and it was really quite moving. I didn't want to train, but when I came to England – and, again, still same husband, same problems – I picked up this magazine, and there was the name of this man who said he'd trained in biosynthesis and suddenly I thought, "Oh, he knows that person and that connects back to Switzerland." and, when I spoke to him, I said, "Have you any experience of Asia?" and he told me he had lived ten years in India, so that was the second one.

130.   And then, after about a year, I just felt like… I was getting so fed up and feeling that this wasn't getting anywhere. I said to myself, "The money is so much, why don't I just do a year of training as a counsellor and learn how to counsel myself!" And then, after the year, I thought, "I quite like this! I might as well go for it." because it turned out I was quite good at listening. And so, then I went on training, and then I moved to a third counsellor.

131.   This was to see the person-centred approach models, and this was a woman and she was English, and it was great. And I worked out a lot of stuff about my mother with her, because I didn't really know my mother, who had left at

ten, until I turned 21. So that's basically it. My therapist story.

132. I: So, did your engagement in training... you're practising now, right?

133. CR6:   Mm hmm.

134. I: How do you feel it's impacted your sense of ethnic or cultural identity? Or impacted your understanding of it?

135. CR6:   Well, in the training there was nothing. Actually, I used to teach English as a foreign language, and I think that had much more impact on my ethnic identity in Switzerland, for a long time. And I had a big group of other teachers who were all somehow in mixed marriages; either with Swiss or had funny backgrounds.

136.   Like I knew this guy who had grown up in Japan, but he was American, so he felt really uncomfortable in America. He was a big, tall guy and he spoke perfect Japanese, but he wasn't Japanese. So, I feel that increased lots of positive ideas about this mixed identity. But the training group itself and the counselling had nothing of it. It wasn't an issue. It wasn't an issue for them, so it wasn't an issue that came out in the group.

137.   I kind of felt they were all very liberal and tolerant and open towards me, but that's not being able to share the issues. There was no development at all.

138. I: Was there a desire from you to want to bring that out more?

139. CR6: Yeah, but you can't. I mean, there would have to be another person in the group, wouldn't there? There wasn't anybody else, so there was nothing to talk about. I mean, we looked at different things like gender, and there were a couple of gay people, so those other differences, and differences of class, but no differences of race.

140. I: So, there was a sense that it wasn't a right forum to bring these issues out, because there was nobody there willing to enter into a dialogue with you?

141. CR6: Yeah. Because it wasn't part of our group, our group had no interest. So, then I kind of took the opportunity to explore other things which were present in the group.

142. I: And, in terms of just thinking about these sorts of things on your own? Did that happen?

143. CR6: No, but I think it through with my clients. I get a lot of clients who chose me for exactly the description I bring. I have a lot of clients from outside, so they feel like they're foreigners.

144. I: Do you advertise yourself in that sort of way?

145. CR6: No. There is a line where I think I say I'm mixed race. A lot of people choose me because my name is a Muslim name, so I get Muslim clients, I get... I don't know why I

get Australian and New Zealand clients. And mixed race. Particular people who say, "I'm mixed race." Normally half white and half Afro-Caribbean or Asian.

146. I: And how about your modality, your psychotherapeutic approach that you work with?

147. CR6:   Well, right now I'm using narrative therapy and that works really well for me, because it's looking at not just the individual, but by looking at the stories we grow up with. Not just my individual story or not the client's individual story, but shared stories.

148.   And also, being somehow *making* your identity rather than having an identity. I make choices to go this way or that way, and I kind of think my clients also, they make choices of things that they want to bring up and grow in themselves. But I haven't done much training, though, I have a supervisor, and I'm interested in power. Power relationships. And victimisation, like, "There's something wrong with me." Then we look at it together, "Well actually, that's a situation. What other choices do you have, in that situation?"

149.   For example, someone who was given away for adoption, and feeling rejected. And then thinking through, "Well, what might have been going on around at the time of the adoption." And thinking, well, actually, 30 years ago you

didn't have very much chance of keeping a baby if you were Muslim and it was some affair and neither family was supportive. And there was documentation of this and then it puts it in a different light. It's not a personal issue anymore.

150.   But there are lots of social forces that impinge on people, and I know there are lots of social forces that have made lots of problems for me, and they're not located in me. But I did the best I could, out of those social forces. So that's what I'm working on now. That 'the problem is the problem' and not 'the person is the problem'. And any persons in that problem situation, what can you do?

151. I: Yes. I see what you're saying. You're sort of locating the problem a bit wider and taking into account more factors.

152. CR6: Yeah.

153. I: And you mentioned choice a few times. About the narrative that we make for ourselves. Are you saying that perhaps people aren't necessarily aware that they're making their own narrative at all?

154. CR6: Well, they don't realise they have the power to make their own narrative. They receive lots of narratives, so I would say that, if you grow up in a colonial country, then you probably are going to receive a story of, you know: "Your country was so primitive until we came along and civilised

I am me: the lived experience of a mixed-race identity
by Haran Rasalingam

you." might be one story. Which is, for many, many colonial countries, not true.

155. I: But it's ingrained in the…

156. CR6:   But you're taught this. "Oh, they're very clever in the West and they have all this science, and what did we have?" It's not true. And there was this woman who was saying, "Oh when I did research into black history…" or even listening to the 'History of the World', that current BBC thing at the British Museum. All these amazing things! And they come from all these other cultures, thousands of years ago.

157.   It just, for me, is very empowering, because it's not just the white history at school and what we learned was very much white history, even though we were independents, it's strong, it's strong. I don't know, you probably grew up in this country, so it's different.

158. I: Yes, I grew up here.

159. CR6:   But then it would be even stronger. You would hear the stories that tell about the greatness of Britain.

160. I: Yes. You'd never hear the downsides or the greatness of others, particularly!

161. CR6:   Yeah, yeah. The greatness of, I don't know… African countries, whatever.

I am me: the lived experience of a mixed-race identity
by Haran Rasalingam

162. I: Yes. It just doesn't feature. So, in what way do you think you're focusing back on race and ethnicity again? That part of your identity. To what extent do you think that may have influenced your choice of how you work as a therapist?

163. CR6: The way I work. So, first with person-centred, I guess. There's some of that, locating yourself in trying to understand the client's frame of reference. And that fits exactly with it, and then continue with narrative therapies. Just that there are other points of view and other ways of looking, is really, really important.

164. And letting people trying to find themselves, because that fits in too.

165. I: So, did you start out as a person-centred therapist?

166. CR6: No. I was very interested in Jung, because he kind of tells the stories as universal, and then I'm not sure. And then when I saw Yoshi – the first therapist – we looked at some Japanese creation stories and the women are quite strong. Japanese culture is very different. I just kind of muddled through and whatever has happened has happened. Maybe I chose, but with a kind of naïve choice, not an informed choice. Even now, I just kind of sense "I think that one's better than this one."

167. I: And do you feel that you stick to a particular approach, or
              are you quite fluid?

168. CR6:   Yeah. I try to stick to an approach and get the most out of
              it because, otherwise, I'd confuse myself. I don't if I'm
              going to stay in one, because things change.

169. I: Did you move from person-centred to narrative?

170. CR6:   Now, I'm trying to move. I would say I'm still pretty much
              person-centred. But I'm still looking at solution focused,
              because I'm quite interested in power, and people finding
              power in themselves. Person-centred, sometimes, is a little
              bit – maybe not as… Sometimes the person-centred
              people will argue, but the reflectiveness; I sometimes
              actually do put myself in and ask a question. I say, "This
              is how I see it…", because I think that that gives a clear
              contrast between "…and maybe you see it differently."

171. I: What is it that you think prompted you to want to move
              towards the narrative therapy?

172. CR6:   I did an online course and, because we were doing a lot of
              writing, I looked at narratives and I just discovered the
              website, and it just seemed so amazing and so
              international. I'm working with disempowered groups,
              and they're based mainly in Australia, so it's working with
              aborigines and working a lot with anorexics – it just seems
              all these cultures haven't had a voice – and it's community

based, sort of linking up a communal self, not just an individual self. So, I think that maybe comes back to think that identity is not just about me, it's about where I fit in. Identity changes as the group you are in changes. I think narrative therapy takes some account of the fact that we have social selves. And a healthy social self, not just a healthy individual self. Mental health, just by myself, is… where I'm in can also help me be mentally healthy, or my clients.

173. I: I could see a sort of parallel between that and the sense that your ethnic and cultural experiences are, to a large extent, governed by the situation you are in, if you are in *[rural area in England]*, or if you are in Malaysia.

174. CR6:   My idea of an indicator of mental or social wellbeing is being able to connect and fit in. So, I think people really go crazy when they can't. So, either the society has to give and kind of say "Well, we have connections with this individual, or the transvestite.", or, I don't' know "Has kinky hair, and we've all got straight blonde hair." Or the person has to go and find a place where he *does* connect with that community. You could get sick if you don't have a community, or a family. And this is what my client way saying to me; "I've grown up in a white family" and she'd

found another family. And family is about sharing. You
can share characteristics.

175. I: Do you feel you have a community?

176. CR6:   Oh yeah. Definitely. Many.

177. I: So, you don't feel like an outsider.

178. CR6:   Uhmm…

179. I: They're not necessarily opposites, even though I made it
sound like they were.

180. CR6:   Yeah. I think that's exactly right. It's a continuum, and
sometimes it's also like a combination. Sometimes with
very little of feeling inside, and sometimes it's very little
of feeling outside. I think that's happening all the time to
everybody, even the most, sort of, pure person. I don't
quite fit in on some level.

181. I: I've got maybe a couple more questions, to finish up,
really. What frustrates you most about the attitudes of
others towards your identity?

182. CR6:   It's not frustration. I'm amused. Sometimes I just go
"God, how can you think that?" They just would have no
clue, then I… Mostly I'm interested. I'm interested in how
people can think so differently.

183. I: Could you give an example, maybe?

184. CR6:   Nothing recent. I remember, one time, with my ex
American boyfriend, we were going to rent a flat, and he'd

found a flat and met this woman and said "Oh, it's great, she really wants us, dah, dah, dah, dah... Just wants to meet you." And we walked in and I just knew, I just knew; she went something like "Oh no!". And he was chatting away, being his bubbly self, and then... and I didn't say anything. And then she turned around and said "Oh, there's a change of plan." That maybe her nephew, or something, was going to stay. And, all the while, he wouldn't even consider that. "How could anybody...? It's not that, it must be something else." And I didn't argue the point, but I knew that she'd... I knew, I just knew. As soon as we... she looked at me and I smiled, but I thought "I'm so sorry, but we're going to lose this flat." And that, I just think, shows... I don't know, I just find it... Was I upset? Not really; I wouldn't want to have lived there, if she's not interested. I felt so sorry for him, because I think it was on the edge of his consciousness, but he didn't really want to admit it. How horrid, how horrid! And, for her, I would say it was so horrid. For them it was like all this yucky, yucky horrid stuff. And I'm just thinking "You're making this yucky and horrible, you can't look at it." And I just thought "But I'm not going to ram it down your throats." So that is a kind of... Why couldn't he consider the fact that maybe somebody wouldn't want me just because I'm

I am me: the lived experience of a mixed-race identity
by Haran Rasalingam

not American, or English? And why would she consider it unacceptable that I might live in that house? So, I suppose one could have asked, "Why?" But at that time in my life, I wasn't that interested. I just thought "There are people who do that and there are people who don't, and I don't care about it. I'm not here to explain to anybody."

185. I: So, you kind of accepted the scenario, the situation, really.

186. CR6: Well, maybe now, older. I was only in my twenties. Now, maybe. And he was much older than me, so I would kind of just go along with whatever he did. Maybe now I would actually say something. I would say it out. Yeah. I would just say it; I would just say "Well, I'm sure she changed her mind because she saw that I wasn't American or English." But I learned to get through it. "People aren't like that. You're just imagining it." Yeah…

187. I: So, conversely, what makes you happiest about people's attitudes towards your identity?

188. CR6: The question doesn't quite fit me. What makes me happy about people's attitudes towards my identity? It's more like, when I meet somebody, it's great. You can have an exchange. Yeah, so I'm looking for exchange with people. And I enjoy exchange. Like, they give, and I have an opportunity to give. And, in that example, with my boyfriend and with that landlady, somehow, the door was

closed. They'd be like "Well, whatever it you have to give, we're not interested." And, also, they don't want to give... open up and share with me whatever they have to give. And that might be a bad opinion. It might be an opinion like "Shit. I'm not going to have any non-English person here, because I believe that this neighbourhood should stay white." Now, that's ok, because then they're giving me something, and we can get into a dialogue. So, I would just say... that makes me reflect and think that I did exactly the same, I just shut down and just said "Well let's not talk about it." None of us talked about it. A willingness to talk and an invitation to talk makes me happy. So, the other person who invites me and the other person who is willing. And I suppose gives some sort of security that they'll be open, they'll invite me and be open when I do say something. Does that make sense?

189. I: That makes amazing sense.

190. CR6:   Yeah, that would be positive.

191. I: Fantastic. It was lovely to hear your story.

[End of interview]

RESEARCH FINDINGS

Introduction

Below, I present my research findings in terms of overarching themes which have emerged through my analysis of the data as common threads running through the narratives of the co-researchers.

Thematic Analysis

Theme 1: Parental silence on racial background

All of my co-researchers were born of parents who considered themselves to be, and were generally considered by the communities around them, to be of different cultural/ethnic/racial backgrounds from each other. Despite this awareness by the parents, a strong theme running through the research narratives was that parents did not discuss this topic and, instead, were conspicuously silent and avoidant of it. For example, CR3 experienced his mother as being extremely vague whenever he pressed her for details of where his father was actually from, while CR2's mother effectively made the discussion of CR2's father a taboo topic for discussion.

Co-researchers seemed to experience a lack of empathy from their parents for the identity issues that the co-researchers grappled with, the most extreme example being that of CR2's mother who felt that she would be betraying 'her people' if she condemned their shocking racism towards CR2. The resulting situation for CR2 and other co-researchers was that they were left completely on their own to deal with social attitudes towards them. CR1's mother appeared to be focused on her own discovery of her 'black' identity, which involved a radical and hostile rejection of all things she considered to be part of 'white' culture, such as reading books and gaining a good education. This seemed to have influenced CR1 to some extent as she expressed feeling guilt for enjoying 'white' privileges, and it was something which she was in the process of questioning.

One exception regarding a lack of parental empathy may be CR6's upbringing in a family and a society which seemed more comfortable with accepting a pluralistic environment. In that sense, she experienced a certain normativity to her identity, since there was a greater familial and societal awareness of different cultures and customs acknowledged as being something which not only others have.

That the details of their children's needs were underestimated by the parents also seems to have followed through with the relationships between mother and father as well. The parents of all the co-researchers separated after initially been drawn to each other either as a perceived chance to improve their status and/or as a result of what CR6 described as 'exoticism'. The fact that the parents of the co-researchers separated meant that most were largely deprived of one of their parents from early on in their lives which prompted not only a yearning to know that absent parent, but also a yearning to seek out a mysterious culture/ethnicity/race which was felt to be part of them and yet concealed. CR3's experience was particularly acute in this regard as, to this day, he has next to no knowledge of anything about his father's origins or roots, while CR5 who, despite having contact with both parents, feels considerable regret at not being 'exposed' to Nigerian culture enough and thus finding it alien, when she believes that she should feel at home with it.

Negative views of 'mixed marriages', 'mixed children' and the perceived inferiority of other cultures/ethnicities/races seemed to make the topic a taboo within the households of most co-researchers and it is apparent that a considerable amount of shame, embarrassment and guilt was displayed by the parents and sometimes internalised by the co-researchers themselves. The taboo nature of the topic seemed to be compounded by the fact that the parent who was not absent may have been experiencing resentful feelings towards the absent parent. This especially seemed to be the case for CR2's and CR3's mothers.

CR4 and to a lesser extent CR1 took a stance of mainly embracing the culture of one parent and rejecting that of the other. CR4 experienced the wrench of identifying with the Ashkenazi mentality and feeling repelled by the Sephardi mentality while feeling that she looked much more Sephardi than Ashkenazi. CR1 appeared to be in a phase of transition towards embracing her father's English background a little more but did feel a little uncomfortable benefitting from 'white' privileges which she was all too familiar with having to fight against as a person with a 'black' identity.

Theme 2: Societal obstacles to sense of identity

All co-researchers to varying degrees experienced others trying to classify them in some way according to pre-established cultural/ethnic/racial constructs. This 'what are you?' questioning was often felt as an unpleasant and denigrating experience described in various ways such as 'boxed in', 'labelled', 'pigeon-holed' or 'pegged'. It seemed to be an experience which was felt to somehow strip away at least a part of their identity and their humanity, their specific particulars squashed, and their individual uniqueness ignored.

Labelling as exclusion

Such labelling was often felt to be excluding. CR3 took great exception whenever asked where he was from. Generally, he felt it to be a fairly direct way of excluding him from belonging to a 'native English' category of which he clearly felt himself to be a part:

> 'What they're saying is, "You're not white. Where are you from in the world? Because you're obviously not from here" - that's what they're saying.'
> (CR3, 61).

CR1 felt that she was identified as 'mixed' by her black friends to account for her empathy, which her friends did not share, for a white girl dancing in a way that they were ridiculing:

> 'it made me feel like they looked at me and … that they might think
> *(whispers)* "it's cos she mixed".'
> (CR1, 156).

Thus, creating a sense of exclusion. CR1 also commented on the widely held view by her family's black neighbours when she was growing up that she would somehow be at an advantage over their black offspring, telling her mother: 'your kids'll be alright cos they're mixed' (CR1, 114). CR1 also explained about the need of others to put her into a 'black' or a 'white' category:

> '… on the estate I don't think there was many mixed-race kids and
> then people were always kind of trying to decipher which side of the
> fence you sat on: whether you was white or you was on the black
> side.'
> (CR1, 6).

In CR2's case, throughout her childhood, her overriding experience was of not being seen as a person and only as a label:

> I wanted to be just seen for who I was, not for what they thought I
> was, not for the colour of my skin, not for the label. Just for being a
> little girl. That's all I wanted.

(CR2, 165).

This experience of labelling had a profound effect on CR2, and she refuses to label people herself which also carries across into her psychotherapy work.

A mixed identity may mean that one does not equate oneself with one or both of the cultural/ethnic/racial backgrounds of one's parents. For CR4, the fact that her father was a Sephardi did not mean that she considered herself as a Sephardi and she strongly rejected Sephardi culture (CR4, 92). Nevertheless, she felt this stance to be somewhat dishonest as she considered herself to be lying when she denied being Iranian (CR4, 164).

Labelling as intrusion

CR3 found others' attempts to place him culturally/ethnically/racially could lead to very intrusive questions which could oblige him to reveal that he did not know who his father was:

> 'sometimes, I'll say, "I'm mixed race, but I'm half English." The problem is … then … they ask, "Where's the other half from?" I have to say, "I don't know". "Why don't you know?" And actually, to somebody I don't know very well, I have to say, "Well, I don't know my Dad… Mum was a single parent…", it's quite a personal story.' (CR3, 62).

CR5 reported that she had become very skilled in answering 'what are you?' questions and felt that she could tell when the questioner was being intrusive and also explained that what she objected to most was when people *told* her what she was. CR6 experienced such questions in a less hostile way and felt comfortable explaining her 'make-up' to people to help them make sense of it.

<u>Negative attitudes to racial mixing</u>

CR5 commented on how people seemed to assume that mixed people would rather not be mixed and that they must be confused:

> 'a black person asked me, "Would you recommend it? Would you like to marry a black, so your blackness comes back? I heard that mixed people are confused". And I was so surprised that someone young asked me that.'
> (CR5, 258).

Theme 3: Impact of appearance on ways of relating

Having tight, curly hair was significant for three co-researchers and was a key marker for being identified as 'black'. Care for this kind of hair was also a key part of forming a sense of identity. All three reported that they grew up in a household in which the knowledge of how to look after this type of hair was not present and not passed down. CR2 reported that her white mother despaired as to what to do with CR2's hair and had no cultural knowledge about it (CR2, 28). CR1's mother, although also having such hair, grew up in a white foster home and never learnt culturally significant knowledge about haircare, such as how to canerow (or cornrow) hair (CR1, 104). For CR5, growing up in Spain and not having a skin colour which stood out as darker than that of those around her, her hair was the feature which singled her out as different:

> 'I've been told so many times, "If it wasn't for the hair, I wouldn't have noticed."'
> (CR5, 154).

CR5 experienced her hair as problematic and she longed to have a different type of hair (CR5, 158) and all three experienced a positive strengthening of identity when they were able to gain access to this cultural knowledge specific to their type of hair which was generally considered to be 'black' cultural knowledge.

The discovery that their hair type made them part of a shared experience took away shame and embarrassment for them. Indeed, shame and embarrassment about appearance was a common theme throughout the narratives. For CR6, she was conscious of being much taller than her classmates and that it made it more difficult for her to get a boyfriend (CR6, 42). CR3 felt like an outsider in his otherwise 'white' family and remembered his grandparents being eager to prevent him from looking like a Sikh (CR3, 26).

CR4 found her strong dark hair to be unattractive and a distinctive identifier of being a Sephardi Jew (CR4, 255). CR2 felt that she had internalised the view that her appearance made her unacceptable which led her to wishing she looked different (CR2, 150). CR1 seemed to be the most comfortable with her 'racial' appearance and explained that her weight as a child was far more of an issue because she felt it made her less attractive (CR1, 94). CR1 embraced a 'black' identity from early on and felt it to be important to 'anchor' herself, to choose a racial category for her identity rather than 'sit on the fence' (CR1, 11).

Such experiences are all due to having to find a way to live with societal norms and the attitudes that others had towards them as a result. Another deeply rooted assumption that the personal experience of most co-researchers contradicted is that one has a single, unchanging skin colour throughout one's life (no doubt reinforced by the popular belief in race realism). My co-researchers were fully aware that their own skin colour/tone and hair colour had varied throughout their lives. CR5, in particular had experienced a lot of variation going from darker to lighter to golden skin and from blond to darker hair and back. For the most part, the trend seemed to be that their skin had become lighter as they got older, but that their self-image was still very much influenced by the darker skin they had as children. CR3 commented that when he looked in the mirror, what he saw was not how he imagined himself to be (CR3, 37).

Theme 4: Gaining a sense of identity as a long and continuing journey

All co-researchers had thought profoundly about matters concerning identity and, although it was not necessarily a dominant issue in their lives all of the time, it was nevertheless something they had all reflected on in quite some detail and, judging by the ease with which they talked about such matters, appeared very much to have a heightened awareness and perception of them.

All had grappled with various different stances towards identity and all had experimented with different stances. There were times when they might think about identity purely in terms of two cultures, one from each parent, and they would think about blending them, or choosing one over the other. For CR2, having spent a childhood being rejected for not being 'white', she went through a stage of embracing the 'black' only to find that she was being objectified in a different way on the grounds of having lighter skin and looser hair. From here, she moved to a new point in her understanding of her identity:

> '... it was like, "Well black people don't want me, white people don't want me. I don't know what I am." And then, somewhere in there, I kind of found that ... it doesn't really matter what other people want to label me. *I'm me*. I don't say I'm black or I'm white. I will say I'm mixed heritage, if I have to say anything.'
> (CR2, 102).

From this, it seems that CR2 reached the conclusion that attempts to try and pin oneself down to some category or common group of belonging is ultimately always going to prove inadequate and that all definitions fall short.

CR1 had long deliberated over the question of whether she was 'mixed race' or 'black' and had some difficulties with both, but she found Barack Obama's words helpful:

> 'I bought Obama's ... second book ... "The Audacity of Hope" (Obama, 2008) ... and at the beginning he defined himself as: "I'm a black man with mixed-race heritage" ... and you know what? I thought: "that's it, I like that", yeah, I like that ... I can work with that ... '
> (CR1, 39).

CR1 had also considered that the idea of race was a nonsense, for example, she says:

> 'I did anthropology at uni and the woman said: "there's either millions of races or there's one race" ... well flippin' 'ell! ... well what am I talking about, then? The human race and done! ... What's wrong with that?'
> (CR1, 169).

For CR5, I gained the clear impression that she was on a journey to become as aware as possible of all the parts of her heritage and clearly wished she had been exposed to Nigerian culture more when growing up. CR6 seemed to have already been on such a journey but had accepted that it was never really complete (CR6, 68). For CR3, the continuing journey for identity had repeatedly led him to want to gain more information about his father's background. Such attempts had been invariably frustrated, with the only realistic source of such information being his mother who was consistently vague on the subject. This had led CR3 to fantasise about what he might have liked his father's cultural background to be and he seemed to have a preference for a Mediterranean background more than anywhere else.

CR4 appeared to have rejected her Sephardi background fairly consistently, but on the other hand she was very conscious of the complexities of her background which not only encompassed the Ashkenazi-Sephardi dimension but also the fact that her parents were born in different countries (Sweden and India) whose parents in turn were from elsewhere again (Eastern Europe and Persia/Iran). This led to CR4 feeling that she could pick and choose elements of each as she pleased.

Theme 5: Being used to standing out, standing alone and challenging norms

A key characteristic of experience shared by co-researchers was the feeling of standing out all alone against norms. Such an experience often proved difficult to bear particularly earlier in life and this would often lead to a strong desire to try and fit in, to blend in, to belong or to hide. CR1 seemed to be particularly successful at gaining a strong sense of belonging through her concept of 'anchoring', which meant that she strongly identified with a sense of being 'black' and belonging to a cultural community which also identified with this sense, while at the same time always being 'mindful' that this was not the whole story, as it were. As mentioned above, she found Barack Obama's description of his own identity to resonate with her stance: 'a black man of mixed heritage' (Obama, 2008:10, paraphrased by CR1, 39).

CR2 stood out in her childhood not so much for being 'mixed' but for being seen as 'black' in a 'white' community. She recalled the day when she was singled out as different when she had hitherto considered herself to be simply another child in her community. The extreme levels of racism she experienced meant that her standing out reached unimaginably painful levels and left her isolated to such a degree that she recalls shutting down altogether psychologically to detach herself from the constant hostility surrounding her. As CR2 grew older, her personality developed around the unavoidability of standing out and learned how to turn it to her advantage and become more independently minded and more comfortable being in opposition to the norm.

CR5 found that her standing out varied from context to context, but she generally found it to be less desirable as an adolescent when she felt it more important to fit in, but as she got older, like CR2, she used it to her advantage and felt that this made her far more open-minded than most people.

CR3 also had a strong sense of standing out and it was clear that this was something that he was comfortable with and which he considered to be a part of his identity, both because of his appearance and his sexual orientation (CR3, 136). CR6's sense of standing out was perhaps the most fluid and she seemed the least in need of having to find stances to cope with it actively, while CR4 found herself in the dual position of wanting to blend in to the Ashkenazi community and the broader community outside of the Jewish community, but at the same time hold on to a distinct Jewish identity which differentiated her but not in too overt a way.

It seemed clear to me that all co-researchers found that standing out could be tough, but also rewarding, and that it had, for the most part, a positive effect on their personality and inner strength. Being forced into standing out prevented my co-researchers from nestling easily into what Heidegger (2007) termed the *everyday* mode of being and led them to wish initially that it were not the case, but then to develop more nuanced approaches which led them to think and reflect more deeply on societal assumptions and to be comfortable challenging them without feeling their self being 'squashed'. It seemed that this made for personalities which were used to creative and sophisticated thinking and awareness around identity and interpersonal interaction.

A particularly powerful point was the sense that a mixed-race identity was a problem *for* other people and created *by* other people. It was striking to witness an absolute clarity on this point that, despite any potential difficulties presented as a result of having a mixed-race identity in a society, the problem was very much located externally. Despite occasions where co-researchers may have felt shame due to their status or a desire to look differently to make their lives easier, ultimately, the belief was unequivocal that the problems were created by the misinformed or prejudiced attitudes of others.

Theme 6: Fluidity of identity

All co-researchers seemed to experience and recognise that their identities were fluid and dependent on circumstances, context and their own chosen stance to their context. Furthermore, in the case of CR1, being considered 'mixed' also seemed to cause those around her to insist that she should clarify her identity, requiring that she decide 'which side of the fence' she was on. As mentioned above, CR1 took a very active stance towards 'anchoring' herself and embracing a 'black' identity. On the other hand, she felt that while she had a choice between seeing herself as 'black' or as 'mixed', it was unthinkable for her to choose to see herself as 'white' and felt that that would somehow be a denial of her 'blackness' which was not the same when reversed – namely that seeing herself as 'black' did not deny her 'whiteness'. This seemed to come down to a sense that her appearance made it acceptable to be called 'black' but not 'white'.

CR2 recalled surprise at realising how much she identified culturally with her hometown after she moved away, when she had been so used to being the outsider in that context. She found that she could slip quite easily and comfortably into 'black' contexts, but that ultimately, she was not keen on seeing herself as part of any group, preferring to think of herself as an individual with a unique identity.

Choosing identity

CR4 explained how, with a slight sense that she was not doing the right thing, she would pick and choose cultural elements from either her Ashkenazi side or Sephardi side to suit her needs. It seems that she would sometimes feel the need to draw on cultural norms to provide validity to her position.

Another side to choosing identity was the decision to embrace the culture of one parent and reject the culture of the other. CR4 seemed to largely reject all that she felt represented Sephardi culture and embraced all that was Ashkenazi and seemed to have a fairly negative view of Sephardim and saw their culture as inferior and 'caveman-ish' (CR4, 16).

CR1 had a strong awareness of her identity and that by its nature it cannot be described by a simplistic label. What comes across in the excerpt below is a clear sense of fluidity and context:

> '... if I go to join a gym and, on the application, they ask ... I might not even tick a box I might put "human species" ... because like I feel freer ... because like in the gym they're not gonna refuse me membership, but if it's an application form for work, I might tick ... I don't know ... I'll probably tick ... "mixed" ... "Caribbean" ...

I am me: the lived experience of a mixed-race identity
by Haran Rasalingam

depending on my mood ... or I might tick "black" ... depending on
how I'm feeling ...'
(CR1, 110).

CR3 commented that he often did not feel conscious of standing
out 'racially' living where he did in a large city, but he noticed that in a
different context, this was not the case:

> '... I visited ... my aunt in a small town in [county in the UK] ... and
> people were literally staring at me on the street, because I wasn't
> white ... I remember going back home and just suddenly
> appreciating, for the first time, that [large city in the UK] was this
> great place where everybody was really different, and nobody
> looked twice ...'
> (CR3, 110).

For CR6, her understanding of her identity took in a wider range
of factors from the genetic to the cultural to the religious. It also
encompassed her life experience living in countries in adult life which
were not connected to her family such as Switzerland.

Theme 7: Inadequacy of psychotherapy training with understanding identity

I gained quite a strong sense that the world of psychotherapy training
and psychotherapists did not provide a particularly good forum for my
co-researchers to raise any issues around cultural/ethnic/racial identity.
Therapists seemed to have reflected very little on cultural/ethnic/racial

issues and seemed ill-equipped to handle the complexities brought by my co-researchers to the extent that some co-researchers felt the need to hold some things back which they felt their therapist could not cope with.

Experiences with therapists

CR3 and CR1 in particular recounted examples of experiences with therapists which left them having very little faith at all in them. CR3 took great exception to the words of one therapist he was seeing, when CR3 described himself as 'mixed' and the therapist's response was: 'I didn't realise you were black' (CR3, 19), perhaps indicating an extremely superficial familiarity with cross-cultural counselling theory. CR1 reported that one therapist was clearly over-compensating and was conspicuously hung up on having a 'black' client. CR2 remembers 'holding back' in therapy because she did not think her therapist could take it, while CR4 also felt the need to hold back from touching on issues relating to Israel and Palestine.

Experiences in training

Co-researchers found that their psychotherapy training did not cover cultural/ethnic/racial issues in anything more than a very brief and superficial way. Both teaching staff and other students seemed unwilling or incapable of addressing such issues and co-researchers were often frustrated if they tried to raise such issues because they were ignored, angrily shouted down or equated to much more minor issues of discrimination. CR1 reported extremely angry reactions when she brought up the issue of race in training and felt that cultural/ethnic/racial majorities simply did not wish to confront such matters. CR4 felt hostility towards her on account of being Jewish and had an especially awkward interaction with an Iranian Muslim lecturer where she felt there to be mutual dislike and negative transference. CR3 reported being pigeon-holed by having a leaflet on black and Asian issues being thrust at him from a lecturer. CR5 felt that the taboo status of race in the UK was a significant barrier to the subject being raised to good effect. CR2 and CR6 both accepted that their training would not help them in this regard and resigned themselves to going alone.

On the other hand, it seems that CR1's willingness to bring up the subject proved beneficial, citing the example of the 'tall dark man' (CR1, 209), whom the tutor did not trust and found to be scary, as an example of how raising her objection brought about clarification and an improved understanding all round.

Conclusion

Co-researchers' experiences of having mixed-race identities were strongly tied to the environments in which they found themselves. Social attitudes, parental attitudes, the assumptions of any particular Zeitgeist, its links to history and the ways in which my co-researchers lived with these *facticities* (Sartre 1943; Heidegger, 2007) of their existence defined what it meant to live as a mixed-race individual. At the same time, the interviews suggested that all co-researchers exerted some choice as to what their identity was.

Co-researchers reported going through different stages with regard to their identity and wrestled with different stances. There was a tension between, on the one hand, trying to accommodate social attitudes and to try and find a way to be accepted by society, and on the other hand, resisting, rejecting and fighting against social norms in order to reclaim personal validity and uniqueness.

The research data pointed to the fact that issues of identity around culture/ethnicity/race are largely absent within psychotherapy training courses and that there is little appetite to focus on such issues, and even hostility to such issues being tackled in an adequate way. This led in many instances to the co-researchers being warned off the topic and simply reaching the conclusion that psychotherapy training was not a suitable forum for these issues. There was strong evidence of denial that there was even an issue to tackle among some students and lecturers.

Furthermore, there was some evidence that qualified and practising therapists with whom the co-researchers had been clients had not reflected sufficiently on issues of culture/ethnicity/race, leading to oversimplification, overcompensation and giving the impression of being unable to cope with some of the material that the co-researchers wished to work on.

A number of deeply embedded social assumptions were challenged by the very existence of my co-researchers in the world. These include the following beliefs: that one has a fixed identity and 'true' self, that one's skin colour is constant and representative of one's behaviour and culture, that being mixed is something to be pitied and that it leads to confusion, that there are distinct races in the world which are grounded in biological reality. Such social assumptions permeate the world of psychotherapy and we can see from the research data how such assumptions are not challenged without a considerable degree of bravery and determination.

DISCUSSION OF RESEARCH FINDINGS

Introduction

My co-researchers have experienced gaining a sense of identity as ongoing journeys which have been long, complex, sometimes painful and sometimes exhilarating. These journeys preceded any engagement with psychotherapy and have continued largely without direct assistance from the world of psychotherapy. The level of perception of identity issues of my co-researchers appears to be heightened as a result of their mixed-race identity experiences far beyond the level of perception of those around them both in and out of psychotherapy.

Their journeys have all involved battles with negative social attitudes which permeate their families and even their own parents and this has also led to some internalisation at times of this negativity towards themselves. The problems they have faced have been largely experienced as failures on the part of those around them to adequately understand the complexities of identity.

It is worth returning briefly to the common themes identified by Miville (2005) in her review of literature and comparing them with the themes from this study. To recap, Miville noted: 'ambivalence and fluidity regarding social group and self-definitions, the search for an overarching community, crossing bridges/loosening social boundaries, and transcendence of or use of multiple racial labels as part of one's identity' (Miville, 2005:314). The theme of fluidity certainly appears to be a common factor, perhaps there is also the sense of breaking with the norm in Miville's findings which has parallels with this study and searching for an overarching community seems to me to be similar to the theme of identity as a continuous journey.

Outcomes and Implications for Psychotherapy

Culture/ethnicity/race as context-dependent

The data from this research strongly support the view that a person's experience of his/her own cultural/ethnic/racial identity is heavily context-dependent and is strongly determined by factors which include parental attitudes, the type of exposure one had to the culture/ethnicity/race of one's parents, the culture/ethnicity/race of the surrounding society, one's childhood allegiances and the attitudes of others during childhood and the way in which one's look blends in or not with a society's expectations of racial categorisations. Through a combination of personal experience, of the literature I have read and of the accounts of the co-researchers, I feel very strongly that the concept of 'race' is bound up with social and historical factors which seem to get forgotten, leading to the illusion that racial categories are concrete and immutable across space and time. I think that the co-researchers show vividly how their struggles have revolved around what stance to take toward a social construct which excludes them.

I believe that this research provides a strong impetus for therapists who previously bought into simplistic labelling, such as the use of the term 'black' to refer to any minority, to reconsider their stance and develop a more nuanced understanding. In the world of psychotherapy, I think that we are used to challenging norms and questioning the foundations upon which our belief systems are based, but when it comes to such a taboo subject as race, there is plenty of evidence, both in the research data from this study and from the literature reviewed here, that this concept goes unchallenged and remains neatly packaged and untouched.

The experiences of the co-researchers appear to correlate well with an existential-phenomenological understanding of the world (Sartre, 1943; Merleau-Ponty, 2006; Heidegger, 2007), in that to understand their stories one has to appreciate their interactions with the world around them. From this starting point, an existential-phenomenological approach encourages the therapist to resist the temptation to rely on illusory essences (Spinelli, 2004), such as racial stereotypes or general cross-counselling theories which could clumsily lump the client into an ill-fitting, pre-ordained framework. Instead, an existential-phenomenological stance would mean that the therapist would strive to understand the unique structure of a client's relationship with the world around him/her (ibid).

The need to move away from race fetishism in cross-cultural counselling theories

Much of the literature in the field of cross-cultural counselling/multicultural counselling falls prey to the seductive and fetishistic pursuit of simplistic labels and thus rests on the premise of large, sweeping generalisations (e.g.: Lago & Thompson, 2002:3-5), grouping people based on a social construct whose basis lies in a deliberate division between, for example, black and white, colonised and colonisers. By approaching cultural/ethnic/racial issues in this way, the field of cross-cultural counselling/multicultural counselling is in danger of reinforcing such fallacious and ingrained historical divisions and being an obstacle to the psychotherapist's ability to meet a client deemed to be culturally/ethnically/racially different to the psychotherapist.

I would like to elaborate on the question of race fetishism in psychotherapy. I would not want to suggest that race and racism are not realities of our society, but I would like to emphasise that they are not the only realities. To focus on them to such an extent raises questions about the kind of therapists who focus on them. What is their agenda? Are they aware that their focus on this blinds them from other considerations?

A further problem of race fetishism is the danger that therapists may either inadvertently or deliberately encourage the mixed-race client to conform to racial norms in the belief that this is the right path to psychological health. As can be seen from the co-researchers here, such a course of action was a stance which was for the most part adopted by only two of the six co-researchers and was actively rejected by the others.

White awareness and cultural encapsulation

Considering that CR3's therapist told him: 'I didn't realise you were black' (CR3, 19) I was tempted to think that any counsellor who had read about cross-cultural counselling might actually be at a greater disadvantage in working with clients with mixed-race identities than a counsellor who had read nothing. It seems to me that coming from a kind of naïve stance, what leading author of existential psychotherapy, Spinelli, terms *unknowing* (2006a), is more conducive to working with a client with a mixed-race identity than someone who had digested huge amounts of theory based on splitting people up into blacks and whites. From the interviews, it can be seen that the co-researchers are used to thinking 'out of the box', of being suspicious of normative thinking and of finding that people struggle to grasp what it is to be 'mixed'.

I should point out, however, that my view on this is modified slightly by some points which I will expand on here. Firstly, the question of being white aware (Lago, 2002) is an interesting one. Given that the co-researchers often yearned to blend in and not to be conspicuous, it led me to consider that to be blissfully ignorant of a 'racial dimension' might be an ideal way to be! For example, if the normativity of 'whiteness' allows the 'white' person to lead a comfortable 'raceless' existence, is it right to insist on white awareness when racial constructs can be seen to be spurious as Rattansi (2007) argues? But the question of being white aware refers to white *therapists* – given that the research data seemed to point to a poor awareness among therapists regarding racial identity issues and racism, it would seem to be an important awareness for a therapist to have in order to be able to be competent in working with such issues when raised by clients.

The second point regards Wrenn's concept of *cultural encapsulation* (1962). It seems to me to be straightforward to assume that a therapist who is not aware of his or her own cultural biases, norms, racial prejudices and assumptions is going to fail to understand difference to any satisfactory degree and this would be a barrier to understanding identity issues connected with culture/race/ethnicity. Such a therapist is likely to see whatever s/he does, thinks, believes, looks like, to be normal and neutral and everything else to be a deviation from that norm. A further point to note on cultural encapsulation is that some of the co-researchers seemed to have parents who, despite having had a child with someone from another cultural/ethnic/racial background, showed poor awareness and low levels of concern for the cultural/ethnic/racial background of their partner and of the significance of this for their children. A client who has experienced such an attitude from his/her parents would likely find this mirrored by the culturally encapsulated counsellor.

Awareness of racism and attitudes to miscegenation

The research points to a need for psychotherapists to examine their own assumptions around race and attitudes to racial mixing. Due to the prevalent social attitudes around race, which generally contradict findings in both the natural and social sciences, a fundamental starting point seems to me to be the necessity for therapists to have a grasp of the idea of race as a social construct. Without this, it would raise the question of how a therapist might appreciate a sense of fluidity and context-dependency in the identity of a client.

I think that becoming informed of the history of the concept of race would need to form a part of gaining a good understanding of this area, but at the same time, given that we have seen that such knowledge can become simplified and over-generalised, it would also seem necessary that therapists remain acutely aware that this is a backdrop and not necessarily representative of the unique personal experiences of the client. For me, this is where an existential-phenomenological approach comes into its own, where the practitioner attempts to bracket his/her own prior assumptions in order to avoid broad brushstrokes which blind us from seeing variations, subtleties and complexities. To take an example, I used to live and work in Spain for a number of years, but it had never crossed my mind that one of my co-researchers would have been of Spanish-Nigerian background, given that my impression was that immigration in modern times from Africa to Spain is very recent and that any integration between migrant and non-migrant groups was practically non-existent. This is a purely speculative stereotype which I had in my mind based on the vaguest of anecdotal evidence.

The data suggests that race is still a difficult subject to broach in psychotherapy training and this seems to mirror the wider society. Furthermore, we have seen that attitudes to 'racial mixing' can veer towards the negative. Consequently, I would also suggest that therapists ought to consider what their own attitude is to this and to be aware of the still relatively acceptable view that it is undesirable.

Meanwhile, the word 'half' can easily be thought of in an excessively quantitative way, as CR1 very clearly expressed:

> '... you hear people saying: "well I'm half Indian and I'm half-" what is "half"? How can you be half of something? Do I learn half of my Mum's Jamaican culture? Half of my Dad's English? I don't know, it seems more like an integration, really.'
> (CR1, 187).

The best way that I can make sense of the persistence of racial categorisations and all the attitudes which go with it is by using both the French existential philosopher, Merleau-Ponty's notion of *sedimentation* (Merleau-Ponty, 2006) and Wittgenstein's concept of bewitchment (Wittgenstein, 2001). Merleau-Ponty describes sedimentation, for example, as the situation when: 'an attitude towards the world, when it has received frequent confirmation, acquires a favoured status for us' (Merleau-Ponty, 2006:513). If a configuration of cultural and genetic factors come together repeatedly in our experience, we are likely to develop a sedimented view of that configuration against which we will compare new configurations. If a person does not fit any sedimented configuration, they are likely to be subjected to the 'what are you?' question.

The self and identity

I gained the clear impression from the interviews that the sense of identity which each of the co-researchers had was strongly linked to their experiences as people who did not fit socially recognised racial categories. This was probably to be expected since I had judged that for co-researchers to come forward to participate in this study, their sense of mixedness needed to be an issue for them in some way. But the point I would like to make here is that it would seem that their sense of identity had emerged through their interactions with the world around them. Such a perspective correlates well with an existential-phenomenological understanding of identity which sees the self as a construct borne of relatedness (van Deurzen-Smith, 1996; Spinelli, 2004) and so I would tend to agree with Spinelli's criticism of humanistic models of the self which are based on the fundamental premise of there being a 'real self' which somehow exists independently of the world (Spinelli, 2006b). In short, a mixed-race identity appears to be wholly dependent on a particular socio-cultural context and this view coincides with an existential-phenomenological one.

Strengths and limitations of the research

The main strength of this research is that it highlights the complexity and variability of identity development and strongly challenges any attempts to theorise based on stereotypical cultural/ethnic/racial boundaries. The co-researchers demonstrated the uniqueness of their identities, the choices they made and stances they took with regard to their *facticity* (Sartre 1943; Heidegger, 2007) – that is their particular situation in terms of when and where they were born and grew up, their specific appearances, the attitudes of the people around them and so forth – and the fact that these choices and stances could change throughout their lives according to their ever-evolving attitudes, life experiences and current situations.

I hope that this research will have dispelled certain myths about mixed-race identities. There was little sense that any of the co-researchers had any desire to be different from what they were and so stereotypical beliefs that mixed-race individuals are to be pitied and that being of a single race is to be preferred seem unfounded. Also, the co-researchers were unanimous in locating any identity problems which they encountered externally, in the attitudes and prejudices of others. I think this is a reminder that having an existence which might be challenging in some way does not necessarily lead to wanting to be different.

As this study employed IPA, the data was collected from a small group of people and therefore the findings cannot be used to make generalised claims on the subject of the study. Another limitation of this research I see as being a lack of targeted analysis of particular phenomena within the psychotherapeutic setting. Here, in my attempt to address an absence in psychotherapeutic literature on specifically mixed-race issues, I felt the need to be quite general within that area to give the best chance of bringing out key themes which could each in turn lead to more in-depth research on those themes.

I had also hoped to get a more detailed sense of mixed-race issues in relation to psychotherapy, but there was relatively little data on this. There were few descriptions of how the co-researchers made sense of their identity from within any formal psychotherapeutic framework. In hindsight, I think that perhaps this was possibly due to three factors: i) the questions I asked around psychotherapy came towards the end of interviews when there was less time; ii) the questions themselves were not formulated in a way which would bring out such data; and iii) the world of psychotherapy had not contributed much to their making sense of identity in any obvious way.

Future studies

It is, I believe, essential that this research was carried out using a phenomenological approach in order to bring to life the rich complexity of the identity development of the co-researchers. The co-researchers were effectively randomly selected and there was great variation between them in terms of the type of lives they had had. But with a small data size, the field of psychotherapy could benefit from further studies along similar lines.

In addition to this, there are many potential directions in which future studies in this area could take. For example, as my sense is that existential therapy seems to be an appropriate fit for such issues, I believe that it could be fruitful to take this question further. Which approaches are based on theories of identity which would fall short and which ones are suitable? It would be useful to know what assumptions about identity psychotherapists have and to what extent they would clash with a scenario presented by clients such as the co-researchers of this study. It would be interesting to find out more about the understanding of the concept of mixed race among psychotherapists and about the question of how psychotherapists who experience themselves as having a single cultural/ethnic/racial background can relate to those with a dual or multiple background.

CONCLUSION

By conducting this research phenomenologically, I hope that I have captured the lived experience of my co-researchers and shed light in such a way as to enrich the reader's understanding of mixed-race issues in particular and the cultural/ethnic/racial dimension of existence in general. For me, personally, I felt that I shared many of the concerns of my co-researchers. For example, I strongly related to the experience of an ongoing tension between trying to fit in and embracing standing out; I shared with my co-researchers the incomplete and never-ending journey of discovering an identity for myself; and I shared the clear sense that the primary cause of discomfort was in the misunderstandings and ignorance of others.

But the variety of situations and stances taken by my co-researchers challenged me to take on board new factors and to reconsider some fixed notions which I had. For example, I was struck by the importance of hair for three of the co-researchers and the significance of specific 'black' cultural knowledge with regard to it; I was challenged by CR6's comfort in dealing with 'what are you?' questions and her acceptance and curiosity of the way people responded to her; and I had to accept that CR1's very interesting concept of 'anchoring', while something I have resisted personally, seemed to provide CR1 with a great deal of strength and sense of belonging.

I concur with Eleftheriadou's assertion that an existential-phenomenological approach is very suitable when working in a

I am me: the lived experience of a mixed-race identity
by Haran Rasalingam

transcultural context due to the premise that we are all 'embedded in a socio-cultural reality' (Eleftheriadou, 2002:31), while the limitations of the principle of ethnic matching are highlighted and magnified if a client (or therapist!) has a mixed-race identity, because the idea of an ethnic match might be meaningless.

Although the situation is changing, I have seen that mixed-race issues are under-researched within the field of psychotherapy. Further research would be valuable for at least three reasons. Firstly, if they continue to be treated as a marginal case within cross-cultural counselling literature, many of the specificities of mixed-race issues will be missed by those studying cross-cultural issues and the tendency will be to encourage thinking towards normative single-race minority issues. Secondly, because mixed-race identities appear to be possible only through an interaction with socio-cultural factors, they call into question many assumptions about the self and identity, regarding ideas such as *real self* (Horney, 1991; Reber & Reber, 2001) or *true self* (Winnicott, 2006), which may either be embedded in formal psychotherapeutic theory or in the general assumptions of therapists. Thirdly, research into mixed-race issues offers the possibility for therapists to consider more deeply, and to develop a more nuanced understanding of, cultural/ethnic/racial issues.

Those of us with a mixed-race identity are increasingly drawing attention to a dimension of existence which for many blends into the background. The very presence of mixed-race people demands of society to sit up, look and wonder about its assumptions. And as each census shows that the number of people of a mixed heritage is rapidly increasing, the common way of thinking today will soon be outmoded.

APPENDICES

Appendix I: Co-Researcher Recruitment Advertisement

PARTICIPANTS FOR MA RESEARCH NEEDED

"Mixed Race"
Are you a qualified or trainee psychotherapist?
Do you think of yourself as having a "mixed-race" identity?

Do you think of yourself as "mixed race" or some other term which suggests that your identity crosses racial, ethnic and cultural lines, due to your parents/ancestors originating from different racial, ethnic or cultural backgrounds?

Have you ever thought of yourself in these terms?
Do others think of you in these terms?

I am carrying out research on "Mixed-race identities and the implications for psychotherapy"
This topic is very close to my heart: my father is Sri Lankan and my mother is English.

I am me: the lived experience of a mixed-race identity
by Haran Rasalingam

Appendix II: Written Consent Sample

CONSENT FORM

Research question:
What is the lived experience of a mixed-race identity and what are the implications for psychotherapy?

Aim of the research
To raise awareness and to enrich understanding among therapists of what it might mean to experience a mixed-race identity.

Participation in this research – what is involved:
- I will conduct a one-hour interview with each participant.
- I do not have fixed questions, but I have a selection of questions that I will choose from with the intention of bringing up particular topics or themes.

Ethical considerations:
- Confidentiality – As this research requires information about personal experiences, I emphasise that all personally identifiable information will remain confidential both of the participants and of any other people mentioned in the interview.
- The right to pull out – you may decide at any point up until submission of my thesis to inform me that you wish to pull out of the research. This would mean that any material that I had gained from you for this research would not be used and would be destroyed.
- Informed consent and the impact of participation – Participation in this research could potentially bring up difficult issues.

Strategies for dealing with any difficult issues potentially arising for you:
- follow-up session: I will be available for a follow-up debriefing session should you wish
- you have the option to hear the recording and to read the accompanying transcription of our interview
- I can provide if desired recommended reading and/or the names of therapists to look at anything that may come up from participation in this research

'I agree that the purpose of this research and the nature of my participation in this research have been clearly explained to me in a manner that I understand. I therefore consent to being interviewed about my experiences of mixed race. I also consent to a recording being made of this discussion and to all parts of the interview being transcribed for the purpose of this research.'

Signed _____   Date _____

REFERENCES

Ahmed, E. (23rd April 2010). 'Is the truth about being a mixed-race Briton really so simple?' *Mail Online.* Retrieved 10th February 2011 from the World Wide Web: http://www.dailymail.co.uk/femail/article-1268375/Is-truth-mixed-race-Briton-really-simple.html

Ali, S. (2005). *Mixed-Race, Post-Race: Gender, New Ethnicities and Cultural Practices.* Oxford: Berg.

Alibhai-Brown, Y. (2001). *Mixed Feelings: The Complex Lives of Mixed-Race Britons.* London: Women's Press.

Anthias, F. (1990). 'Race and Class Revisited – Conceptualising Race and Racisms'. *Sociology Review*, 38, pp.19-43.

Ardenne, d', P.M. & Mahtani, A. (2004). *Transcultural Counselling in Action.* London: SAGE.

Ashworth, P. (2006). 'The origins of qualitative psychology'. Chapter 4 in Smith, J.A. (Ed). *Qualitative Psychology: A Practical Guide to Research Methods.* London: SAGE.

Aspinall, P.J. (2008). 'Ethnic Options of "Mixed Race" People in Britain: A Report for UK Census Agencies on Preferences for Terminology and Classifications'. *Economic and Social Research Council.* Retrieved 26th June 2011 from the World Wide Web:

http://www.esrc.ac.uk/my-esrc/grants/RES-000-23-1507/outputs/Download/57ac0cbf-0cf4-4547-9af4-af0dae798a8f

Baldwin, T. (6th November 2008). 'Barack Obama, America's first black president, turns focus to challenges ahead'. *The Times.* Retrieved 6th February 2011 from the World Wide Web: http://www.timesonline.co.uk/tol/news/world/us_and_americas/us_ele ctions/article5093813.ece

BBC News Online. (18th June 2008). 'S Africa Chinese "become black"'. Retrieved 12th February 2011 from the World Wide Web: http://news.bbc.co.uk/1/hi/7461099.stm

BBC News Online. (22nd June 2011). 'Changes for mixed-race adoption policy'. Retrieved 14th August 2011 from the World Wide Web: http://www.bbc.co.uk/news/education-12513403

Beauvoir, de, S. (2008). *Le Deuxième Sexe.* Paris: Gallimard.

Bennett, M.R. & Hacker, P.M.S. (2003). *Philosophical Foundations of Neuroscience.* Oxford: Blackwell.

Broyard, B. (2007). *One Drop: My Father's Hidden Life – A Story of Race and Family Secrets.* New York, NY: Back Bay Books.

Channel 4. (2009a). *Race and Intelligence: Science's last taboo.* London: Channel 4, 26/10/2009.

Channel 4. (2009b). *The Event: How Racist Are You?* London: Channel 4, 29/10/2009.

Channel 4. (2009c). *Is it Better to be Mixed Race?* London: Channel 4, 2/11/2009.

Choi-Misailidis, S. (2010). 'Multiracial-Heritage Awareness and Personal Affiliation (M-HAPA): Understanding Identity in People of Mixed-Race Descent'. Chapter 26 in Ponterotto, J.G., Casas, J.M., Suzuki, L.A., Alexander, C.M. (Eds). *Handbook of Multicultural Counseling.* Thousand Oaks, CA: SAGE.

Cohn, H.W. (2002). *Existential Thought and Therapeutic Practice: An Introduction to Existential Psychotherapy.* London: SAGE.

Colaizzi, P.F. (1979). 'Psychological research as the phenomenologist views it'. In Valle, R.S. & King, M. (Eds). *Existential-Phenomenological Alternatives for Psychology.* New York: Oxford University Press.

Cooper, M. (2003). *Existential Therapies.* London: SAGE.

Creswell, J.W. (2007). *Qualitative Inquiry and Research Design: Choosing Among Five Approaches.* London: SAGE.

Dalal, F. (1997). 'A Transcultural Perspective on Psychodynamic Psychotherapy: Addressing Internal and External Realities', *Group Analysis*, 30, pp.203-215.

Dalal, F. (2006). *Race, Colour and the Processes of Racialization: New Perspectives from Group Analysis, Psychoanalysis and Sociology.* London: Routledge.

Damasio, A. (2000). *The Feeling of What Happens: Body, Emotion and the Making of Consciousness.* London: Vintage.

Deurzen, van, E. (1988). *Existential Counselling and Psychotherapy in Practice.* London: SAGE.

Deurzen-Smith, van, E. (1996). 'The Survival of the Self'. *Journal of the Society for Existential Analysis,* 7(1), pp.56-66.

Eatough, V. & Smith, J.A. (2008). 'Interpretative Phenomenological Analysis'. Chapter 11 in Willig, C. & Stainton-Rogers, W. (Eds). *The SAGE Handbook of Qualitative Research in Psychology.* London: SAGE.

Eleftheriadou, Z. (1994). *Transcultural Counselling.* London: Central Publishing House.

Eleftheriadou, Z. (1999). 'Assessing the Counselling Needs of the Ethnic Minorities in Britain'. Chapter 5 in Palmer, S. and Laungani, P. (Eds). *Counselling in a multicultural society.* London: SAGE.

Eleftheriadou, Z. (2002). 'Transcultural Counselling and Psychotherapy: A Philosophical Framework'. Chapter 3 in Palmer, S. (Ed). *Multicultural Counselling: A Reader.* London: SAGE.

Ellicott, C. (25th January 2011). 'White children in Birmingham "a minority" this year because of immigration'. *Mail Online.* Retrieved 6th February 2011 from the World Wide Web: http://www.dailymail.co.uk/news/article-1350087/White-children-Birmingham-minority-year-immigration.html

Eshun, S. & Gurung, R.A.R. (Eds) (2009). *Culture and Mental Health: Sociocultural Influences, Theory, and Practice.* Chichester: Blackwell.

Fanon, F. (1986). *Black Skin, White Masks.* Trans. Markmann, C.L. London: Pluto Press.

Fanon, F. (2004). *The Wretched of the Earth.* Trans. Philcox, R. New York: Grove Press.

Fears, D. (2004). 'People of Color Who Never Felt They Were Black'. In Fiske-Rusciano, R. and Cyrus, V. (Eds) Experiencing

Race, Class and Gender in the United States. Maidenhead: McGraw-Hill.

Fernando, S. (2002). *Mental Health, Race and Culture.* Basingstoke: Palgrave.

Fonagy, P. (2001). *Attachment Theory and Psychoanalysis.* New York: Other Press.

Freud, S. (2001). 'New Introductory Lectures on Psycho-Analysis'. In *The Standard Edition of the Complete Psychological Works of Sigmund Freud, vol. XXII.* Trans. Strachey, J. London: Hogarth Press.

Gadamer, H-G. (2006). *Truth and Method.* Trans. Barden, G. & Doepel, W.G. London: Continuum.

Gaskins, P.F. (1999). *What Are You? Voices of mixed-race young people.* New York: Henry Holt.

Giddens, A. (1987). *Social Theory and Modern Sociology.* Cambridge: Polity Press.

Gilroy, P. (1993). *Small Acts: Thoughts on the Politics of Black Cultures.* London: Serpent's Tail.

Giorgi, A. (2002). 'The Question of Validity in Qualitative Research'. *Journal of Phenomenological Psychology,* 33(1), pp.1-18.

Giorgi, A. & Giorgi, B. (2006). 'Phenomenology'. Chapter 3 in Smith, J.A. (Ed). *Qualitative Psychology: A Practical Guide to Research Methods.* London: SAGE.

Gregory, I. (2003). *Ethics in Research.* London: Continuum.

Heidegger, M. (2007). *Being and Time.* Trans. Macquarrie, J. and Robinson, E. Oxford: Blackwell.

Hook, D. (2004). 'Frantz Fanon, Steve Biko, "psychopolitics" and critical psychology'. *LSE Research Online.* Retrieved 12th February 2011 from the World Wide Web: http://eprints.lse.ac.uk/961

Husserl, E. (1998). *Ideas Pertaining to a Pure Phenomenology and to a Phenomenological Philosophy, First Book: General Introduction to Pure Phenomenology.* Trans. Kersten, F. Dordrecht: Kluwer.

Horney, K. (1991). *Neurosis and Human Growth: The Struggle Toward Self-realization.* New York, NY: Norton.

Israel, M. & Hay, I. (2006). *Research Ethics for Social Scientists.* London: SAGE.

Kingsley, K. (2003). *Opening to Life: Reconnecting with Your Internal Source of Energy, Wisdom and Joy.* Lincoln, NE: iUniverse.

Krause, I-B. (1998). *Therapy Across Culture.* London: SAGE.

Lago, C. & Thompson, J. (2002). 'Counselling and Race'. Chapter 1 in Palmer, S. (Ed). *Multicultural Counselling: A Reader.* London: SAGE.

Lago, C. (2006). *Race, Culture and Counselling: The Ongoing Challenge.* Maidenhead: Open University Press.

Laing, R.D. (2010). *The Divided Self: An Existential Study in Sanity and Madness.* London: Penguin.

Langdridge, D. (2007). *Phenomenological Psychology: Theory, Research and Method.* Harlow: Pearson.

Latour, B. (2005). *La science en action: Introduction à la sociologie des sciences.* Paris: La Découverte.

Legrenzi, P. & Umiltà, C. (2009). *Neuromania: il cervello non spiega chi siamo.* Bologna: Mulino.

Lynn, R. (2006). *Race Differences in Intelligence: An Evolutionary Analysis.* Augusta, GA: Washington Summit.

MacAskill, E., Goldenberg, S. and Elana Schor, E. (5th November 2008). 'Barack Obama to be America's first black president'. *The Guardian.* Retrieved 6th February 2011 from the World Wide Web: http://www.guardian.co.uk/world/2008/nov/05/uselections20084

Malik, K. (2009). *Strange Fruit: Why Both Sides are Wrong in the Race Debate.* Oxford: One World.

Marx, K. & Engels, F. (1985). *The Communist Manifesto.* Trans. Moore, S. London: Penguin.

Masterson, J.F. (1985). *The Real Self: Developmental, Self and Object Relations Approach.* New York, NY: Brunner/Mazel.

McCormick, E.W. (2008). *Change for the Better: Self-Help through Practical Psychotherapy.* London: SAGE.

McLeod, J. (2001). Qualitative Research in Counselling and Psychotherapy. London: SAGE.

Merleau-Ponty, M. (2006). *Phenomenology of Perception.* Trans. Smith, C. Oxford: Routledge.

Milville, M.L. (2005) 'Psychological Functioning and Identity Development of Biracial People: A Review of Current Theory and Research'. Chapter 16 in Carter, R.T. (Ed). *Handbook of Racial-Cultural Psychology and Counseling: Theory and Research, Volume 1.* New Jersey: Wiley & Sons.

Moustakas, C. (1994). *Phenomenological Research Methods.* London: SAGE.

National Statistics Online. (April 2001). 'Ethnicity and Identity'. Retrieved 10th February 2011 from the World Wide Web: http://www.statistics.gov.uk/cci/nugget.asp?id=455

National Health Service. (2011). *The GP Patient Survey.* Ipsos MORI. Retrieved 14th February 2011 from the World Wide Web: http://www.gp-patient.co.uk/onlinesurvey

Nazroo, J. (2000). *Ethnicity and Mental Health: Findings from National Community Survey.* London: Policy Studies Institute.

Nietzsche, F. (1998). *On the Genealogy of Morals.* Trans. Smith, D. Oxford: Oxford University Press.

Obama, B. (2008). *The Audacity of Hope: Thoughts on Reclaiming the American Dream.* Edinburgh: Canongate Books.

Obasogie, O.K. (4th July 2009). 'Return of the race myth'. *New Scientist,* Issue 2715.

Okasha, S. (2002). *Philosophy of Science: A Very Short Introduction.* Oxford: Oxford University Press.

Oliver, P. (2010). *The Student's Guide to Research Ethics.* Berkshire: Open University Press.

Olumide, J. (2002). *Raiding the Gene Pool: The Social Construction of Mixed Race.* London: Pluto Press.

Palmer, S. and Laungani, P. (Eds). (1999). *Counselling in a multicultural society.* London: SAGE.

Palmer, S. (Ed). (2002) Multicultural *Counselling: A Reader.* London: SAGE.

Pearce, A. (2002). 'Investigating Biases in Trainee Counsellors: Attitudes to Clients from Different Cultures'. Chapter 18 in Palmer, S. (Ed). *Multicultural Counselling: A Reader.* London: SAGE.

Pedersen, P.B. (Ed). (1987). *Handbook of Cross-cultural Counselling and Therapy.* London: Praeger.

Pena, S.D. (11th September 2009). 'Do pensamento racial ao pensamento racional'. *Ciência Hoje Online.* Retrieved 10th February 2011 from the World Wide Web: http://cienciahoje.uol.com.br/colunas/deriva-genetica/do-pensamento-racial-ao-pensamento-racional

Phoenix, A. and Owen, C. (2000). 'From miscegenation to hybridity: mixed relationships and mixed parentage in profile'. Chapter 3 in Brah, A. & Coombes, A.E. (Eds). *Hybridity and its Discontents: Politics, science and culture.* London: Routledge.

Phillips, A. (2010). 'What's wrong with essentialism?' *Distinktion: Scandinavian journal of social theory, 20.* ISSN 1600-910X.

Polkinghorne, D.E. (1989). 'Phenomenological research methods'.
In Valle, R.S. & Halling, S. (Eds). *Existential-Phenomenological*
Perspectives in Psychology: Exploring the Breadth of Human
Experience. New York: Plenum Press.

Prasad, A. (1st November 2009). 'It's a wonderful, mixed-up world'.
The Telegraph. Retrieved 26th June 2011 from the World Wide Web:
http://www.telegraph.co.uk/comment/6475543/Its-a-wonderful-
mixed-up-world.html

Rasalingam, H. (2009). 'Language-Games: Race and Bewitchment'.
Existential Analysis, 20(2), pp.319-328.

Rattansi, A. (2007). *Racism: A Very Short Introduction.* Oxford:
Oxford University Press.

Rawson, D., Whitehead, G., Luthra, M. (1999). 'The Challenges of
Counselling in a Multicultural Society'. Chapter 1 in Palmer, S. and
Laungani, P. (Eds). *Counselling in a multicultural society.* London:
SAGE.

Reber, A.S. & Reber, E.S. (2001). *Dictionary of Psychology.*
London: Penguin.

Reid, K., Flowers, P. & Larkin, M. (2005). 'Exploring lived
experience: An introduction to Interpretative Phenomenological
Analysis'. *The Psychologist,* 18, pp.20-23.

Ricœur, P. (1977). *Freud and Philosophy: Essay on Interpretation (Terry Lectures)*. Trans. Savage, D. New Haven & London: Yale University Press.

Ricœur, P. (1997). *La métaphore vive*. Paris: Seuil.

Root, M.P.P. (Ed) (1992). *Racially Mixed People in America: Within, Between and Beyond Race*. Newbury Park, CA: SAGE.

Root, M.P.P. (Ed) (1996). *The Multiracial Experience: Racial Borders as the New Frontier*. Thousand Oaks, CA: SAGE.

Rushton, J.P. (2000). *Race, Evolution & Behavior: A Life History Perspective*. Port Huron, MI: Charles Darwin Research Inst.

Sartre, J-P. (1943). *L'être et le néant: essai d'ontologie phénoménologique*. Paris: Gallimard.

Sartre, J-P. (1985). *Réflexions sur la question juive*. Paris: Flammarion.

Sartre, J-P. (1997). 'Return from the United States'. Trans. Sharpley-Whiting, T.D. Chapter 5 in Gordon, L.R. (Ed). *Existence in Black: an anthology of black existential philosophy*. London: Routledge.

Sashidharan, S. (2003). *Inside Outside: Improving mental health services for black and minority ethnic communities in England.* Leeds: NIMHE.

Sayyid, S. (2000). 'Bad faith: anti-essentialism, universalism and Islamism'. Chapter 12 in Brah, A. & Coombes, A.E. (Eds). *Hybridity and its Discontents: Politics, science and culture.* London: Routledge.

Sewell, H. (2009). *Working with Ethnicity, Race and Culture in Mental Health: A Handbook for Practitioners.* London: Jessica Kingsley.

Silverman, D. (2010). *Doing Qualitative Research.* London: SAGE.

Smith, J.A. (1996). 'Beyond the divide between cognition and discourse: using interpretative phenomenological analysis in health psychology'. *Psychology and Health,* 11, pp.261-271.

Smith, J.A. (2006). 'Validity and qualitative psychology'. Chapter 11 in Smith, J.A. (Ed). *Qualitative Psychology: A Practical Guide to Research Methods.* London: SAGE.

Smith, J.A. & Osborn, M. (2006). 'Interpretative phenomenological analysis'. Chapter 4 in Smith, J.A. (Ed). *Qualitative Psychology: A Practical Guide to Research Methods.* London: SAGE.

Smith, J.A., Flowers, P. & Larkin, M. (2010). *Interpretative Phenomenological Analysis: Theory, Method and Research.* London: SAGE.

Smith, L. (6th September 2006). 'Absent Voices'. *The Guardian.* Retrieved 10th February 2011 from the World Wide Web: http://www.guardian.co.uk/society/2006/sep/06/guardiansocietysupplement1

Spencer, R. (2004). 'Assessing Multiracial Identity Theory and Politics: The Challenge of Hypodescent'. *Ethnicities*, 4.3, pp.357-379.

Spinelli, E. (2004). *The Mirror and the Hammer: Challenging Orthodoxies in Therapeutic Thought.* London: SAGE.

Spinelli, E. (2005). *The Interpreted World: an introduction to phenomenological psychology.* London: SAGE.

Spinelli, E. (2006a). *Tales of Unknowing: Therapeutic Encounters from an Existential Perspective.* Ross-on-Wye: PCCS Books.

Spinelli, E. (2006b). *Demystifying Therapy.* Ross-on-Wye: PCCS Books.

Spinelli, E. (2007). *Practising Existential Psychotherapy: The Relational World.* London: SAGE.

Suarez-Kurtz, G. et al. (2007). 'Self-reported skin color, genomic ancestry and the distribution of GST polymorphisms'. *Pharmacogenetics & Genomics*, 17.9, pp.765-771.

Sue, D.W. and Sue D. (2008). *Counseling the Culturally Diverse: Theory and Practice.* Hoboken, NJ: Wiley.

Winnicott, D.W. (2006). *The Family and Individual Development.* Abingdon: Routledge Classics.

Wittgenstein, L. (2001). *Philosophische Untersuchungen/Philosophical Investigations.* Trans. Anscombe G.E.M. (Bilingual edition). Oxford: Blackwell.

Wrenn, C. G. (1962). 'The culturally encapsulated counselor'. *Harvard Educational Review,* 32(4), pp.444-449.

Yardley, L. (2000). 'Dilemmas in qualitative health research'. *Psychology and Health,* 15(2), pp.215-228.

Young, R.M. (1994). *Mental Space.* London: Process Press.

Zahavi, D. (2003). *Husserl's Phenomenology.* Stanford, CA: Stanford University Press.

Printed in Great Britain
by Amazon

47614866R00225